Never The Same River

New Thoughts on . . .

9·1·2020

For

Susan

Well met at MNTA!

Never The Same River

With every good wish

ANTONY WOOD

Antony

Berkshire Community Foundation and 1ˢᵗ The Queen's Dragoon Guards Benevolent Fund will benefit from sales of this book.

© Antony Wood, 2013

Published by Wood Ant Publishing

A CIP catalogue record for this book is available from the British Library.

ISBN 978-0-9926318-0-2

Book and cover design by Clare Brayshaw

Prepared and printed by:

York Publishing Services Ltd
64 Hallfield Road
Layerthorpe
York YO31 7ZQ

Tel: 01904 431213

Website: www.yps-publishing.co.uk

Dedication

This memoir is for Ursula, James, Ellie and Hattie as well as Louis, Audrey, Digby and Dashiell. In a wider sense, however, it is dedicated to all the family – past, present and yet to be.

'No-one can step into the same river twice, for new waters will always be washing over them'

- Heraclitus

'Life can only be understood backwards; but it must be lived forwards'

– Søren Kierkegaard

'The woods are lovely, dark and deep,
But I have promises to keep,
And miles to go before I sleep,
And miles to go before I sleep'

– Robert Frost

Contents

CHAPTER ONE

Elstree: The Story Starts

'For many people life is a struggle and for most it's a mystery'

– Charles Handy

This is the story of a nervy, dyslexic boy who grew up in a country vicarage and who, through nobody's fault, was part of a dysfunctional family. He has been shot at; twice been made redundant; faced bankruptcy; had children; been lucky enough to fall in love and stay in love (and have love returned) and had five careers (perhaps this is a sixth?).

I decided to write these memoirs a long time ago but, as I now realise, I faced the usual inexperienced writer's block of lack of confidence and failure to find my 'voice'. However, these are just excuses for not getting on with it, and now here I am in a car park in Brighton looking at the soft September sunshine and ready to write the first page.

Ask any storyteller and they will say that good stories have a beginning, a middle and an end. Whether this story is a good one or not is open to debate. What is not in doubt is that it has a beginning and a middle but no end and I admit there is even a bit of a problem with the beginning. It's the bit I don't really want to write or think about. It's not that I have completely sublimated unhappy memories from my days living in the Rectory at Elstree. I think I have a pretty sure grasp of what went on and have, over the years, confronted it, but it has taken quite a while to get the right balance.

I developed slowly after an indifferent start. I was essentially a sunny, lively and rather sweet young boy who had to endure an unhappy childhood as part of what would nowadays be described as a dysfunctional family. I still have characteristics of intensity and a sharpness of manner and, although these are clearly part of my innate personality, I believe that my formative years didn't help; there is still, I suspect, a small but pretty angry young child inside me. At some point before I left home, I recall looking up to the sky and saying: 'One day I'm going to tell people how horrible this is.'

My birth certificate confirms that I was born in Datchet, Berkshire, near Windsor, where I now live, on 2 September 1941. I believe the birth took place in a nursing home and we were in Datchet because it was wartime and my Father, Lawrence Wood, was chaplain to an anti-aircraft battery based in the woods near Burnham Beeches. Apparently I nearly didn't survive my birth as my blood group was B Rhesus positive and my Mother's was different. Nowadays this sort of thing is sorted out as a routine pre-birth issue but for some reason in my case the problem was overlooked and I languished for some days and very nearly died. Since then I have always attributed my lean frame – I was really skinny as a young boy – to this poor start, together with naturally light bones, an overactive metabolism and, maybe, wartime rations. However, in this, as with almost everything, I may be wrong.

For the next four years or so my Mum, Sylvia, whose maiden name was Barker, was well, and apparently had little problem looking after my elder brother Michael and me. I think these years were passed up north with relatives, possibly in Knutsford or Alderley Edge, roughly the area from where both my parents originated.

But of these years I have no recollection. As you read these pages you will quite quickly realise that I did many things late. My first early memory is of when I was nearly four; I couldn't read till I was about eight; proper sex didn't occur until I was about twenty-one and I got a Higher Degree at fifty-nine. I have long regarded myself as the latest of late developers and within this light-hearted comment lies a truth. I believe that I have best used my talents and fully developed as a person after the age of fifty. On this basis there will be no stopping me when I'm ninety.

While my Mother, my brother Michael and I were seeing out the war, my Dad was heavily engaged fighting in it and I am immensely proud of what he did. He clearly must have been someone with a very strong physical and mental constitution. After a number of postings he was sent to India in 1943, where he joined the Duke of Wellington's Regiment and eventually found himself out in Burma, as a padre attached to Chindit Column 76. He was part of the second wave of Chindits flown in to operate in the jungle behind Japanese lines. These columns were the first military units to be totally reliant on air drops.

None of us can imagine the demands this cruel arena of conflict made on the men involved. For a start it was the 'forgotten war' and the forces felt ignored and neglected. The weather, especially in the rainy season, was unimaginable and the terrain impossible. The columns had to hack their way through primary jungle in very humid conditions or fierce rain. They carried 80lb packs on their backs, which, of course were even heavier when sodden with rain.* The enemy had a fearsome reputation for cruelty and Japanese troops came to be regarded as invincible, indeed almost super-

---

* For more detailed information on what the Chindits did and what this particular column went through, see W. A. Wilcox's book *Chindit Column 76*, where Dad is mentioned as the 'Bish'. A very fine, factual description of the campaign can be found in George MacDonald Fraser's memoir, *Quartered Safe Out Here*. I particularly love the last few pages, which haunt me still.

human. Anyone captured could expect to be tortured and to die from starvation or be sent to terrible prisoner-of-war camps.

However, the most debilitating element was disease, which was rife and killed far more soldiers than the enemy. I only recall my Father talking about the war once, when he told me about how he eventually got away from the fighting zone when the column was disbanded. He and a handful of other sick soldiers were guided out by local Naga tribesman who carried the soldiers on stretchers. My Father's diarrhoea was so bad that the force of it pushed his shorts several inches away from his backside. By the time he limped back into base camp (with, in addition, an injured ankle) he also had malaria. When the Medical Officer examined him he said: 'Why aren't you on a stretcher? You are the sickest of the lot.'

I am so proud of Dad's achievement in this most terrible theatre of war and this pride is doubled when I recall that throughout his time behind enemy lines he was unarmed, as chaplains don't carry guns. However, I think the campaign took its toll in ways in which neither he, nor our family or anyone who knew us was able to recognise at the time. I sense the effort involved left him prone to periods of depression and that physically and emotionally he returned in no state to cope with Mum's illness and slow deterioration.

However, I like to believe that the thought of his two small boys back home sustained him and I have no doubt he absolutely adored me. As I grew up, this love became more tangible and it almost certainly helped me to survive difficult times.

My Dad was a handsome man, with a strong face and I always picture him with a pipe in his mouth. (The cabinet in which he kept his tobacco is by my desk and if I open it now, many years after he last smoked his pipe, I can still smell the distinctive aroma.) During and after the war, life became quite tough for him and I think it showed in terms of the person I remember. He could be taciturn and look somewhat preoccupied, and in these moods you couldn't be sure what he was thinking. Like a lot of people born soon after the turn of the century he had a well-developed sense of duty and did everything he could for his children, especially in terms of our education. I think he was essentially a private man, so strangers might have found him difficult to get to know but this trait was offset by a good and lively sense of humour.

Thinking about Dad and what he was like brings back my first real memory which connects him, Burma and the war. I recall sitting on a double bed and my Father in uniform, newly returned from the Far East, arriving with presents such as a pair of red leather slippers and bananas. Where was this? My gut feeling is that it was while we were in Cheshire but it might have been in Bredon (in Worcestershire) since my Father had taken a curacy there in 1945 soon after he returned home. This was only a temporary post while he sought a permanent parish.

We must have had some connection with Bredon via Dad's Mother – Bessie Wood – as her husband (my paternal Grandfather) Mark Stuart Wood was buried there following his death in 1945. Bredon is also the focus of my other two very early memories. The first is of me sitting in a pony and trap with a nice lady in a hat. We are going up one of the hills in the village, to deliver laundry to people. Mike, my brother, who has a wonderful memory, tells me the lady in the trap was Mrs Wilkinson. My second early recollection actually features Michael, who is five years older than me. I can see him now standing beside the River Avon, which flowed behind Bredon Rectory. He was using an old air rifle to take potshots at tin cans floating in the water. I guess if one had the chance to choose where to start one's conscious existence, then a famously beautiful village in the heart of the English countryside at the end of a terrible war, with my Dad safely returned, would be hard to better. Sadly, it didn't last.

Sometime in 1946 my Father became Rector of the parish of Elstree in Hertfordshire. Elstree is now famous as the home of the international film studios but to be precise the studios are actually in Borehamwood, some two miles away. Although Elstree lies only eighteen miles from Piccadilly Circus, at the time it was a small, essentially rural village, with some big houses and a station. It had a main street containing a line of mock-Tudor, white-fronted houses; a pub called the Plough; and a grocer's shop called Hawes Bros, run by Charlie Moore. On Sundays, after the 11.00 a.m. service, Charlie, who was a sidesman, used to come and count the collection, using a green baize card table in the Rectory study. I was fascinated to watch the coins zipping into his hands as he flicked and counted them off the edge of the table into neat piles of silver and copper coins. Later Dad conducted the marriage service between Charlie's daughter, Betty, who was considered the local beauty, and John Puncheon, the Scoutmaster of the church Scout pack I was in. As you might expect, I sang in the choir (which I joined at the age of eight). The going rate for a choirboy singing at someone's marriage was five bob (two silver half-crowns).

My rather circumscribed life revolved round three things: the church, school and our wonderful garden. I shall talk about these in much more detail, but first I should explain the nature and impact of my Mother's illness.

My Mother and her twin sister Marguerite were born in 1909 into the Barker family, which had apparently been well off. The story I heard from my Mum's younger sister, Aunty Jill, is that Ernest Barker, my maternal Grandfather, placed his money with the local solicitor who embezzled it and ran off to Australia. Mum (Sylvia) was one of six children. The others were Marguerite, Noel, Kenneth, Theo and Jill, the youngest.

It is interesting to note that the first time I met my Aunty Jill was six years ago, only two years before she died, when I was sixty-four and she was in her nineties. She was still playing golf most days and was in fine fettle, but even though I was desperate to know about my Mum's early life she gave away nothing. It seems that Aunty Jill lived for many years with a bookmaker in Reading, and, because she didn't want the family to know, she kept away from family things.

I never met Kenneth at all, or Theo, who sadly died young of TB. Also, I only remember seeing my maternal grandparents, Florence and Ernest Barker once, and the same applies to my Uncle Noel. Similarly, the one time I met Aunty Marguerite was when I went up to stay with her and this turned into a disaster. Such visits were all due to the fact that my Mum couldn't cope and so we had to be farmed out. As a result, my lasting impression is that most of our relatives didn't really want to know about my poorly Mum living down south with her struggling vicar husband.

Mum's illness may have been inherited. The story is that Florence herself suffered from depression, and no doubt the combination of the family losing its money and her youngest son coughing his young life away in a TB ward can hardly have helped.

Increasingly my Mum suffered from bouts of manic depression. I believe she had her first breakdown in her late teens, which would have been in about 1926 or 1927. She and my Father must have met around 1933, probably in Harrogate, where Dad had his first curacy, and they were married in 1935. Things appear to have gone well up to and including Dad going to Burma in the middle of the war. Mike, my elder brother, was born in 1936 and in those days being the wife of a vicar (or curate) meant a house, a reasonable income and guaranteed social status.

My Father always claimed that the Barker family never told him about Mum's first breakdown, and he felt let down. That may have been wrong of the Barkers, but we should remember the extreme social stigma in those days with regard to mental illness – especially among middle-class families, for whom respectability was a religion of its own. It was a world in which, for example, people noticed if a man was or wasn't wearing a hat, and in which it would have been quite a social error not to tip the said hat to a lady passing in the street. This preoccupation with social respectability and being 'correct' made life even harder as my Mum's illness grew worse and attacks more frequent. Over time the vicar's wife's 'mad' behaviour became a topic for 'secret' discussion for everybody.

I can't recall how and when the deterioration in our family life began or even how it developed. Moving to Elstree and the harsh times everyone endured at the end of the war (bitter winters, poor food and power cuts) clearly didn't help a lady of frail disposition and no great physical strength. I am looking at Mum's picture now as I write, trying to see in her face what it was that led to so much unhappiness. Of course a black and white photo of a girl, taken in the 1930s, can't tell you much. The most obvious thing, however, is how beautiful she looks. Her thick auburn hair runs all the way down her back and her face reflects a sweet-natured, rather delicate person who was probably artistic (she had a lovely singing voice) and who needed looking after. Above all, you get the impression of someone who was not yet mature and who has probably just left school. That would be fine if it weren't for the fact that I'm fairly sure this photo shows a woman in her early twenties.

My Father always said that Mum would have been OK if she had lived in a world where money could have protected her. This may be true but only partly so, because it's clear that during the two years Dad was away fighting in India Mum coped pretty well on her own with two small children. I now only remember her beautiful qualities, half seen through the mists of constant illness.

Although my Mum had trained as a physiotherapist I don't think she ever worked after she was married, which was quite usual in the 1930s. Certainly she never worked after I was born. Elstree parish was seen as a good living for a vicar, but gradually a shortage of money and lack of sufficient help in a big, shambling old house must have begun to wear Mum down. I guess there may have been other things as well, including money. Dad's income in 1946 would have been about £1,000 per annum which was OK. However this was roughly what it had been in 1896 when Canon Eales (Dad's predecessor) arrived, and at that time the same salary would have paid for indoor servants, gardeners, a stable boy, a coach house and a very active social life. So the Rector of Elstree's salary of £1,000 a year stayed the same while the Church of England declined and prices increased. Looking back, you can see how this combination of factors worked to undermine my Dad's ability to cope and my Mum's resistance to the 'black dog' of depression, ultimately her nemesis.

Incidentally, because Canon Eales took over the parish in 1896 and stayed so long, Elstree only had three vicars during the whole of the twentieth century. Dad followed Canon Eales at the end of World War II and his successor didn't depart until after 2000. This may be some sort of a record and reflects the power of 'parson's privilege' at the time.

Despite our family troubles I felt much loved, and my view years later is that my parents were simply dealt a rotten hand. Although I still have some residual anger about the family, overall I just feel so sorry that life was not kinder to them.

After World War II, things were very tough in England. The country was broke and in hock to the Americans, with major cities still showing bomb damage ten years after the war and cars a relative rarity. A trip to the cinema often meant a walk, a bus and then another walk, and the same in reverse to get home again. In 1947 Britain had one of the coldest winters on record and there was a power strike. The year before the government had introduced the 'austerity loaf", along with bread rationing, which hadn't happened even during the war. To help alleviate famine in parts of Asia and defeated Germany, the extraction rate of flour from wheat was increased until it reached 85 per cent. For two years the already grey British loaf got even greyer. My early memories of going to school are set against a background of drab clothing, basic food, very few outings and a 'Sorry, we're closed' mentality to most things.

In the midst of this, my Mum tried to run a huge house which was poorly carpeted, draughty, dirty and dilapidated. We had some nice pieces of furniture (given, I think, in the 1930s as wedding presents) but my recollection is that the Rectory was generally cold, with worn lino and large rooms decorated (many years before) in a severe Victorian style. I used to kick a football against the wall in the empty 'red room' and downstairs we had a flagstoned scullery with a dark larder with hooks hanging from the beams for carcasses. Upstairs the bathroom had green shutters, a wobbly basin and a hot, square green tank in the corner, on which I used to warm my clothes. The lighting when we arrived was gaslight, and this was only changed when some German prisoners of war came to dig up the drive, which ran alongside St Nicholas's Church, in order to lay the cable to the house for electricity. I used to enjoy going to watch them at work.

Though we didn't know it, we existed in that worst of all states, genteel poverty, or, more accurately in our case, middle-class pretensions, with all the unfulfilled aspirations that phrase implies. At that time it really mattered how people thought of you and how you acted socially was of great importance.

While Mum's family had had money and a comfortable upbringing, my Dad's relatives were directly connected to the aristocracy through Granny. Her side of the family went back through some of the great families of Britain: the Beauforts, Howards, Galloways, Murrays, Stanley's and on to royalty, via the Tudors, Of course, this stuff mattered to my Grandmother and my Father and his family because, in their day, being well-connected meant the prospect of a good job, or inherited land and a comfortable life.*

I have talked already of my Mum's siblings. On my Dad's side, the family looks a bit of a mess as well. I believe one of his brothers was imprisoned (or probably just charged) for homosexuality (or maybe bankruptcy?). This brother certainly had a drink problem. I think one of Dad's sisters married a leper and his youngest brother had a breakdown. Another sister married a quite successful textile salesman and another, I think, was a missionary in Japan.

Returning to my Mother's family: after the war my Mum's twin sister Marguerite married the Director of Music at the BBC. He was called Maurice Johnstone, and he wrote various pieces of music, including a melodic orchestral rhapsody called 'Tarn Hows'. They must have stayed away from us (or were they kept away?) as I only saw them once. This was when my Mum was so ill that my brother and I had to be sent up to Cheshire to stay briefly with my maternal grandparents and later with Aunt Marguerite. All went well for a while, though I suspect I was merry and noisy and I recall energetic games of French cricket with Mike on summer evenings in a nearby park. Anyway, one day I must have got filthy and, being constantly impetuous, rushed into the house to wash my hands before drying them in a cursory way on a nice white, fluffy towel and dashing out

---

* Granny Wood's family had included Queen Victoria's Personal Ambassador to the Heads of Europe and Granny's mother was a member of the Antrobus family. They owned Eaton Hall in Cheshire, which was a stately home until Tarmac bought the site for its land and gravel pits and then pulled the house down in 2005.

to play again. Later I was summoned to a confrontation in the study with two severe adults holding a filthy white bathroom towel, which had a child's dirty hand marks all over it.

'Did you use this towel?'

Terrified and near to tears, I lied: 'No.'

That was enough. Tired of caring for someone else's wayward children, they sent us home.

I am trying hard to remember any other moments of contact with what amounted to some eight or nine aunts and uncles and attendant cousins – but that really is it. To this rather limited experience of relatives I should add that during most of my childhood very few children of my age came to the Rectory. There was virtually no 'tea after school' or 'come round to play tomorrow'. Mum was ill, so there would be no tea – not for visitors, that is, and I suspect we felt ourselves a touch socially superior for me to go round to someone else's. So I didn't.

Set against these rather general impressions of what life was like, I do have certain very specific memories of living in Elstree village just after the war. I say village because that's what it was then, and our life was set against quite a rural background. We had, for example, a village blacksmith called Albert Sands, who had a German ex-prisoner of war working for him. In the holidays I used to walk along to the forge and watch the two of them shoeing horses, mending lawnmowers or making things out of wrought iron. Fancy having been born in time to still see the bellows pumping an open fire and watch red-hot metal being beaten into the shape of a horseshoe with huge hammers, which made the sparks fly.

I went for a couple of years to the local C of E primary school, where I principally remember endless playground games and having to drink warm milk. The playground was also the place where fist fights sometimes took place, and kids would go home minus a tooth or with a black eye. I only got involved in one such fight but it was frightening, particularly the speed with which a ring of chanting and yelling children formed, egging us both on.

There is a picture taken of me when small clutching my favourite soft toy, a golly, though my affections were soon transferred to a rather threadbare dog called Spottie, who went everywhere with me. However, despite the comfort of cuddly toys later I went through a period during which I was a bit disturbed. I became very interested in lighting fires, mostly in the garden where I could cook potatoes in the embers, but all this got a bit out of hand and on one occasion I set light to a whole heap of comics under my bed and caused a small fire. Something not quite right there.

We weren't entirely solitary: at times I used to go off with my brother to David Bell's house where we played in the 'brickfields' and the woods. However, when Mike went to boarding school in 1949 – when I was eight – these visits dried up. Also at some point a boy called Tom Lowenstein came to stay for a few days and we had a riotous time making a raft for the swampy, green, mosquito-ridden Rectory pond. In return I went for a weekend to their cottage in East Anglia, where I sense I was seen as disruptive.

Once Michael and I went to Broadstairs for a week by the sea, with a family called the Gullivers. Peggy Gulliver and her husband lived in Elstree parish with their three children in a big house near Munt's Farm. I knew they were well off because they had a large nursery containing a huge rocking horse with a long swishy tail, as well as this second house at the seaside. It was all very Enid Blyton and included the others getting itching powder from rose hips, (- the little seeds inside these hips are very itchy), and putting it down my neck. At breakfast I was interrogated in front of the other children as to whether I had been to the loo.

'Have you opened your bowels this morning, Antony?'

'Yes,' I would lie.

* * *

Peter Gulliver made colour ciné-films of the garden parties my Dad put on in the Rectory garden in the late 1940s and early 1950s. These exist still and as we've put them onto disc you can now see the stuttering, soundless pictures of another age. Peter Gulliver also came in once when Mum was in hospital and completely redid our rather slummy kitchen, painting it and putting in new equipment. I was taken to see it and remember thinking, 'at last everything will be all right'.

Given my rather limited experience of others of my own age – apart from school – it strikes me now that mine was a cloistered and somewhat solitary childhood, posited on a rather Victorian view of the world and how children should be brought up. At the heart of this unsatisfactory state of affairs was Mum's illness. She would now almost certainly be diagnosed as having bipolar disorder. From the late 1940s until her untimely death in 1959, aged only fifty, she had a series of nervous breakdowns. Mostly, when she was not in a psychiatric ward in Shenley Hospital (or Napsbury as it was then called), she lay in bed refusing to come downstairs. This would go on for months on end. One of the most poignant moments of this ghastly saga came when I was about ten. We had been offered a seaside holiday – at a time when holidays and going away at all were a rarity. I knelt at my Mum's bedside with tears pouring down my face saying, 'Mummy, do please get up – do please, otherwise we can't go away.' We didn't. The unhappy story continued with a series of increasingly unhappy incidents as my Mother's illness meant that she swung between being depressed (permanently in bed) and manic, rushing around the parish creating rumours or broadcasting stories about her husband the Rector.

Children hear things in these kinds of situations which they don't understand but which they recognise, after a fashion. Certain phrases or words echo down the years and resonate with incidents and feelings of long ago. One such for me is 'sodium amatol'. This was the medicine prescribed at the time for those suffering from depression. I have no idea if it was any good long term. In the short term, if Mum didn't take her pills, life got tough. Longer term neither the pills nor a series of electric-shock treatments seemed able to save her. Although there were short periods when the illness regressed and for a bit she would be our Mum again, I think we sensed the 'good' times wouldn't last. These periods became fewer and shorter. Meantime, during my teens, the rows grew worse, more violent and longer.

When I was about ten, an incident occurred that really frightened me and which highlights the stress we were all under. From time to time I used to get out the old petrol-driven lawnmower and cut the grass. It required a starting handle to get it going and used to puff out large clouds of blue smoke as I steered it across the lawns. However, even if it was a bit much for me to handle I enjoyed the responsibility and used to be engrossed in the work. On this occasion I was happily mowing the grass when two large stones flew past my head and landed in the pond. I was both startled and very frightened and, looking up, saw my Father, clearly distraught and very angry, standing some way off by the house, getting ready to throw more rocks in my direction. So I switched the machine off and ran to see why he was so furious. Apparently he had been trying to attract my attention because he needed me to do something and thought I was ignoring him. Of course, nothing about this incident makes sense now, for if he needed me why not walk over? If I couldn't hear him, it was because the mower made so much noise. At the time I just felt fearful and a bit aggrieved, given that I was only trying to help.

In 1948 Mum became pregnant again and my sister Nickie was born. Nickie was thirteen years younger than Michael (who at this time was away a lot) and eight years my junior. Mum was better for a bit after the birth but then things got bad again. Dad lapsed into his own kind of torpor. I can see him now with his pipe in his mouth, one elbow on the landing window, staring out at the sky for long periods.

Before she left home, apparently on the advice of doctors, Mum would come down in the evenings in her dressing gown. Her face was sad and sunken with over-bright, rather wild eyes and her hair unkempt. She and my Father would start to argue loudly, and I remember on numerous occasions going down and shouting at them to be quiet as I couldn't sleep and had school in the morning. Terrible times.

I had to help out a great deal at home. The weekly grocery order would come from Hawes Bros. and, as one of my household duties I would check the bill against the contents of the box: it usually came to less than £1 for the week. Then, later, I would try to cook the evening meal of which fried kippers (on their own) and chocolate pudding would often be the staples. At some point Nickie would need putting to bed and, in the morning, I would change her nappy and sometimes clean the mess off the side of the cot. I was nine or ten years old with a sick Mum, a struggling Father, no close friends but plenty of absent relatives, trying to cope in a huge Rectory. In today's terms I think I would be called a young carer, and my heart goes out now to all those in the same position.

And yet, despite all this I was a sunny, energetic, even hyperactive child. Because there was not much on offer I threw myself, often impetuously, into anything that came along: choir, Cubs, Scouts, school, sport, even the Church Garden Party. I was eager to be involved in everything and to please.

* * *

Another example of my curious existence was having to be farmed out at regular intervals to be looked after by other people. I know I stayed for a while at the house of the headmaster of the local Church of England Primary School. His name was Mr Adcock, and he once ticked me off for my mischievous (and probably noisy) behaviour in the choir during morning service: 'As your Father's son you should know better!' I got the impression that John Adcock had had, as they say, a good war. His face was brown and leathery with a large nose, which gave him quite a fierce expression. He liked music and when the choir sang an anthem he used to sing tenor solos in a light, quavery voice. His wife was called Doreen (or was it Dorothy?) and was a bit like a hospital matron. I recall her as a large-bosomed, rather intimidating women with her hair done up in a greying bun, who liked to do the right thing.

The Adcocks had two daughters, Jennifer and Demaris, both of whom I fancied and I used to watch them over the churchyard wall when the whole school was out for playtime. So, once when I was lodged with the family, I thought it would be fun to see the girls going to bed (all right, undressing). I therefore hid under one of their beds but Jennifer noticed and told the formidable Mrs Adcock. Thus I was discovered and sent puce-faced and ashamed from their bedroom.

Another time I stayed with the well-off Mrs Murray-Fyson because Mum was in hospital again. This was a carefully regulated and very proper existence as Mrs M-F was a classic blue-rinsed Tory, who was well aware of the class structure and was doing her bit to keep it in existence. Hers was a world in which children went to the nursery and if they weren't there then they 'should be seen but not heard'. I fear I was mostly seen *and* heard.

She had a maid called Annie who wore the standard maid's uniform of bobbed hat, black dress and large white pinafore apron and who served all the meals, as well as doing the cleaning. Meals were announced by a banging of the gong and we always ate in the dining room, with its polished table, napkins and plenty of silver. Knowing what I was like at this time, I would guess these rather adult mealtimes induced me to be both boisterous and overawed. It was the sort of place where people insisted you should have a rest after lunch, but no one ever quite explained why.

The bed I slept in had a scented air (lavender, I expect) and immaculate white sheets with big cosy pillows. The strange thing, however, was that no one thought to send any books with me (picture books that is, since I didn't learn to read till I was eight). Instead, I was given huge, great hard-backed annuals of World War I to look at. Pictures of dead soldiers in trenches and gun carriages madly fleeing enemy shelling were the staple diet of my stay and who knows how they shaped my subconscious. To this day, if I'm reading a detective story in which a country house features I see in my mind the hall, stairs and garden of that house. Thus, at the end, when Poirot or Miss Marple summon the suspects for the denouement they are always brought together in Mrs Murray-Fyson's sitting room.

I'm not surprised I took so long to learn to read. From about the age of six or seven till I went to secondary school I was a bundle of unfocused energy, and I'm sure my concentration level was very low. My writing was (and some say still is) a mess; my spelling was non-existent; and I felt I didn't have time to read. It hardly helped when the family told me I should be reading more (meaning fewer comics) and ticked me off for not getting stuck into Victorian novels such as *Lorna Doone*. I argued vehemently and stoutly against this nonsense and resisted for all I was worth. This long-running argument displayed, in a rather foolish cause, two perfectly good characteristics of mine: determination and stamina.

Another example of my being foisted onto generous (and possibly press-ganged) families was my regular Sunday visits to Charlie Moore's home, behind Hawes Bros grocery. If Mrs Murray-Fyson's was a final glimpse of the wealth and stability that provided maids, well-tended herbaceous borders, croquet and gongs for dinner then at Mr Moore's I just caught the tail end of what 1940s, not very well-off Britain looked like.

For Sunday lunch the Moores always had roast beef, gravy, roast potatoes and Yorkshire pudding. This was cooked on an open range next to the sink against which was a table just big enough for a family of four and me, so, on these occasions, we were all jammed round it using three chairs and a bench seat under the window. That was it – this room was their home in terms of downstairs. The rest comprised two tiny bedrooms accessed via a winding wooden staircase with a door at the bottom, through which I never went. There may also have been a small rocker in which Charlie would read the Sunday newspaper (the *News of the World*, I think) or take his regular Sunday nap. I recall this house (actually this room), as snug, worn, small and full of people and the smell of food.

Outside there was a cobbled yard with tall green gates that were opened during the weekdays to allow the bulk delivery of goods. Also in this yard was the outside loo which had a green door and a peep-hole two-thirds of the way up. I can't be sure if it had a flush mechanism or not but I guess so. I was glad of the food, the warmth and the aura of family at Charlie's, and it never struck me as odd that 'vicar's lad is going to Charlie and Joan Moore's again for lunch'. And that was the point of all this, of course. Nothing was odd. What happened was normal and only as I grew older did I begin to see the curious nature of our existence; how limited it was and that what I was doing, compared with other children, was surviving. These slow realisations only occurred in flashes and when they did I might feel angry or sad, but normal children adjust quickly and, in this sense, I was a normal child.

There was one other great blessing in my life at this time which I believe was a very real antidote to the oddness of our existence and the unhappy background against which I grew up. One of the things that came with our shabby Rectory was a very large and, ultimately, rather rundown garden. But children don't mind a garden being a mess. If it's big enough to turn into the prairies of North America or the jungles of the Far East, that's fine. And the Rectory garden at Elstree was big and, for an eight-year-old, very exciting. It had two big lawns large enough to hold the five or six hundred people who came to the Church Garden Party every summer – plus stalls, tents for the various display artists, Church Army bands, dancing teams and, one year, even a full-size boxing ring.

In addition to the sizeable lawns, there were a couple of shrubberies, two big vegetable gardens and an overgrown pond with an island in the middle. The Rectory also had a small wood attached to it, and a walled garden, next to which was a pigsty with two pigs in it called Hamlet and Bacon (Mike's clever suggestion), and a chicken run which held a fair few Rhode Island Red hens. The stable block backed onto this and had stalls for four or five horses with enough room inside for a carriage to be parked. But the glory of this fabulous play area was the trees. I learnt to climb many of them and was quite fearless in getting as high as I could. My favourite was a huge copper beech that had a rather high first branch but after that was easy to climb. Ever since then the copper beech has been a favourite tree of mine and I'm glad to say the one I climbed is still thriving in Elstree, albeit as part of a residential development. My other special tree was a sycamore which overlooked the 'New Churchyard' (i.e. only fifty years old) and it was great fun to watch secretly from its branches as visitors walked up the path with their flowers and watering cans to visit the graves.

Lansbury, who, officially, was the sexton hired to look after the two churchyards, also did one day a week in the Rectory garden. He was quite young, probably in his thirties, and a personable chap with thick, black Brylcreemed hair. I used to spend a lot of time with him in the holidays and he spun me yarns about how he had killed German sentries in the war by creeping up behind them and strangling them with the straps of their helmets. Of course I believed him and he became a bit of a hero to me. He was also goalie for a local club and in the holidays when I was bored we used to play 'three goals and in' between the trees at the far end of the churchyard. Once we were doing this during the middle of the morning when Lansbury should have been doing some task or other and my Father discovered us. Dad looked disapproving and, though not a word was said, Lansbury abruptly stopped playing and walked off with a guilty look. Despite my youth I knew he had been caught out.

Whatever the arguments going on round me, the old Rectory garden was my absolute delight and when I say 'my' I really mean it was mine. After Mike went off to school I cannot picture anyone else in it. I peopled it with pirates, cowboys, Germans and every villain from the *Dandy*, the *Beano* and old *Chums* annuals that I could muster. I used to wear wellies, an old pair of jodhpurs salvaged from the church jumble sale, a polo neck sweater and a cowboy's yellow neckerchief plus, of course, a holster with cap gun and reels of caps.

And I would set off on my adventures, baking real potatoes over real fires, wading in the pond, searching the horizon from up a tree or building a den which no one could find. That sublime place was (and still in a way is) my refuge. As a boy growing up I sought it out so I could enact my fantasies and create within it another world. So, now, as a grown man, I return to it in my mind for solace when I'm tired or ill or things are tough.

Looking at a black and white photograph of myself aged about nine, I appear jug-eared, freckled and quite impish – just as an energetic lad should be. It's not an unhappy face; rather, it is open and ready for adventure. The pose in the latter picture is quite confident and I confront the camera with a steady gaze.

For all the unhappiness and pain of the Elstree years, I do not now blame my parents. Nor did I at the time. Of course, I got angry with my Mum's inability to care for us and I remember once emptying all the clothes in her chest of drawers on the floor. I shouted at her from time to time and told her how let down I felt. But at heart I knew she was sick, and just occasionally I got beautiful glimpses of the gentle, feminine, kind and generous soul who could have been my Mother. As for my Father, he was, as I have said, sometimes stern, quite Victorian and caught up in black moods, but I knew then, as I know now, that he adored me. That, for nearly every child, is enough.

I believe my Mother and Father gave me the values they thought would serve me in a difficult world, and I have spent my adult years keeping some of these values and, in part, working my way to a different set. That I have done so is not to imply that I have flung back what they offered. On the contrary I sense I am where I am because of what they gave me in good faith. As Sir Isaac Newton said: 'If I have seen further it is by standing on the shoulders of giants.' My parents may not have been giants but they were my Mum and Dad and I hold them dear in my memory.

CHAPTER TWO

The Learning Curve

'Nothing that is worth knowing can be taught'

– Oscar Wilde

After a short period at St Nicholas's Church of England Primary School, Elstree, and a short, unhappy period at a very academic prep school I went to two other schools: first, a prep school in Hampstead, called The Hall, and then, when I was just thirteen, to Aldenham, a boys' boarding school about two miles from home.

Mike went to a prep school in Mill Hill called St George's, which I also attended briefly. He did well there, as he was very clever, and in 1949 he won a scholarship to go as a boarder to Haileybury. I, however, struggled and I can vividly remember being hit by the headmaster's massive Dutch wife for getting my sums wrong. I can see my crumpled and scruffy Maths exercise book with its many hopeless rubbings-out and the splodges where my tears had made the ink run. One day, Mike took me off after school to cheer me up, possibly to see a film, and my parents were frantic with worry, not knowing where we were. Dad beat us for what we'd done which was, I think, the only time he hit me.

I can remember St Nicholas's C of E Primary School in Elstree well. It had high ceilings, block wooden floors, large Gothic-style windows, a coal-burning brazier in the main classroom and row upon row of wooden desks, all with inkwells and lids. The school had outside toilets, a hard playground and large classes. I'm pretty sure we learnt some things such as our tables by calling them out and repeating the same thing over and over again. The school was run by Miss Best, a classic Victorian headmistress.

But (as I found out much later, when I was grown–up) I was dyslexic and it all meant very little to me so I couldn't write very well or spell or do sums; indeed, I might as well have been learning Arabic. I am now passably literate and can think and work things out, but until I was in my mid-teens that seemed a rather unlikely outcome of my education.

That my schooling did in the longer term produce results must, in part, be due to my Father's decision to put me into private education, regardless of the expense. How he afforded it I don't know, and the fact is that I only went to The Hall because Dad's churchwarden was Mr Murray-Fyson, who taught Classics there and was able to secure reduced fees for me. Later there were the fees to meet at Aldenham, but the fact that I was a day boy saved about 50 per cent of the cost (which, if I remember rightly, was about £60 a year). Nonetheless, by the time I came to leave The Hall, Dad was in serious financial difficulty and owed a lot of money, with no house to act as collateral. Sending me to private school caused him much worry and it took years for his finances to recover. In short, he broke the bank to give me a good start and also, I think, to prevent any sense of Mike being given preferential treatment.

I lived in Elstree at the Rectory from our arrival there in 1946, when I was five, until I left school and joined the Army, aged eighteen, in 1959. My existence was very limited by today's standards and family problems contributed to this. But it was home and, though a somewhat wobbly base, being brought up in a Rectory, with its emphasis on church, duty and service, gave me a set of values early on in life, which was no bad thing. My schools also gave me clear values, particularly The Hall (which I entered at the age of eight) and Aldenham.

Thinking about my journeys to The Hall, I can see now that I caught the tail end of a twilight period, in this case wartime Britain, albeit now at peace. It was a time of half-day closing on Wednesdays for most shops, when people worked all week and Saturday mornings as well and office workers wore suits, black shoes and white shirts, coloured shirts being almost unknown till the 1960s. I remember boiled sweets in jars – indeed, nearly all sweets were in screw-top jars – and every bus had a driver and a conductor who gave you a ticket, generally costing threepence (pronounced 'thruppence') or sixpence, from a little wooden hand-held rack with the tickets kept in place by metal springs. Cars, such as there were, were mostly black, the class system was firmly in place and not many women worked. It would have been unthinkable for my Mother, as the Rector's wife, to have earned money, though money was a constant worry to just about everybody, largely because Britain was broke after two World Wars and this was reflected in a general shortage of cash.

On my journey to London in the late 1940s and early 1950s I would pass lots of bomb sites, some of which would remain as unsightly scars until twenty to twenty-five years after the war had ended. Cinema was the major regular treat and queues would form right round the block for good films at evenings and weekends. As young lads we were generally fed on a diet of Westerns, war films and thrillers. The whole programme changed on Thursdays and again on Sundays and for your money you got a main film, plus a 'B' feature and, of course, a Pathé newsreel, which cheerfully and quite incorrectly stated that Britain and the Brits were the best and doing well. I also devoured comics, and used to buy my daily ration from Annie Fields who lived opposite the bus stop. You went into a darkened room by pushing open her front door and there on a table were laid out a host of comics and papers. Annie herself was in another room sitting by an open fire in an armchair with her legs up on a stool. She was (or appeared to be) very old and her legs were swathed in yards of bandage, which was quite a common sight at the time. Whatever her shop was, it wasn't W.H. Smith.

I believed for a long time that being English, singing in the church choir and belonging to the Cubs (later the Scouts) was as good as it got. Nobody I knew ate out; if you did you went to a hotel to be patronised and put in your place by head waiters, who managed to deliver indifferent food as if royalty were in the next room. I never went abroad until I was eighteen, travelling as Second Lieutenant A. S. Wood on an Army troop train across Germany. I hardly recall actually staying overnight in a hotel or catching a taxi until I was well into my twenties, and the first time I watched television on a regular basis was when I was posted to Bovington Camp in Dorset in 1967 and the Officers' Mess had a colour set. By and large I now realise that black and white TV and I hardly ever met. In my youth a telly was something rented by those who had one from Radio Rentals and was pretty much an unknown in our family.

There was merit to the pretty simple existence we had then, but it also contained no end of nonsense. Families spent their time trying to be 'normal' to the outside world. Women had nothing like enough help in the home. This led to lots of drudgery and frustration in a world where there was far less colour than now and I mean literally colour: clothes, cars, houses, streets and homes were, in comparison with today, quite drab. Things were made to last and the idea of throwing anything away was anathema. This approach was nicely encapsulated recently when a friend of ours, clearing out his Father's home, found a tin with a label on it saying 'pieces of string too small to be any use'. To this day I am famous in the family for scraping round jam or marmalade jars so as to collect every last morsel of the contents. I once had a pair of shoes that lasted nearly twenty years.

My journey to school took me from Elstree to Hampstead and back and was quite a challenge. I suppose the whole journey was only fifteen miles in all, but there were no school buses in those days, so it had to be done by foot and public transport and took well over an hour each way. I carried my Mother's yellow leather briefcase full of school books and sports kit on my term-time commute. This took the following course: walk down the Rectory drive to the bus stop; catch a number 141 bus to Edgware tube station; then on the tube for five stops to Golders Green; out to the bus terminus for another bus ride – this time down the Finchley Road to alight at Swiss Cottage with a final five-minute walk to The Hall. In the afternoon I would repeat the process in reverse.

At one point it all became too much and I nearly fainted on the journey home. Somehow I staggered back and was desperately ill for some days with a very high temperature and what may have been polio. If it was, I was lucky to escape because at the time quite a number of young people didn't survive this terrible disease, or were paralysed.

Despite my long journey each day, I continued to buzz round in my usual highly charged, impetuous way: roaring round the playground, throwing myself into sport, chattering in class, smearing my work with blotches and crossed-out wrong spellings. I was cheerful in a rather desperate, merry way, indulging at times in odd activities. For example, one of my more eccentric pastimes after school was to go with friends into John Lewis in the Finchley Road and practise running up the down escalators.

Once my exuberance almost got me into serious trouble. I formed a friendship at The Hall with an American boy called Hank, who invited me to stay one weekend at his parents' house in north London. It was early summer, with the London trees already in bud and the warm air inviting us out to play. Hank knew a bomb site nearby where we could build a den, so the two of us ran down the street. The area had grass sprouting through the concrete and trees forcing their way through the shattered remains of old walls. It had atmosphere, and we explored it happily until we heard the shouts of other boys at play. Suddenly a piece of brick came our way and we realised we were under attack. Of course we retaliated, and my cricketing skills came into good effect, until we heard a howl of pain from our adversaries, followed by shouts of outrage. Clearly one of our missiles had scored a direct hit and they were out to 'get us'. We ran as fast as we could to the wire fence that seemed to be miles away as the boys chasing us got nearer and nearer. I leapt up and was almost over when I felt a hand pulling me back to the ground. When I looked up I saw that in his other hand my captor was holding a rather large knife with which he threatened me. 'Woz it you who threw the stone what hit my brother's head? If so I'll do you.' It was a very frightening moment, as it looked as though he meant it. Although I can't now remember how I got out of the situation the memory of it is still pretty vivid.

Returning to The Hall. I believe it took its name literally from the school hall, which was pretty imposing. It had a balcony all round the first floor from which classrooms radiated out and under this was a painted frieze depicting Victorian propaganda about the creation and retention of the Empire. On my first visit to the school, the headmaster, Mr Wathen (the son of the founder), asked me to identify various people depicted in the frieze. I knew none of them (including, I now realise, Queen Victoria, and Nelson, who is normally a bit of a giveaway). Had he asked me who played right-half for Hendon or centre forward for Arsenal I probably could have told him. Despite my ignorance and unsuitability (he didn't seem fussed about my journey), Mr Wathen agreed to take me at almost certainly reduced fees. So my Father was over a barrel. The only real chance of educating his daffy but loveable son was to send him on a daily commute long enough to daunt a merchant banker, though at much reduced cost. Later, Mr Wathen was to give me three strikes of the strap on my backside, which was the only formal beating I ever had. It did me no good at all and I have never forgiven him.

I use the word 'unsuitability' in relation to myself and The Hall because it was blatantly not the ideal school for me: far too pressured and with many clever boys on the books. In those days, as now, the Golders Green, Finchley and Hampstead areas of London were home to many gifted and well-off Jewish families, quite a few of whom, in my day, must have fled the Nazis. These families often had highly intelligent sons, many of whom found their way to The Hall. With my dyslexic and temperamental disadvantages I would probably have struggled even in a school for 'average' children. At The Hall I found myself up against scholarship material. Looking back at my reports from those days I think it shows.

My long-suffering teachers battled away with me. Mr Earle gave me extra tuition in French irregular verbs in his top-floor Belsize Park flat. What these were; what they did and why they behaved in such a strange way I had no idea. Mr Bathurst, who wore jolly waistcoats and had a Tudor-like pimple in the middle of his forehead, was benign and got me to like history, while Mr Rothwell (Latin and Maths) had a ferocious temper, which displayed itself on a daily basis. Among ourselves we believed it was because he had been bayoneted in the stomach in World War I, and we were probably right. I doubt his temper was improved by my appalling Maths: algebra was a complete mystery to me and geometry revealed that I had no spatial perception whatsoever.

A year before the Common Entrance exam (the passport to entering private secondary schooling) I got zero in a mock geometry exam. Though the years have revealed that I am fairly quick-witted and intelligent, I don't think anyone considered that the thin, twitchy lad behaving badly and talking at the back of the class had anything to offer the world of academia. The system didn't grasp that I was a highly verbal creature who learnt in ways not prescribed by a standard Oxbridge view of the world.

One talent I did have was an ability to sing. Being in the church choir from the age of seven gave me lots of confidence, and I was quite often asked to sing solo. Another of my strengths was that I was very independent-minded. This became particularly clear when I took part in a school debate held, I think, at The Hall in my final summer term. This was a time when Communists were active politically. A recent story in the newspapers had described a young Communist boy who had been told to leave the Scouts as his views were not acceptable. Our debate was as to whether this was right, and I volunteered (for sheer fun, I think) to speak in defence of the boy. I must have spoken quite well, because, to huge cheering, we won the debate. Afterwards the rather earnest and worried master in charge of the Scouts, Mr Earle, sought me out to discover if I actually believed what I had said. I don't know if he was pleased or perhaps more worried when I confirmed that my stance was not at all my own personal view.

Towards the end of my time at The Hall, Dad put me in for the Hertfordshire County Council Open Scholarship. This was an attempt by well-meaning educators to open a path for those who could not afford the fees for a private boarding school. During the process it was agreed my maths was weak (a kind understatement) and my handwriting/spelling needed more work – lots more work. Once again, from a distance of over fifty years, I have to ask: what was I doing having to jump through this kind of hoop? I was in no way scholarship material, nor would a boarding education at an expensive school been a wise move. After the interview, which was probably my best moment, the panel kindly wrote to say that, as I was earmarked for a private school anyway, they would not be offering me a place So I found myself destined for Aldenham as a day boy, which proved to be a very good outcome. A transformation was about to occur.

* * *

My narrow and surprising success as I limped into Aldenham was in sharp contrast to Mike's triumphant academic progress. He not only got a scholarship to Haileybury (where I don't think he was very happy, as he ran away at least once), but also, later, an Exhibition to King's College, Cambridge, together with a state scholarship. At the time King's was the *nonpareil* of the academic arts world, and when Dad got the news of Mike's scholarship to Cambridge I recall him breaking down in tears.

Nonetheless, the move to Aldenham proved to be very good for me, and I blossomed. Aldenham is in Hertfordshire, about twelve miles from London and roughly three miles from Watford. I arrived in September 1954, and my first memory is of the new boys' tea in the headmaster's home. The relatively new head was Geoffrey Mason and tea, which was supervised by his wife Mary (later daringly known as Hairy Mary), consisted of lots of cream cakes and jam doughnuts. The little boy from the Rectory in his herringbone tweed suit (all three buttons done up as was mandatory for new boys) had got off to a good start.

The heart of the school is set round three sides of a fine cricket field including, at the time, five boarding houses and was boys-only, from thirteen to eighteen. In my first year there were 311 pupils, of which only about fifteen were day boys. The myth was that day boys were a waste of space, but in fact our immediate predecessors had made a big impact both academically and in sport, and this view began to run out of supporters as my generation continued the trend. Certainly I never felt like a second-class citizen and, significantly, was neither beaten by the staff nor bullied by other boys in a period when such activities were rife. Gradually, and very slowly at first, I began to do a few things well: acting, sport, debating and the Combined Cadet Force (CCF). This in turn fed into my work, where I started to shine in the subjects that Mike did so well, namely History and English. Success at these 'wordy' subjects perhaps depends less on the retention of facts and more on argument and the use of words. And I was good with words.

Aldenham provided for me an upward, virtuous spiral based on providing opportunities: have a go – have some success – try something else. This seems to me to be as near the provision of an ideal educational system as we are likely to get. I was never 'brainy' or 'an intellect', but because of the confidence I got from doing other things well my work improved term by term. By the time I reached the Lower Sixth (Year 12) I was having a go at almost anything. I became stronger physically; no doubt a ten-minute bike ride rather than an hour's commute helped in this respect. Though the situation at home was often intolerable, I sense I even became happier and I don't think I ever suffered from a sense of low self-worth. So, looking back, my constant enthusiasm for everything school could offer stands in sharp contrast to the feelings of many of the boarders, who, quite naturally, longed for home, some personal freedom and time away from the academic and sporting treadmill.

My approach to school was not typical. But school was for me better than home for at school I could do things – some of them quite well. Consequently, in contrast to the other day boys, I stayed there as long as I could. Up at about 7.30 a.m. I would swallow a quick breakfast and set off down the drive on a much-loved, brand new Hercules bike, for the two-mile ride to school. Dad bought my dark green three-gear pride and joy from Harrods for £13, and I used to clean it every Sunday after tea.

My route took me in all weathers past the house where Charles Dickens used to stay (visiting another secret mistress?), past Aldenham Reservoir; past the farm, past the gates of Aldenham House (now Haberdashers' Aske's Boys' School), past Butterfly Lane and the Battleaxe Pub, then up the slight hill to the school gates, arriving in time for chapel at 8.40. I say 'all weathers' because I was sometimes lucky enough to cycle home on summer evenings when the heat of the day had gone, or at the beginning of a fresh spring day when everything was full of promise. At other times I was perfectly happy crunching along my empty rural byway with snow and frost as my only companions. If the weather was bad I ignored the pelting rain, and if it was good I felt alive three times over.

Cycling could lead to dramas. On the first day of term I found we had forgotten to take my straw boater with all my other kit to the school in our second-hand Austin Seven the day before. So I duly plonked it on my head and cycled off down the Rectory drive. Unfortunately, as I hurried onto the main road past people queuing at the bus stop, a sudden gust of wind caught my brand new 'public school' straw hat and it floated unceremoniously into a puddle. What a lovely easy laugh that was for those waiting patiently to go to work.

A short service started the school day at 8.40 and, if pushed for time, I used just to prop my bike against the school wall and join the hundreds of boys walking along the path to chapel. Quite often I was last in, and it never worried me that I would sometimes enter with more than three hundred people facing me. I wasn't late and hadn't missed the service, so there was no problem. This approach to time-keeping has guided me all my life.

The school day would proceed with a mixture of lessons, sport, hobbies, free time and other activities such as choir, the CCF and drama. Of course, at the end of the day there was also Prep (homework). Prep lasted from 7.00 (after the evening meal) until 9.00, and I always stayed on to complete the day. Thus I wouldn't normally get home till between 9.30 and 9.45, just in time for bed. So my term-time day was regularly 8.00 a.m. to 9.30 p.m.: a thirteen-hour working day. Nor were Saturdays in term-time very different. Chapel on Saturday morning was once again at 8.40, followed by the usual mixture of lessons and sport (and increasingly there were away matches to go to by coach). Then, if there was a debate, a film or a play rehearsal I was always up for any of these, with the result that a Saturday homecoming could be even later than the weekday.

Sunday, it's true, would be different. I still had to go into school, and Sunday Service was at around 10.30 or 11.00 and was compulsory, but when the other day boys used to go home I would to stay for anything that was going, including, or especially, Sunday lunch. School House, which I was in (my 'bit' was called Evens, as opposed to Odds!), used to have a special Sunday pudding made of jelly, custard, tinned fruit and cream. It was served from a huge metal tub and was nicknamed by us 'Baby's Bath'. I envied the boarders their tuck boxes and would hungrily observe boys sitting by their little stores of food, eating tinned fruit. However, that was about all I envied them. The dormitories were spartan, with ten or twelve boys to a room. They had wooden floorboards with wooden, waist-high partitions between beds. A cold-water wash in the morning was the only option, and boys slept on cast-iron beds. My home was hardly luxury accommodation but it was better than that. Boarders in those days got three exeats a term, which meant that they could join their parents for a half-day out after Sunday Chapel. Not a brilliant option if your family came from as far away as Dorset or Yorkshire, which many did. So on Sundays, after kicking a ball around or some athletics training on my own, I would take it easy and go home at about teatime. Then I would do schoolwork, especially during my two years in the Sixth Form, when I had a lot on.

One aspect of my schooling which set Aldenham apart from the state sector was the amount of time made available for sport. We had time for 'Games', as they were called, every day. On Monday and Wednesday afternoons we played a variety of sports until 4.00 p.m., then, after a short break, we had three lessons until 6.30. In the winter the main sport was football. Hockey took over in the spring term, and we had athletics, tennis and cricket in the summer. All year round you could do sailing and squash (a minority sport at the time), or Eton Fives. This is played in a three-sided court with four players wearing special gloves with which they hit a hard rubber ball. On all the other days of the week, Tuesday, Thursday, Saturday and Sunday, you could play sport all afternoon and follow this with some sort of activity or hobby. Friday afternoons were reserved for things military and the CCF/Naval Section.

Given, therefore, that sport was played every day of the week, there was plenty of time to get through the complex system of inter-school and inter-house matches. As there were five Houses it worked out that there were roughly sixty boys in each House. For inter-house games each would be expected to field a junior and a senior team, thereby involving a minimum of some twenty-two boys competitively in major sports, more if you included minor sports. Under the House system there was an opportunity for everyone to get involved, albeit sometimes reluctantly. Athletics, which very much became my major interest, would be a case in point.

An athletics team rarely comprises fewer than twenty people. And, of course, given the nature of the sport, a big, unathletic fifteen-year-old would be more likely to take part in a field event for his junior side, despite the claims of a talented but much younger and smaller new arrival. So, even those with a moderate aptitude for games might get their chance to shine. I'm not extolling here the virtues of competitive games. All I'm saying is that with this system everybody had a reasonable choice to get fit, develop skills and take part in the business of learning how to win and lose. I think we were lucky in this respect.

As for me, so much sport was a godsend. My build, combined with my having inherited Dad's stamina, meant I could keep going. By dint of constant practice, which I loved, I also got better at hand–eye coordination, for I was not a natural ballplayer. At school I played every sport except squash for my House in both the junior and senior competitions. At the same time I also worked my way through most sports for the various school teams: Under 15, Colts, Second XI and First XI but, though I loved my cricket (and still do), when I got older I had a glitch.

At The Hall I was a useful fast bowler and this continued at Aldenham until I became Under-15 captain. Then my form deserted me and I decided that not only did cricket take too much time (all day on a Saturday, for example) but that I was better at athletics. So I stopped playing seriously and together with Mr Barnard, the science master, we founded the school's Third XI. We only played on Saturday afternoons, and as captain my mantra was 'the Third XI never draws a match' – win or lose was our credo. This was some twenty years before the advent of limited-overs cricket!

My best moment came a year or so before leaving school. My House (Evens) was playing McGills in the Senior House Final and McGills had wily left-arm spinner called Peter Rotheroe, who rather fancied himself and his spinning ability. He had a hidden action that was all twists and twiddles, designed to make you think he was good. Well, coming in fifth wicket down I hit him and his buddy for sixty-four in about ten overs including a straight pull for six through the library window. As I type this, I look at the Aldenham School picture on my mouse mat and it shows exactly the pitch I batted on and the window that was on the receiving end of my six. Great.

I was also lucky enough to play in probably one of the best football teams Aldenham has had. In the 1958–9 season we didn't lose a match against another school, and on our tour of Liverpool, competing against much bigger schools, we did really well. That season Ron Greenwood (who later became England manager) brought the Arsenal team to Aldenham for an exhibition match and at some point I wore a real Arsenal shirt for twenty-five minutes. Ron Greenwood had helped the school some years earlier in his role as an FA Youth Coach. He trained our Under -15 team when I was playing left half, and reportedly said that Alan Arthur and I were the best two young half backs he'd seen that season.

So I got my colours for football; captained the Third XI cricket; played in the Seconds at hockey; and ran the mile for the school for two years in succession. I also captained the athletics team and in my penultimate match only missed the record for the mile by two-tenths of a second (4 minutes, 49.4 seconds), which was a pity.

In case all this effort seems easily won and the telling of it a little vainglorious, I would plead not guilty, as the background to all this exertion was still pretty grim. For example, I never took my sports clothes home to be washed as there was no one to do it. The sports clothes stayed rank and sweat-ridden, scrunched up in my wooden sports locker all term. No wonder that during my mid-teens I suffered from regular attacks of boils on my neck. On one occasion I lost my admittedly filthy towel and 'borrowed' someone else's. Unfortunately the owner came in and, recognising mine as his, took it from me, even though it was wrapped round my waist after a shower. Not good, but fairly typical of my housekeeping arrangements. There is a picture of me straining to get round the final lap of a mile race which rather makes the point. My legs are thin; my kit rumpled and my face looks too drawn. I have a rather hollow-eyed look.

I mentioned earlier about cycling to school in the morning, but coming home, especially in the winter, was often more fun. This was because after Prep another day boy called Mike Woods and I used to cycle part of the way home together. There was no lighting at all in our country lane so, come 10.00 p.m., it was a haven for courting couples to snuggle down in their cars. They thought they were out of sight but we were only too happy to disabuse them. At some point we had learnt an oratorio in the school choir containing a chorus which had, we thought, very appropriate lyrics. Starting in unison but breaking into perfect harmony for the last line we serenaded our furtive couples with the words:

♫ ... And to give light

[Pom, pom]

Unto his people

[Pom, pom]

For the remission of their **SINS** ♫

with heavy and lingering emphasis on the last word.

From this distance I can't now separate the various terms of the school year and therefore cannot be quite sure exactly what happened when. As my work improved, I found myself able to take on seven subjects at O-level (now GCSEs). My two best subjects were English (taught by Mr Parren) and History (taught by Chris Wright). I also took French (taught by Mr Stokes), German, Scripture (now known as RE, taught by Mr Stott), Latin (taught by Mr Kennedy, son of the author of the famous *Kennedy's Latin Primer*) and Maths (taught by Mr Fletcher, known as Gaff). The latter two subjects were my weakest. I failed Maths first time round and went on regularly taking and failing it for the next two years. I still don't have the equivalent of GCSE Maths, even though my number skills are not bad. Very strange. As for Latin, I only passed the O-level by one mark and that was a very close-run thing

The teacher who got me through this Roman hurdle, Bill Kennedy, had a strange but hugely effective style of teaching. For the first twenty minutes or so of the lesson he would tell us stories of his time as an infantry officer on the Punjab/Afghan border, where there were lots of skirmishes and daring incidents. Suddenly he would change tack and roar through pages of Latin irregular verbs and pieces of translation. He would finish by setting masses of homework and the standard he required was tough. I wonder what your average school inspector would make of his lessons now, but the fact is that he was brilliant and I doubt anyone else could have got me through.

I prospered in the Sixth Form when I was able to concentrate on my strengths: English and History. I found I was good at remembering quotes and I had outstanding teachers in Donald Parren and Chris Wright. In fact, Fred Clitheroe and I started the English Sixth at Aldenham. Before 1957 English was not on offer at A-level, and we were both the first and only pupils for the next two years. In contrast to Donald Parren in style, but just as stimulating and interesting, Chris Wright set out his stall in our History lessons as a strong socialist in an English public school, and used to engage us with an outrageously left-wing slant to the goings-on of history. We loved it, and learnt a lot as we tried to challenge his approach.

In my penultimate year (1957–8) I also edited the school magazine and enjoyed acting as secretary to the Debating Society.

Being editor of the magazine involved writing three leaders a year, and the best one I did was handed to me on a plate. One morning Donald Parren came to me and said, 'Take a notebook and pen when you go to the lecture hall this afternoon. The Head and Governors are greeting someone called Stanley Spencer. He's an artist and has recently finished a painting to go in the School Chapel. I think you should take down what he says.' What a clever piece of advice that was. Although Spencer was quite well known in the UK at the time, his paintings contained figures with distorted limbs, religious themes and a mantra that God can be found anywhere, 'living in humble places', and were not then that much in vogue. After his death in the 1960s he became even less popular, but latterly opinion on his work has changed and his paintings are now displayed in many leading art galleries.

On this occasion, I dutifully went along and did my best to capture verbatim what Stanley Spencer said that day about his new picture of the Crucifixion, but it wasn't easy. Firstly, he had a very strange way of talking: he spoke quite fast with a staccato delivery and disjointed sentences, which I represented as strings of words joined by dots. Thus: 'Mr Martineau very kind man ... drives too fast ... beauty flashing by ... no good.' Or 'as the choir comes in ... processing ... I saw their open hymn books ... white bird's wings ... beautiful.' The second disadvantage I had in my self-appointed task was Stanley Spencer's physiognomy. He was quite short, and rather gnome-like, so not very much of him was visible above the lectern from which he spoke. He had a grey fringe cut close above his eyes and made quick, urgent movements as he talked. I did my best to catch his words, and my unedited record of what he said that day went out as planned in the form of the leader for the next edition of the school magazine.

There the matter rested until the school hit serious financial difficulties in the late 1970s. In order to prevent the school closing the governors decided to sell the Stanley Spencer. The complete work of art was actually a diptych: two pictures comprising a main one to go behind the altar and another smaller, subsidiary picture to go underneath. The main painting shows the Crucifixion taking place in Cookham High Street, with the cross mounted on a pile of rubble dug up by the gas contractor. I believe the man banging in the nails was a local workman, who died long after Spencer did the painting. The school must have put their Spencer on the market at a time when the artist's reputation was on the up, as it raised £3 million. As a result Aldenham survived and has, I'm glad to report, become a flourishing co-educational establishment for children from the age of three right up to university entry at eighteen, and a small boarding section.

Mr Martineau was the school governor who had originally bought the picture for the Chapel and he paid less than £800 for both the main painting of the Crucifixion and the smaller one. This smaller painting showed worshippers at a service of Matins in Cookham Parish Church at the turn of the century. Speaking of it, Stanley Spencer said, 'and that's my Mother there, with my brother and here is me as a little boy'. So my leader for the school magazine has played a small part in the provenance of this extraordinary work as it identifies the painter as one of the figures in part of his painting. Not long ago, Tate Britain ran a Spencer retrospective, and the picture that we once gazed at each day in morning Chapel was among the fine pieces on show. I sent them a copy of my school magazine article for their records.

During my years at Aldenham I also got very involved in school drama and in class, when we were doing novels like Thomas Hardy's *Under the Greenwood Tree* or plays such as George Bernard Shaw's

The Devil's Disciple. I tended to be asked to read. So from my early days at Aldenham until I left, I performed in many school plays. In 1956 Aldenham put on Ronald Duncan's *This Way to the Tomb*, a special production to celebrate the opening of the New Hall and stage. A photograph of the whole cast and back-stage crew of *This Way to the Tomb* was taken at the time and there I am – stage left, in a wig, pink glasses and black shoes, dressed in a frock and nylon stockings. Yes, folks, it's Miss Philippa Form, American chanteuse and leader of the astral group (whatever that may be) who visit the island of Zante.*

Next was R. C. Sheriff's *Journey's End* which I adapted and put on as a House play. I followed this on Visitation Day by performing the Inquisitor's monologue from Shaw's *St Joan* which, as it extends over two pages, was a bit of a *tour de force*. However, as is sometimes the case, this achievement was soon followed by disaster. I was chosen for the lead role of Khlestakov in Gogol's *The Government Inspector.* Halfway through the play I had to act Khlestakov getting drunk, and this I just couldn't do. No matter how hard Donald Parren tried to demonstrate unsteady steps and a slightly bleary look, I always ended up behaving like some manic rubber doll. Suffice to say with only five weeks to go and having learnt most of the lines I was summoned to the Headmaster's study at ten o'clock one night and thrown out of the play. The manner of this dismissal hurt and I really felt a failure.

Thinking about it now, it's possible that Mr Parren did try to make up for this blow. One day, about two terms before I left, he

* The local paper, the *Herts Advertiser*, wrote up the play quite extensively under the headline 'Large Cast Handled in a Skilful Manner'. 'While I normally dislike applause to disrupt the theme of a play I could not help but agree with the spontaneous appreciation of A. S. Wood's singing spot as the American chanteuse Miss Philippa Form.' That's as may be, but the whole thing played to my strengths. I guess I was a pretty boy (naive might be a better word) and a frock and a handbag easily completed the illusion of being feminine. I have always been able to do a broad, rather annoying American accent and the singing merely extended what I had done in Elstree Church choir since the age of eight.

gave me an envelope and told me that I should use the contents to travel, possibly to Europe and maybe to help some of the many World War II refugees still in camps in Germany and Austria. In those days I was happy to mouth the mild xenophobia with which most English kids were brought up, and I think he wanted me to meet people from other countries. Mr Parren's envelope contained four £5 notes, which was a serious amount, equal to over £300 in today's money. Not knowing what to do with it, I gave it to Dad to look after. I think it was eventually spent on a new suit which I could wear for job interviews.

In the 1950s, as indeed now, Shakespeare was the order of the day for sixth-formers. So I did my bit. First I played Gadshill in a shortened version of *Henry IV, Part 1*, then the lovely role of Mercutio in *Romeo and Juliet*. This was a very enjoyable production, and the only blip was a slight piece of over-acting by me. In the play, Tybalt kills Mercutio with a sword thrust. I managed to portray several emotions before falling to the ground, and uttering loud groans followed by the words: 'I am hurt.' At this statement of the obvious the audience happily burst into a roar of laughter.

My theatrical career at school was rounded off during my final term when we put on our Leavers' Concert, known as the 'The Rec'. This took place between the end of A-levels and the start of the summer holidays, which almost everybody involved remembers as a golden time. As we were almost exclusively a boarding school, all the Upper Sixth stayed on at school after examinations, so we had something like four or five weeks to rehearse full time and put on a good show. There was an orchestra, songs and lyrics were written by members of staff and there were, of course, lots of in-jokes and digs at the teachers. I played the Headmaster – 'Head Ned', it says in the programme, and I believe the Head himself wasn't too pleased with my weaselling speech and cringing interpretation.

So my school days ended in a haze of rehearsals, athletics matches, concerts and end-of-term parties. The thing I remember most from my drama experiences was the sheer fun of it: the ease of learning the lines, the dressing-up and the shock and delight of actual make-up (greasepaint, lipstick and eye shadow all have a particular smell that are foreign to boys). Being able to get up on my feet in front of audiences stood me in good stead in later years.

Learning lines for plays at Aldenham led to my life-long love of poetry and quotations. That gift alone would be enough to justify my five years at the school. Donald Parren taught us in the Sixth Form always to try and support what we said in an essay with examples from the text, and I found no difficulty in recalling these – even under pressure in the exam room.[*]

The poems and the fragments I have by heart are things that last a lifetime. You can turn to them either for solace when things are tough, or in times of joy. It could well be that learning some poetry is a good tool for developing the memory, too. It certainly exercises the brain and, if done in small chunks when we are still young, ought to contribute generally to our development. For example many years later, when I was in Aden putting together a radio show for the Christmas period, I was able to recite the whole of another much-loved poem: Walter de la Mare's mystical *The Listeners*.

Sitting next to my old poetry book is a dog-eared copy of my first dictionary, *Chambers Etymological Dictionary of the English Language*, which I still like to use. It's held together now by black masking

---

[*]   As I write I have my battered copy of *The School Book of English Verse* (edited by Guy Boas) by my side. Inside the fly-leaf it is inscribed 'A. S. Wood 22/Sept/54' and there is a note that reads 'What's our history prep tonight?'. This is linked across to the other page via a huge ink blot to the answer which someone has written in green ink, 'Make notes on Agricultural and Industrial changes 1815 – 850, pp 92–98 and (if time) learn about political reform 1815 – 32'. More interestingly, perhaps, inside the back cover are two inept drawings – one of an aeroplane and other, strangely, of a girl's top and skirt. I still know lines from many of the poems in this book, and The Highwayman by Alfred Noyes and Tennyson's *The Lady of Shalot* were favourites during my school days and still are.

tape, and a badly drawn cat is staring out somewhat mournfully from the front cover. I also see that underneath I have been practising different signatures. As I produce these artefacts from my time at school, I realise that one of my characteristics is to be a bit of a hoarder. I still have my milk teeth and a cocoa bean that I was given when going round the Nestlé Chocolate factory in 1955. Another prized possession from my teens is the plastic comb given to me by Helen Gresford-Jones at the Bishop of St Albans's Christmas party to which all the clergy children were invited!

Another big part of my life at school was the Cadet Corps. Friday afternoon was when the Corps, or CCF, or Combined Cadet Force paraded, and in those days most public schools had a CCF. The Corps was compulsory, and the whole school would therefore be on parade, dressed in tickly barathea khaki uniforms which were generally too large (or, even more amusingly, too tight). No Goldilocks around to say '… and this one is just right'. We wore black army boots plus gaiters and belts which were made of webbing. This had to be blancoed (scrubbed with light-green powder to give uniform cover). Anything leather or brass was polished. Dressing schoolboys aged thirteen to eighteen in all this stuff produced something akin to a Whitehall farce, particularly since the whole outfit was topped off by a floppy black beret, which looked so French that pictures of onion sellers came easily to mind. Still we soldiered on, more or less happily, and wildly energetic boys such as me loved it all. We learnt field craft, how to assemble a Bren gun, the parts of a rifle and so on. Once a term we had Field Day when we ran round Berkhamsted Common, completely lost, firing blank rounds from our rifles and eating our packed lunches by 10.30 in the morning.

I must have taken to all this as during my last year I was made CSM (Company Sergeant Major) which, in terms of the Corps, was senior boy. My forte was acting as drill sergeant and organising the weekly Friday parade. I've always had a loud, clear voice, so giving out orders was easy as long as I gave the command at the right moment. I wore a peaked, officer-style cap and carried a short cane with a silver school badge on the end.

The custom at Aldenham was for you to get a study when you joined the Sixth Form. These had to be furnished with your own kit, which seemed a worry at the time but I raided the Rectory and in the end I was thrilled to get a desk, a comfy chair, a table light and even a radio. It all made me feel very grown up and aware that, in a short while, having somewhere to live would be down to me. A year later, I was sitting in school assembly thinking about nothing in particular when I heard my name called and realised that I had been made a praeposter, or prefect, of which there were only eight or nine in the school. It was a genuine surprise to me as my work was only fair, and I was a day boy to boot. However, I duly donned my regulation black jacket, with a silver tie and flannels, and tried to do the job. Quietly I suspect it did a lot for my confidence.

In those days as a prefect you were allowed to use the 'boying' system, which involved getting younger boys to run errands to help run the school. (Most private schools at the time had a similar system – unfortunately referred to as 'fagging'). If you wanted someone you stood and just shouted 'Boy' and several small pupils would have to stop what they were doing and run to be given instructions. Sometimes, I fear, we took advantage of the system and I well remember when I was down on Cooke's Fields, about five minutes' run from the main school, being greeted by an out-of-breath, pink-faced junior obviously carrying an important message. 'Please, Wood,' he panted, 'Reynolds wants to know whether you want Marmite or jam on your toast.' Clearly a system so open to abuse couldn't survive and nor should it but, with this, as with many other things, my generation caught these final aspects of a lifestyle that was essentially pre-war, and I do not regret their passing.

I was a young member of the Sixth Form. When I left school in June 1959, I was only seventeen years and ten months old. I could easily have stayed on for a third year in the Sixth and taken university entrance. Indeed, my work must have showed some promise as I was sent up to King's College, Cambridge, then the Mecca of the undergraduate world, for an informal interview, which could have led to an official application on my part. King's was known as a thoroughly intellectual place and it seems a strange thing to send a boy who was not particularly academic for an interview there. Indeed, only about 3 per cent of students went to university in the 1960s and strange though it may now seem, at schools like Aldenham nobody ever mentioned that there were universities besides Oxford or Cambridge. I, like my friends, genuinely believed that after leaving school you either went to one of these haunts of academia or you got a job.

I imagine that the reason I didn't stay on for a third year in the Sixth Form was that my Father's financial troubles were so dire at this time that he had to cut his expenses; a further year of school fees was not on. Besides, Dad didn't really think a degree was necessary and this, coupled with the fact that he and my undergraduate brother were not getting on, rather settled the decision.

And so my days at Aldenham drew to a close. I look back on the school, the staff, the lovely grounds and buildings with great fondness and gratitude. Although my domestic background was tricky, and although I never distinguished myself academically, I was so involved in everything that life at school passed happily and I grew immensely as a person. I didn't, sadly, make any lifelong friends as some people manage to do, but that was probably due to the generation we belonged to and my home life. However, as I recall it, I got on with most people and had no serious problems with other boys. With one or two fellow pupils like Mike Woods, Percy Vydra, Gerry Beecham, Peter Vaux and Chan Kwong, I had closer friendships, but by the spring following my final year I was effectively out of the country for eight years, so the chances of keeping these links were pretty slim.

The fact is, I think I was lucky to be in a relatively small school, which gave me the chance to have a go at lots of things. Nor did the size of Aldenham mean that its standards were low. We got our Oxbridge scholarships; competed with pretty well everyone at sport and held our own with most local private schools in such things as music and drama. So for me small was indeed beautiful.

There was one incident from my schooldays that I felt at the time was quite unusual, and still do. One summer evening I was cycling back from school, and nearly home. My journey took me past a bridle gate at the bottom of Hunt's Fields, from where you could look up and see the spire of St Nicholas's Church, Elstree, silhouetted against the setting sun. It was very quiet, very rural and the only sound was of the birds singing. Briefly, very briefly, I had a premonition of some benign spiritual force looking after me. It was only transitory but it was both powerful and beautiful. As Julian of Norwich prophesied: 'And all shall be well and all manner of things shall be well.' As I look up from writing these words I can see a picture painted by our friend Gina Fermer on the sitting-room wall with those very words inscribed round it.

CHAPTER THREE

Three Ladies, the Church and Me

'Hey ho, if love were all'

– Noël Coward

It's impossible to think of Elstree without thinking of church life. I was a true son of the manse, with all the connotations that phrase carries. When my Mum was well, we went to church every Sunday. As you would expect, my Father performed all the usual duties of a priest: writing sermons in his study, calling in on parishioners, visiting the sick, taking services including marriages, baptisms and funerals, organising the annual Garden Party and producing the church magazine. Every month I used to help bundle copies of the magazine up into packs for delivery. Dad taught me a clever way of breaking string without using a knife – a trick he had learnt during a spell working in a warehouse.*

My joining the church choir at the age of eight meant that church-going increased to twice on Sundays: Matins in the morning (this eventually became sung Family Communion), then Evensong in the evening. Together with compulsory chapel during term-time this meant that I was steeped in the liturgy, dogma and practices of

---

* I'm afraid I now can't remember how this neat piece of work was done save that it involved twisting the string back on itself and giving a sharp tug.

the Church of England, so even now if a hymn is being sung I find I know many of the verses without looking at the book. However, I am immensely glad that my young sensitivities and easy acceptance of religion didn't lead me to becoming a vicar. My Father, though respecting my seriousness about spiritual things, quietly discouraged me from a clerical vocation, and my life in the Army opened my eyes to the narrowness of the view I had imbibed.

On the other hand I'm sure Dad's Mother, Granny Wood, would very much have encouraged me to pursue such a vocation as the Church was very important to her. Granny (Bessie Wood) must first have come into my life when we were living in Bredon, near Tewkesbury. While Dad was in India, my grandfather, Mark Stuart Wood, and Granny were lodging in Bredon Rectory, which was built in 1430 as the Summer Palace of the Bishop of Worcester and was enormous. Brother Mike remembers Mark Wood preaching at Evensong as a lay reader, which he (Mike) looked forward to as Grandpa had false teeth and used to do whistling s's because his dentures didn't fit! He died from a heart attack in 1945 and is buried in Bredon Parish Churchyard.

My next recollection of Granny after our Bredon days is when she fell on hard times and came to live in draughty old Elstree Rectory. This must have been in the late 1940s, when she would have been over eighty and I picture her dressed in black. She used a walking stick with a handle carved in the shape of an elephant's head, complete with small ivory tusks. She used to read to me under the apple tree. I think I annoyed her by always asking for the same rather trite stories about sportsmen who failed initially and then triumphed. Granny would have preferred me to have read something more improving and, as people did with young children at the time, told me so.

Granny was essentially an ascetic who preferred simple and probably poor living conditions. I suspect her tastes were somewhat puritan and that faith was much more important to her than love. She drank the water the cabbage was boiled in, which, she claimed, prevented arthritis; went for long walks at a great age, and everybody told me how wonderful she was, which I didn't get at all. Now that I know more about her life, though I admire her I have to say that I do not share many of her views.

Bessie Bryans was born in 1867 into a rich, titled and locally influential family; her Mother was a member of the Antrobus family.* Granny was both very beautiful (I have a picture of her in her twenties with her sister) and very determined. Too determined for her own good, I suspect, for when she was in her early thirties she became a missionary in Africa (not a job for faint-hearted ladies) and preached the gospel in the Dark Continent. According to her memoirs, she was a teenager when she first saw Mark Stuart Wood (then aged eight), fell in love and vowed to marry him. Much later on, when he had become headmaster of a large private school in South Africa she followed him out and, against the wishes of the family, married him in Pietermaritzburg Cathedral in 1901, when she was thirty-four years old. By this time I imagine the Boer War must have moved up country, otherwise I don't see how the marriage service could have happened.

Granny's family were angry at the marriage and in retaliation cut her off. Thus, in the classic way, an important source of material comfort and security was lost for ever. After they had moved back to England Bessie and Mark had five children, of which my Dad was the second youngest. For the next twenty or thirty years Mark

* One member of the Antrobus family was reputed to have been Queen Victoria's personal private messenger in Europe and since Queen Victoria was related to (and in her view in charge of) most of the crowned families of Europe he must have been pretty busy galloping all over the continent.

Wood continued to lose money in various enterprises and to have a series of adventures. At one time, he and Granny bought a farm at Over Peover in Cheshire, but had to give it up as Grandpa proved to be a poor farmer. The only pictures I have seen of Mark Wood show a short, very dapper man with highly polished shoes who, frankly, looks a little dodgy.

Granny was a strict moralist and very devout. The story goes that she read the Bible in Greek each morning and as a result forgot to stir the porridge; when her children pointed out that it was burnt she insisted they ate it with the classic line: 'Eat it up. Suffering breeds character.' Her memoirs tell of a vision she had while in the mountains in Europe, which I guess in some way explains the depth of her religious convictions. She used to forbid me to play cards or read on a Sunday. Pubs were off-limits for our family at any time and the implication was that people who went into such places were 'the undesirable element'.

Two things sum up Granny's approach to the world: the one physical, the other a matter of mindset. I can clearly recall being shown that if a piece of toast got burnt you didn't throw it away and make another one. No, it was solemnly scraped with a knife so some of the carbon went into the sink and a brown/black piece of toasted bread with whitish bald patches was served up. What was this all about? Frugality, I guess. I fear also that part of Granny's mindset was an attitude akin to veneration for people of a certain class and breeding, or members of a profession of which she approved. I think this approach was pretty general among the middle classes at the time. Granny's excuse for her husband's infidelities, for example, was that he was 'led astray by wanton women'. This was convenient as it meant neither he nor she was culpable, and hence he could happily continue preaching at Evensong.

No one seemed to make the connection between the state of genteel poverty in which our family existed and the fact that my aristocratic great-grandparents seriously disapproved of their daughter marrying a teacher when she was thirty-four, an age when they presumably felt she was getting too old for marriage. However, in terms of handling life's challenges, having aristocratic relatives and a blood line which went back in a few generations to the Royal Family and ultimately Henry VII was no help to us.

So, perhaps, a rather unflattering portrait of one of the few relatives I knew well. Tough, saintly, determined, intelligent and beautiful, with very clear values, she oversaw an extended family (of which my own family was part) that gradually disintegrated. To be fair, two World Wars and a severe economic recession hardly helped, and I think both Granny's generation and that of my parents lived through most demanding times. Bessie Wood ended her days in an old people's home up Bushey Lane called The Lees, in a very nice area just outside Elstree. I remember going there on 6 June 1953 to watch the Coronation on a quite small black and white TV, surrounded by all the old ladies. I must have lowered the average age by about seventy-five years!

Granny wrote a brief memoir in five old school exercise books (very thrifty) and much of what I have written here is taken from these. At the end she writes, 'and if I had my time again I would like to go back to Eaton Hall to have dinner served by the liveried servants and see the candlelight flickering in that lovely room'.

And so to two other important women who were very much part of my life in the 1950s. Just after I had started at Aldenham (in 1954, when I was thirteen) my Father took a locum in a little village called Winkleigh in the heart of rural Devon; a locum, or parish swop, being an easy way for hard-up clerics to have a holiday. In return for taking the occasional service, clergymen and their families could exchange parishes for a period during the summer holidays. I don't recall much about the two weeks in Devon except that at one point I sampled the local scrumpy and with the help of a little acting put on a consummate performance imitating one of the locals rolling home drunk down a steeply banked Devon lane.

The high point for me was meeting up with a local girl called Margaret Cooper. I don't really know much about Margaret, which is strange since we wrote to each other for the next five years and I met her twice more. She sent me two photos of herself (black and white, of course), in one of which she is wearing a fairly glamorous dress with a black shawl and high heels, standing outside her Mother's bungalow. To my eyes she seemed both very attractive and grown up; mind you in those days most people would have appeared grown up compared to me.

The other photo is of Margaret sitting on a Devon beach in a dark one-piece swimsuit. Though the pose is not suggestive, to my young eyes it was all very enticing. I knew no other girls and to have regular letters from someone I thought of as a far-off beauty was sweetly romantic and rather special. Like any healthy male, I fantasised over this lovely girl who seemed to think I mattered, and maybe this very platonic but powerful relationship was good for me as I grappled with the difficulties of growing up.

Women, sex and relationships are hard enough for any young lad to cope with, but they could produce quite a troubled person when overlaid with the Church's teaching in the 1950s about abstinence and no sex before marriage. I do think the modern view on these issues is much healthier, and had it been prevalent in the 1950s and 1960s it would have helped me avoid much heartache and worry. I must add that eventually I sorted myself out and was significantly helped in this by the Army's altogether red-blooded view of these matters. In particular, I noticed that my soldiers suffered no qualms about such things and were perfectly happy to ask me cheeky questions about my sex life and what I was doing about someone I 'fancied'.

I saw the good Margaret only twice after that holiday when we cycled the Devon lanes and talked endlessly about the future. At some point I travelled down to Devon and met her in Exeter one evening after she had finished her work as a part-time waitress. I can't recall what we did or where we went, but we finished up late that summer evening in a park overlooking Exeter station. To this day I associate this station and the sound of steam trains shunting and hooting (all quite Freudian!) – with the first fumblings of early love and, in my case, passion. After lots of intense kissing I put my hand tentatively on her breast, only to have it gently removed. My reaction to Margaret's kind (and probably sensible) response underlines the fact that I hadn't a clue what I was doing or why. Nor did I understand that I was involved in the age-old game of courtship, where each move carries its own counter-move; 'sexual politics' was a phrase I first learnt twenty or thirty years later. Suffice to say, I felt abashed, somewhat foolish, untutored and (hateful word) 'dirty'. Clearly I had a lot to learn and none of this reflects on Margaret.

I last saw Margaret shortly after I was commissioned in April 1960. I was on leave, preparatory to going out to the Regiment in Germany. My mind was preoccupied with military life and the excitement of going abroad for the first time, so I fear I was in no fit state for an incipient romance. We met in a café in Villiers Street, near the Charing Cross Hotel, and I suspect the conversation was desultory. Margaret was, I think, going off to train as a teacher, and we talked about her coming out to Germany some time, with the vague feeling that this was unlikely. And so we parted and my early romance was over. She was a lovely girl and I have no idea what she saw in me, but I'm glad she saw something.

Why didn't I get off my backside and catch the train and go and see her, certainly later in our romance, when I was in the Sixth Form? The answer to this tells you a lot about middle-class kids and their relationship with adults in those days. First, there was no money. (I didn't get pocket money nor did I have regular earnings of my own, which seems rather pathetic now.) Secondly, as a teenager in the 1950s, you didn't just walk out of the house saying, 'Bye, I'm off to Devon for the week'; if you did there would have been an almighty row. Quite apart from the small matter of where I would stay, children of my age and background existed in a climate where things were organised for you. Adults decided schools, subjects, friends and, up to a point, your job, and our generation mostly had to go along with it. We knew nothing else.

I said this chapter would include three women. The arrival on the scene of Anne Wood, as she became, was an important turning point in our family's unhappy saga, and for me personally. At the time of our first meeting, Anne was holding a demanding job as Nursing Sister on Bland-Sutton Ward at the Middlesex Hospital, then one of the top five hospitals in the UK. This was the male post-operative ward and many seriously sick people straight out of the operating theatre were in the care of her and her team. Hospitals then were much more hierarchical than now and everybody wore a uniform of some sort. The gods were consultants, then the housemen, followed by the matron, with 'Sister' as the most senior person on the ward in the terms of day-to-day efficiency.

Anne's family were parishioners of my Father, which is how we met. I can picture Anne and I standing talking in our uncarpeted, rather scruffy hall, I with my coat still on, having just returned home. Anne showed a real interest in my life at school and my activities, and I felt that something different and special was happening as we talked. From that time on she really became my 'fairy godmother' and I told her so. After my Mum died, Anne brought a caring, feminine presence plus a degree of order to the Rectory, and two years later she and Dad were married. She made him very happy and solved many of the family's problems – not least the small matter of Dad's significant debts. She did this not only through her ability with money but by becoming a working vicar's wife, which was quite revolutionary for those days. As a highly qualified nurse, she was able to get the job of nursing adviser on *Emergency Ward 10*, the large-audience television soap opera of the time, shot live each week at Elstree Studios. The money was good, and from then on things got better and better for them both, which was wonderful.

Not that it was all plain sailing. When Annie and Dad married she became my stepmother, and we know from both fiction and history what a tricky relationship that can be. Despite the huge improvement Anne's presence brought us, I almost certainly resented her. I remember a row we had when my Dad wanted me to say how wonderful it was that the food cupboard now had packets and tins in it. My response, I fear, was churlish and along the lines of 'anyone can go into a shop and buy some stuff', which wasn't very gracious. Later, while on leave, I recall an argument about whether I had lent or given my Father and stepmother a small radio. I had been dismissive about the set, left it behind in the Rectory for them to use, and a misunderstanding ensued. But I only tell these anecdotes in the context of the amazingly good relationship Annie and I have built up over the years. As these relatively trivial stories show, it is not easy taking on an argumentative, independent-minded, only partially house-trained stepson. That we avoided nearly all the pitfalls and are now so close is very much due to Anne, and I love her for everything.

Anne's kindness, thoughtfulness and love gave me the hope that things could improve and a reminder of what the feminine influence brings to a home. And this thoughtfulness continued. Not only did Anne help financially with my fees at Aldenham, but she generously helped with other school fees in later years. In particular, when she retired she gave us all (not just a bit) of her the lump-sum payment, which would otherwise have been part of her pension.

I had grown up in a home where the Mother was more or less permanently ill or absent. My sister Nickie was eight years younger than me and therefore just ten years old when I went to Germany. My education after the age of nine was at a boys' prep school, followed by almost total immersion in a boys' only boarding school, albeit as a day pupil. From leaving school until I was twenty-eight I would be part of the semi-monastic, men-only life of an officers' mess, mostly based abroad. You may therefore imagine that my understanding of women, sex and (much more importantly) love was minimal. In this I was not unlike many men of that time from backgrounds like mine. Looking back, I pity any girl who found herself the recipient of my naive, over-energetic fumblings.

Despite being reasonable healthy, young and with my own teeth I really didn't do well with girls for some time. It must have been clear to them that this keen and impetuous youth had no idea that there was a person attached to their fine cleavage or lovely legs. Most sensible girls quite reasonably object to being 'used', and I fear I was my own worst enemy. I learnt a bit during my time in Germany from the occasional trip to the Bruchstrasse in Braunschweig – convenient and well organised in terms of health and hygiene, as the Germans tend to be in these matters. However, one or two limited and anonymous liaisons there left me more sad than happy and I had the sense to see quite quickly that this wasn't the way forward.

While my sex education languished, I became that most annoying of creatures: the young man who doesn't quite see the point of love, marriage or, by implication, home – and said so! I had made a decision to become a soldier, was dedicated to the Army and declared that I would fulfil myself via the military. For my youthful, rather disdainful, attitude to change it would need a very remarkable girl to come along. Fortunately for me she did, and my views now are very different.

CHAPTER FOUR

Joining the Front Line

'Every man thinks meanly of himself for not having been a soldier'

– Samuel Johnson

'How can I live among this gentle, obsolescent breed of heroes and not weep?'

– Keith Douglas (poet and cavalry officer, killed in 1944, shortly after the D-Day landings)

After the war, an essentially bankrupt Britain still believed it had an Empire to run and a peace-keeping force in Germany to maintain. The Empire role turned out to be a slow, somewhat painful but nonetheless supervised withdrawal, in which I later took part. In Germany, however, we were better placed. Britain was committed to NATO and the rest of Europe to maintain a standing army (BAOR – British Army of the Rhine) of 55,000 men indefinitely. If we reckon that today the whole of the regular Army is less than 90,000 personnel, you can see what a serious commitment this was. We garrisoned the north of what was then West Germany (Hamburg, Bonn, Düsseldorf, Hanover and other cities in the area) while the Americans looked after the larger and more beautiful south. The French also had soldiers posted in West Germany, and all three countries (as well as Russia) shared responsibility for Berlin, about 150 miles to the east down a narrow corridor of autobahn. This ran across Eastern (Russian-occupied) Germany, where massive Russian and East German forces were stationed. This was all part of the Cold War, and everyone seriously believed in the possibility of an attack by the Eastern Bloc, using tanks to race across Europe. There was the sense of a proper job to be done, and the locals very much saw the point of having foreign troops stationed on their soil.

None of this was very clear to me when I applied for a Direct Short Service Commission (DSSC) in the summer of 1959. The DSSC was a new idea. Up to that point, the only way to become an officer was to go to Sandhurst for two years of training. This, it was said, equipped twenty-year-old second lieutenants to run a brigade of about 3,000 soldiers, while their actual first command on being commissioned would be about thirty 'squaddies'. This in-depth training would suit career officers who were intending to stay in the army till they were fifty-five years old. But, in reality, while the Army needs lots of subalterns (junior officers), it only needs a few brigadiers and generals. It was necessary for people to start dropping out at quite an early age in order to create the classic pyramid shape of a few people at the top and lots beavering away at the bottom. Therefore the DSSC was brought in with the intention of giving us six months of training followed by two and a half years of commissioned service. Then we had the choice whether to leave or stay on. It's interesting that I never considered the idea of two years at Sandhurst. Perhaps I knew that the military wouldn't be right for me for ever – not a bad instinct given my relatively unformed personality.

The DSSC was run from Mons OCS (Officer Cadet School) so that is how on 18 October 1959, having passed a selection board, I came to be travelling to Aldershot to take an Oath of Allegiance to the Queen. Having signed my Attestation papers, I was given the number 464803 and sent along to one of the many Nissen huts which made up the camp to draw my kit from the quartermaster.

The point about Mons was that up to this time it had only dealt with National Service would-be officers. In order to maintain our numerous post-war military commitments around the world, Britain used conscription which required men between the ages of seventeen and twenty-one to serve in the Armed Forces for eighteen months. These soldiers were cheap, could be stationed in old, run-down camps with generally poor food and the Army I joined in 1959 still consisted largely of these 'pressed' men. Understandably, very few of them wanted to be there, whether as officer cadets or ordinary soldiers. They had homes to go to, careers to pursue and no wish to fight anyone, anywhere. Morale was therefore very patchy, but despite these misgivings many men did their best and got from National Service what they could.

That first issuing of kit gave me some inkling of the immediate future. The items we got were so cheap and poorly made I couldn't believe it. Children's plimsolls (soft gym shoes) in men's sizes, hairy shirts, trousers that were too big, berets that needed shrinking and for each of us a rough canvas holdall, called a kitbag, which functioned instead of a suitcase. I suspect the best quality item were the boots (with metal heels and toes for drill) but these had to be 'bulled' into a highly polished state, so the very tough leather was, in this case, a mixed blessing. Bulling your boots was something we were required to spend hours doing. One tin of black polish with the lid upside down and full of water. One yellow duster balanced on the end of your index finger. Having spat on the toe of the boot, you then applied innumerable combinations of water, polish and spit, all the time going round and round in small circles with the duster, hence the sobriquet 'spit and pol'. You just carried on doing this most evenings for two or three hours at a time.

Because Mons was designed to assess, train and discard National Servicemen wanting to acquire officer status, it was the classic sausage machine. However, in this case its purpose was not, as you might think, to produce as many sausages as possible, quite the opposite. Far more people applied from the ranks to be officers during National Service (well, you would, wouldn't you?) than were needed. The aim at Mons was to throw out as many people as possible as soon as possible and not waste valuable training money.

There was no subtlety in the system used to achieve this end, which was based on two approaches. The first was to make most of the day, and quite a lot of the night, as unpleasant as possible, so that after a couple of weeks of hell people would say: 'blow this I'm going back to being a lance corporal'. The other approach was to have a series of tasks, tests or grades that you had to achieve. If you failed to meet your targets you could either be put back a month or RTUd (Returned to Unit). I can't remember clearly the hoops we had to jump through but they must have consisted of fire arms competency; a given standard of drill; physical fitness tests; and extras such as being able to jump off a ten-metre diving board into the deep end of the Aldershot swimming pool. Though my memory of these tests is incomplete, I have a much clearer recollection of the methods used to make each day very long and very tiring and to make the individual feel deeply inferior. From hour one on day one it was clear that the world did not hold a lower form of life than the officer cadet.

For a start you ran everywhere, 'at the double', as the drill sergeants had it. You were rushed everywhere, from PT (physical training) to map-reading to small arms training to drill and then back to PT. To change for PT you were given two minutes and the same at the end, having also stood for twenty seconds under a lukewarm dribble called a shower. Too slow and you had to do ten press-ups. If anything went slightly wrong, a big, horrible, hairy face would come within six inches of you swearing and shouting as though you had been discovered plotting to murder the Queen.

Sometimes all this got a little absurd. As a squad we weren't that good at drill manoeuvres, which caused the (Irish Guards) sergeant in charge of us much displeasure. He had to get us up to standard and ready to march off as officers at the next Commissioning Parade, which was only a matter of weeks away. Woe betide him and his confidential report if we didn't make it in the eyes of Regimental Sergeant Major 'Noddy' Lynch, who was a physically dominating, loud-voiced barbarian of an Irish Guardsman. I suspect not bright, but very traditional, and a man to fear in the way that a mafia boss is feared.

The winter of 1959-60 was particularly cold so, as we marched onto the drill square (sacred ground to Guardsmen), we could see our breath and the tarmac beneath our steel-tipped boots was either frosty or icy, and possibly both in some places. That day our drill instructor decided to march us around the square at a pace so fast he could hardly get the words out.

'Left, right, lef', righ', lef', ri', l', r'... HALT. You', he said coming up close to me, 'you lost the step, you useless...'

Back came my voice, uttering a piece of ill discipline so revolutionary that I still can't believe I did it. 'I'm sorry, I answered (totally unforgivable),'but I'm doing my best.'

This so stunned the instructor that he couldn't think of anything to say other than to shout, 'Squad, quick march'.

The bane of my life was not this routine of harassment and uncalled-for abuse. No, it was the extra work we had to do on top of a day that stretched from 6.00 a.m. to 10.00 p.m. – flat out. Every day we were inspected, looked up and down and our uniform checked for cleanliness and smartness. For some reason that I never quite fathomed, my kit was regularly found to have some blemish. Hairs on my beret, dirty belt brasses, poorly polished boots, badly pressed trousers – the possibilities were endless and as soon as I had righted one wrong another appeared. Now the punishment for being 'idle on parade' was extra drills. This meant that at the time when everyone else was settling down to prepare for the next day I and other members of the criminal fraternity – or 'the untidy brotherhood' as we might better be described – were marching stiffly down to the drill hut on the parade ground to be inspected – yet again and drilled till about 8.00 p.m! Then back to the billet to try and catch up on lost time. I say we marched stiffly because moving in highly polished squeaky boots in a uniform that appeared to have been made out of old blankets, while trying not to touch anything that had been polished or blancoed made us look like toy soldiers who had recently come out of the deep freeze.

To be honest, these extra parades were a nightmare and I don't know why I put up with it all. I wonder why I didn't consider leaving; though, of course, a potent factor was that I knew nothing else. I had volunteered to become an officer, and maybe I thought each extra would be the last. I had no idea what I would do if my attempt at working in the Army failed (and I hated the thought of being in an office). I have a cussed streak which means that I don't give up easily and I would have had a sense of shame if I just dropped out. Above all, the problem was that I had no idea how to work the system and give myself a break.

Earnest, determined and naive, I ploughed on in the touching belief that if I genuinely jumped through every mad hoop the authorities asked of me somehow I would accumulate points in the great military lottery. What I really needed to see me through was a wise old 'uncle' by my side whispering, 'Bit of a twinge in the ankle there, son, better see the Medical Officer', or 'Both grannies still alive? Time for a bit of compassionate leave, my boy'. But there was no one like this around, and I ploughed on, determined not to give up or let the side down. Thousands of young boys took the same qualities as these to excess and, as a result, got mown down in World War I. In a sense, I suppose I was just another product of a certain type of English upbringing and went along with the system.

Another part of the process was that everything we had was inspected each morning. Every day the hut floor had to be polished; all the shelves dusted; every cupboard opened and we stood to attention by our black-painted iron beds. The trickiest bits were to get the iron stove in the middle of the hut gleaming and to create a 'bed block' by carefully folding our blankets one on top of the other and then wrapping the sheet (singular) tightly round them. The stove was a challenge because on cold winter evenings it was full of red-hot coke doing its best to heat twelve tired officer cadets. Thus, in order to blacken it, polish it, and paint it (yes, paint it), someone was deputed to get up at four in the morning to put the fire out. By six it was therefore cold enough to begin work on. I shall never forget the *coup de grâce*. Each day shortly before the Inspecting Officer arrived one of us would sit on a stool, artist's paint brush in hand and slowly outline in white paint the immortal words embossed on the door: 'Do not fill stove above fire-brick level'.

On the morning of one inspection, I thought my bed block was looking rather neat and soldier-like, placed carefully as it was at the head of the bed. The whole edifice lay like some piece of woolly layer cake on top of a green under-blanket, which remained in place covering the mattress. Maybe my bed was a good attempt but it didn't save me. All our green under-blankets had a dark line down the middle which was supposed to be straight; unfortunately the officer decided mine wasn't.

'This blanket is not on straight, Sergeant.'

'Very good, Sir,' came the reply.

'Officer Cadet Wood – idle bed.' This meant extra drills. The concept of beds being by their very nature idle was no help to me, as the Army at this stage in my career was not given to an undue amount of metaphysical thought.

Incidentally, there is a famous story which illustrates the kind of nonsense caused by over-inspection, as well as the essentially unthinking nature of many drill sergeants. At Sandhurst, an officer cadet was deemed to be wearing a belt which was too loose. This was noted and the inspection went on. After a while the officer came back down the ranks and unwittingly stopped by the same officer cadet, but this time behind him. 'Loose belt here Sergeant,' he murmured. 'Very good, Sir,' barked the NCO. 'Loose belt ... back and front!'

As potential officers, when out of uniform we had to wear Army-issue white gabardine raincoats, cut in a riding style. These were often too big for us, and thus wearing one was like being enveloped in a small, lumpy and very heavy tent. A hat was obligatory, so you could raise it in acknowledgement of any soldier who saluted you. Most young officers had the sense to invest in a raffish trilby (à la Humphrey Bogart) or what were known at 'ratting caps' of the checked variety worn by race-goers and horse breeders. In a foolish attempt to save money I finished up with a cheap, green corduroy thing, which had the peak sewn upwards into the main part of the cap. It made me look like a lorry driver.

Picture me now on a dark winter's evening about eight o'clock on a Sunday arriving at Aldershot station after twenty-four hours at home, white-faced and wearing my odd hat and issue raincoat. I fear my spirits were low as I moved to the exit to await the duty truck and another punishing week at Mons.

In November we all had to give mini-presentations (what the Army called 'lecturettes'), and I remember the one I did was on the Christmas shopping rush, based on a cutting on spending statistics I had found in *The Times* and which I still have. My other safe stand-by if lecturettes were in demand was a five-minute talk on Stokesay Castle, a fortified medieval manor house just outside Shrewsbury. I still have the postcards and photos I used for this party piece.

At some point in the training cycle I did actually get ill and was taken to Aldershot Military Hospital with flu and a very high temperature. I recall it as a grim place but nonetheless it was a very welcome break from basic training and the endless cycle of drill, PE, weapons instruction, map-reading and the rest. Knowing me, I doubt I took sufficient advantage of this genuine illness to 'buy' myself a proper break.

But, as they do, these tough days passed and after about four months I found myself in G Squadron. This signalled the end of our basic training as foot soldiers and the start of 'specific to arm' training. G Squadron was the place for all those destined to go into the Cavalry or Tank Regiments and was reputed to be quite civilised. No more standing on freezing shooting ranges jamming the rifle butt into your already bruised shoulder and wondering how much colder the metal bits could get as you waited to fire five rounds across the snow and ice towards a wooden target 200 yards away. There was very little, if any, drill and a consequent absence of aggressive drill sergeants. We also got inspected a good deal less, which was a relief. However, life was still tough. By this time about half of our original intake had been sent away and would complete the rest of their National Service as NCOs. Despite G Squadron's deserved reputation for a degree of sanity and reasonable behaviour, it was reckoned to be more demanding about those whom it commissioned than almost any other part of the Army. The emblem of the Royal Armoured Corps is a mailed gauntlet, but maybe it would have been more accurately displayed within a velvet glove.

The truth is that I was still struggling to make the grade. I would do silly, awkward things like saluting an officer when I had no hat on (not done in the British Army); angrily accusing a storeman of stealing a piece of kit which had been issued to me and gone missing; failing to see how two armoured cars could be used as a road block, or regularly getting lost. I was clearly a borderline case. The story goes that after I had indulged in a particular piece of foolishness I was discussed by Trevor Morris and 'Dingo' Stevenson. These guys were not only G Squadron Officers and part of the selection process but also QDG (Queen's Dragoon Guards) officers, who would have a particular interest in anyone earmarked for 'the Regiment', as I was. Dingo was saying that he didn't feel I was mature enough to be commissioned. Trevor wasn't sure. Apparently his wife, Caroline, had met me at a drinks party (where the cadets served rather than consumed the drinks) and found me 'rather nice and quite charming'. So that was it. Thanks to Mrs Caroline Morris, my boyish smile and the British Army's eternal tolerance of foolish young men who might one day make something of themselves, I wasn't slung out. Down the years I salute the good Caroline, though I also like to think that in due course I paid her and the Regiment back in good measure.

At this early stage in my training, however, I suspect I was seen as immature, argumentative and a bit bolshie. However, after I had been at Mons four or five months the powers that be made a decision about my future. This in itself was important but what is instructive is the way the information was handed on to me. Our Troop Instructor was one Captain Flood of the Royal Tank

Regiment. He was a round-faced man with a loud, rather affected voice who managed to give the impression that he was quite pleased about being an Instructor at Mons, a plum posting. He would often visit our barrack block in the evenings, when, as always, we would be cleaning our kit, to lecture us about this or that. I fear the fact that I was underwhelmed by him may have shown, and this wouldn't have helped my cause.

Early in the New Year (1960) we went on a three-day exercise in real armoured cars (Daimlers left over from the war) to Salisbury Plain. Living in or near such vehicles has its benefits as you can carry lots of food and water and you have a 'bivvy' to sleep in. A bivvy is a big piece of canvas like a tent which is designed to hang off one side of the vehicle so the crew of three or four men can rest in a degree of relative comfort. Comfort, that is, compared with the poor foot soldier whose lot was often to live (and sleep) in a waterlogged slit trench, wondering whether his food (when it came) would be tepid or just stone cold.

On this particular night the staff decided to have some fun and attacked us with thunderflashes and blank rounds at about 3.00 a.m. We staggered out to man our vehicles and return the fire. Eventually, after about an hour of chaos and stumbling round in the dark, order was restored and we prepared to go back to our sleeping bags. 'Ah, Wood,' said Flood in his over-rich tones, 'Something I meant to say. We've decided to back-term you for a month to see if you can make the grade.'

'Ah, right, Sir,' I mumbled, not knowing whether to be angry or relieved that I hadn't just been kicked out.

From this distance two things strike me. One is that Flood was probably thankful that by going back a month I would be going to another troop, led by a different officer. Also, I guess the authorities may have been unwilling to throw out people who had volunteered without giving them a second chance. But Flood's choice of time and place in which to tell me I was back-termed was unfortunate, and I think many officers would have handled the situation differently. I saw him some years later when, as a staff officer, he was part of a team running an exercise. He didn't look very at ease. Shortly after that I heard he'd left the Army.

The other major incident that took place while I was at Mons was tragic and happened quite close to Christmas. I was in the barrack room one evening in mid-December when someone told me the Orderly Officer wanted to see me in the Officers' Mess. As this was most unusual, I assumed I was in some sort of trouble. On arrival I was taken in and was told that the news was bad: my Mother had died. The Orderly Officer, who was kind enough, sat me down and offered me a drink. But it was a dark, gloomy, leather-chaired sort of a place. Because it was quite late, they arranged for me to have a train warrant to go home the next day. I remember trying to sleep in the hut that night, very confused and uncertain due to the suddenness of this unhappy news.

Eventually I got home and learnt that Mum had died alone in her flat, and that there was to be a coroner's enquiry. I think the events of the next few days took place just before Christmas but I can't be sure. Certainly my Mum's funeral took place in Elstree Parish Church, with the Bishop of St Albans officiating. My memory of that horrid time is confused, but I was to some extent aware of standing outside myself and seeing an absolutely exhausted young boy in an outsize Army-issue raincoat struggling through each moment numbly. In those days there was an understanding that suicide victims couldn't (or, rather, they shouldn't) be buried in consecrated ground, so the Bishop's presence plus the fact that Mum was buried in Elstree churchyard were statements of support for my Father and indicators that it was generally believed that her death was an accident. This was confirmed by the coroner. Later, my Dad took me up to the mortuary and encouraged me to see Mum where she lay. She looked white and drawn, and you could see in her dead face how hard life had been for her.

We got through all this but our family troubles were not over yet. A disturbing tension had developed between my Father and my brother during Michael's time at King's College, Cambridge, and in Michael's final year at university, after my Mum's death, their quarrels becoming fiercer. It's hard now to fathom what the fundamental cause of this broken relationship was. Certainly Mike drank quite a lot, and spent quite freely, money he didn't really have. It's true too, that though he was proud of Mike's intellectual achievements (and he has the most formidable brain) my Father was suspicious of universities in general. At heart Dad didn't find Mike straightforward or easy to deal with and I'm sure Mum's death brought a number of issues to a head. Mike's behaviour didn't fit with my Father's rather conventional view of the universe and brought out aspects of the over-stern, even censorious Victorian papa in him. I know that the relationship between Mike and my Father was difficult for about ten years after Mum's death – until 1969, when Mike and his wife came to my wedding.

After graduating from Cambridge, Mike went on to be a successful English and Drama teacher at Dulwich College but after his marriage broke up he went to live in Weston-super-Mare. There he stood for the local council and made many friends. However, after a number of years, a combination of drink and ME caught up with him and he went into rehabilitation. He still lives in Weston, where he is now being cared for, and we go and see him whenever possible. I love our phone conversations, because he has such a good memory and a delightful sense of humour despite being still being quite unwell.

Some scars probably remain from the time of Mum's death. For example, when the children were growing up I tended to be rather edgy in the run-up to Christmas; strangely, I only realised this quite recently. My 'un-Christmassy' attitude may have been due to the grey weather, the worry of extra expenses or a deep-down anxiety about meeting the expectations a family Christmas brings. On the other hand it may have been an echo in my mind of the 'old forgotten far-off things and battles long ago' of Christmas 1959.

One way or another I scraped through my Officer Training Course and became Second Lieutenant Wood. There is a picture on the bureau in Anne's home of me wearing my 'blues' uniform, with chain mail on the shoulders, and holding my new dress hat with blue velvet banding and a glinting regimental badge. I was just over eighteen and a half years old, but to look at the photo I look about fourteen and positively angelic: more ready to sing a verse of 'Once in Royal David's City' than to lead 'all the King's horses and all the King's men' into battle. But of all the armed forces in the world I believe the British Army in general is probably the most tolerant towards both its enemies and its newly joined officers. My good fortune was to have this benevolent, uncle-like tolerance extended to include myself – at the time one of the least of its children.

CHAPTER FIVE

Growing up in Germany Courtesy of the British Taxpayer

'Courts and camps are the only place to learn the world in'

– Lord Chesterfield

I didn't know it at the time, but a benevolent attitude towards young (and often foolish) officers was certainly part of the culture of the distinguished regiment I was about to join. 1st The Queen's Dragoon Guards came into being in 1959 as a result of the many regimental amalgamations imposed on the military during a programme of cutbacks, known as the post-Suez reorganisation. Our amalgamation involved two cavalry regiments whose inception dated back to 1685 – the time of Monmouth's Rebellion – a year which historians often regard as the start of the modern Army. The Queen's Bays (The Bays) and 1st The King's Dragoon Guards (KDG) became, in its shortened version, the QDG, with the Habsburg double-headed eagle as its regimental cap badge, which was fondly known by the 'boys' as a silver shite-hawk! This historic symbol of the old Holy Roman Empire was given to the KDG as a gesture of thanks by the Emperor Franz Joseph I during the nineteenth century and, although it was dropped during World War I, it came back into use before and during World War II. I think it is rather typical of the Brits to fight the Germans proudly wearing an Austrian cap badge.

My first trip abroad in May 1959 actually took place on a troop train which left from Victoria, was loaded overnight onto a ferry and then spent the best part of twelve hours pootling across Holland and what was then West Germany. It was early May and the day fine with some spring sunshine. To start with, as we crossed Holland, the countryside was flat, and it stayed flat as we travelled through the Ruhr and I saw with my own eyes how a previously devastated country had been completely rebuilt in only a few years. Rural Germany was looking ordered, calm and well cared for, with tractors, some horses, carts and labourers all at work. What an adventure to be looking through the train window at what not long before had been enemy territory.

As we moved westwards and entered the Hanoverian Plain the countryside remained flat. The train itself being a troop train was run on military lines so, of course, we had to wear uniform and there was also someone called Officer in Charge of Train. I found myself with two captains from the 15th/19th The King's Royal Hussars, who inveigled me into playing poker – fortunately for low stakes. So my entry into military low life and the 'brutal licentious soldiery' was relatively gentle. Eventually, we arrived close to the East/West border, so I got out to collect my luggage and to see what happened next. My baggage was a black tin trunk (still up in the attic) with '464803 2nd Lt A. S. Wood' written on it in white letters, and it managed to look both formal and slightly forlorn all on its own on Bahnsteig 6 at Brunswick station.

In the world of pantomime there is an event just before the last happy scene when the stage is cleared of the previous rather drab scenery of village greens and castle halls and made all sparkly and colourful. This is often known as the transformation scene, and this is how I would best describe these next few days and hours. The signal for this change in the quality of my life was the arrival of the

Orderly Officer, Lieutenant Donald Swann. Donald and I were in C Squadron together and I soon got to know him. He was innately generous, the most cheerful of people, and he and I always got on, which was easy given his lively, amused personality. Besides being a good sprinter and rugger player, Donald loved horses and rode well in three-day events. After he left the Army, he ran a big stable in Northern Ireland, and his son, Charlie Swann, became a popular champion jockey.

At our first meeting, Donald brightened up the rather drab German railway station, as he was resplendent in full blues uniform, spurs, Mess Wellingtons (mid-calf leather boots), tight trousers with a white stripe on the sides, a tunic with chain mail on the shoulders, silver buttons, a silver pouch belt, plus white gloves, sword and blues hat. Very elegant and impressive. To add practicality to this combination of history and theatre, he brought with him a driver who, to my surprise, not only saluted me but picked up my trunk as well. We chatted happily as we drove the twenty or so miles to the small frontier town of Wolfenbüttel and into the modern barracks Hitler had built for the Wehrmacht in the 1930s. As it was getting late, I changed quickly and went down for the meal which was waiting for me. Despite it being late, Donald and I were served our meal by Francis, the ancient German Mess waiter, who had lived through the Depression in Germany in the 1920s and 1930s. As we ate, I looked with interest round the room.

An Officers' Mess is as close to a London gentleman's club as you can get without actually being in one. Lots of leather sofas and chairs, newspapers spread round, a waiter permanently available to provide drinks, plenty of silver on the highly polished tables and many a gilt-framed floor-to-ceiling painting. Two special paintings caught my eye, and these I lived with on and off for several years. One was of the aforesaid Emperor Franz Joseph I and another was of a youthful Queen Elizabeth (the Queen Mother), who was the regimental Colonel-in-Chief. For the next few years I was to get to know and live alongside all the beautiful things the Bays and the KDG had accumulated over three hundred years. But I remember that first night, with the long dark dining table, the silver and the pictures, as particularly impressive. As you might expect, the contrast for me between this oasis of civilisation and gracious living and my existence at Mons was pretty overwhelming. Only two weeks before I had been slaving away in a Nissen hut, ready to be shouted at or thrown out. I have never forgotten that first evening in Wolfenbüttel.

As a final reminder of my changed status, Donald told me that there was a soldier called Goddard waiting to clean my kit. At that time, all officers still had a batman to look after them, and officers' wives each had a soldier who reported daily to help run the household and assist with entertaining. Anyway, even though it was now late, Goddard patiently took my shoes and service dress hat to clean, my belt to Blanco and polish, and I think he also ironed my uniform after the journey. Goddard was short and came from the Midlands, unlike most of our soldiers, who were increasingly from Wales. He was rather serious, with a stutter, and liked to keep out of the limelight, so working in the Officers' Mess might well have suited him as it was hardly onerous. His parting comment: 'What time would you like your tea in the morning, Sir?' put the seal on a remarkable day.

For the first three months or so I shared a room with John Whalley, who had been at Mons with me but not back-termed. (Sadly, John was killed in a car crash soon after he had completed his three-year commission.) During that first day I happened to pop back to the Mess, where Goddard had unpacked my trunk and hung up my things. In those days, and I think it's still true, officers had their uniforms made by top London tailors (often in Savile Row) and I was immensely impressed to have a special fitted 'blues' uniform and service dress. To complete my entourage I had lashed out on a 'Tootal' (spotted red cotton) dressing gown and two pairs of new shoes. There they were, displayed in a large wardrobe, looking rather lonely, with only my old school best suit (the one bought with Donald Parren's money) and my day-time Army issue uniform, (called battledress), to keep them company. Well, it's a start, I thought, until I looked across the room to where John's double wardrobe stood with the doors open. The space was filled with two or three dark suits, three or four country suits, blues, mess kit, dinner jacket, smoking jacket, hunting kit, white tie and tails, plus hats, shirts, ties and shoes galore. Not surprisingly I wondered what I had done in joining a 'crack' (as the tabloids would say) cavalry regiment.

So why and how did I come to choose such a prestigious outfit? After all, horses formed no part of my background. My brother had done his National Service in the Gunners and Dad had been an Infanteer. I think that probably my choice was influenced by several factors, including a chance meeting while at school, and the family's connection with the Regiment through Dad's TA service. For several years while I was in my teens Dad used to have a break from the parish and earn a few quid by going up to London on Wednesday nights for what were then called Territorial Army Drill Nights. As part of the UK's defence plan, all young men who had completed their two years of National Service had to join the reserve for, I think, five years. So, once a week, ex-National Servicemen would go along to their nearest drill hall to wear uniform and keep their training up to date. In due course, Dad was attached as Chaplain to the 'Rough Riders', whose parent (i.e. regular) Army unit was, until amalgamation, the Queen's Bays. Dad therefore knew some of the Bays Officers, and this gave me an entrée that was sufficient to support my application.

However, the key determinant in my choice had, in fact, taken place some years earlier, when I was about fifteen. After a year in the school CCF you were expected to take a simple military proficiency test called Certificate A. So on a rather grey day that winter term I stood by the school armoury, being questioned by an officer from the Blues (Household Cavalry) dressed immaculately in a tailored grey greatcoat and officer's service dress hat. 'So, how would you organise your platoon to get from here to that wood over there across the playing fields?' he asked. I started to explain my cunning plan, and he, quite gently, interrupted me: 'That's excellent. You've obviously got that all sorted. But, you know there's no need really for all this crawling and hiding in ditches. If you were in my regiment you'd be in a tank, and, having driven straight through the armoury building, you'd cross those fields in half a minute with bullets bouncing off the armour plating and crash straight through the wood.' And that really was that. My easily excited youthful imagination got the point and from then on I was sold on the idea that some personal form of Blitzkrieg was much to be preferred to sitting in a damp slit trench and walking everywhere.

The story of my joining the QDG and how I came to fit in, somewhat against the odds, is instructive. At Mons, and probably countrywide, the prevailing wisdom at the time was that to survive as an officer in the Guards or Cavalry one needed a private income. Up to and including the 1960s class was still a major issue in English society (many would claim it still is) so whether you were accepted or not depended a great deal on your school, speech, dress and family background. For example, at my interview (at the Cambridge Hotel in Camberley) Brigadier Tiarks asked me whether I fished, hunted or shot. My answer, that I didn't but that I played lots of sport and would like to have a go at everything, was true, but I feared I might sound unconvincing. He was nice about it, though, and it became clear during our discussion that having to live off your pay and not being particularly into country sports were not pre-conditions for entry to 1st The Queen's Dragoon Guards.

But socially mine was a risky choice and in another, less tolerant regiment I might have had a hard time. For example, having grown up in an effectively teetotal Rectory I had no idea what one drank: was it 'gin and ginger' or 'brandy and tonic'?! Although troops in the British Army of the Rhine had access to highly subsidised petrol, with tax free cigarettes and drink, it was quite possible, if you owned a car and drank and smoked, to get through a moderate private income and more. Fortunately, for me, financial survival turned out to be quite easy. I had no car, decided not to drink very much and bucked the trend by not smoking. This was quite unusual as most of the soldiers smoked, and many officers too. On training courses after every forty-minute lesson the instructor didn't say, 'OK, lesson ends', but, 'OK, smoke break'. Then the cry would go up as to whose 'push' (round for cigarettes) it was. Not smoking was an easy decision, as I knew smoking and sport, especially athletics, didn't really go together.

I survived financially and more than survived in other ways. Over the next ten years I was able to take up pretty well everything that took my fancy. Riding school (briefly, as I was often away in the winter when the school normally operated); squash, including competitions; climbing; golf tournaments; canoeing; football matches; much athletics; sub-aqua; ocean sailing; skiing; mountain walking and trekking; as well as discovering four continents and about ten European countries. Over the next four years, from a position of having never been outside the UK, I visited Holland (canoeing), Belgium (hockey), Germany (travelling all over), Austria (cross-country skiing), Denmark (sailing and on exercise), East Berlin (football tournament and my first nightclub), Switzerland (downhill skiing) and Italy (holiday).

As you can see, my whole Army experience was an enormous extended education, in terms of travelling, soldiering on active service and, above all perhaps, in the leadership of people and of teams (often in quite tricky situations). The Army was my university, my home and my mentor. My Regiment gave me all these opportunities and it also taught me something so important that it has influenced me ever since. The Sandhurst motto is 'Serve to Lead', and, because I was in a good regiment, it was drilled into us as young officers, on an almost daily basis, that our *raison d'être* was the welfare of the soldiers under our command. As the old cavalry motto has it, 'Horses first, soldiers second and yourself last'. In this, at least, the combination of a vicarage upbringing and Aldenham's ethic of duty and service prepared me well for the Army.

Some officers found it easier to try and use the system to suit themselves. This didn't go down well in the Army generally, and particularly in the Regiment I had just joined. For when I use the word 'good' with reference to the Queen's Dragoon Guards, I'm not just using the word in social or sporting terms (though it applied) but in terms of doing our job. We were 'good' professional Army officers in an Army which, after the end of National Service, became one of the best in the world.

By the mid-1960s the Regiment had said goodbye to all our conscripts and, in future, unlike the rest of Europe, the British Army was made up only of long-term soldiers and officers. This improvement, together with better equipment, meant the whole thing visibly improved. Also, at the higher levels many senior officers in the British Army had served in the war and knew about fighting. For example, my Squadron Leader, Tom Muir, and our Colonel,

Jackie Harman, had fought in North Africa and Italy respectively, so there wasn't much you could tell them about 'the Profession of Arms'. Also, I was very lucky in my generation. For a start, we had lots of regimental officers and at one point I think more than seventy were either at Wolfenbüttel or on attachment, which meant it was easier to go off and take part in the many activities available in Germany while still performing excellently on exercise. The point about being good at what we were paid to do is underlined if you reckon that, of the people I served with, five officers went on to be generals.

The link between my generation being professional and the QDG being regarded as one of the best regiments in the Army is reinforced by Field Marshall Slim's dictum about officers: 'There are no bad regiments, only bad officers'. Colonel Jackie Harman, who welcomed me on my first day and who later went on to become second-in-command of NATO, was vexed by the physical appearance of the three ex-Sandhurst men who followed me. So, half-seriously, he ordered the adjutant to send a message to the War Department saying, 'Send positively no more short officers!' Luckily, as a fairly tall man I didn't incur his irritation! Also, during my time in uniform I saw some officers, possibly seduced by the lure of high command, lose this crucial sense of service. I can think of at least two people who were generally reckoned by the NCOs (who are perceptive about these things) to have used the Regiment for their own advancement. I never tried this. Though I can be competitive, and am able to put myself forward, I have never set out per se to achieve high office, lots of money or a high profile.

Conveniently for this memoir, the ten years during which I wore uniform divide themselves into various periods depending on where I was stationed. During the first period of four years, we were with armoured cars in Germany where I literally grew up. Then I had a couple of years split between Northern Ireland (quite passive at the time) and Borneo (a six-month active service attachment). This was followed by more active service with a year in Aden (now called the Yemen) and generally regarded as the backside of the world. Finally, my life gained a degree of civilisation and normality when I was posted to England for two years as an instructor at the Junior Leaders Regiment in Dorset. I started in the regular Army as a second lieutenant and finished as a captain. During this period I received two General Service Medals (for Borneo and Aden) and later served as a major in the Territorial Army.

What was daily life in the Regiment like? The first thing that strikes anyone (military or otherwise) visiting a cavalry regiment is the relaxed atmosphere. There is not a lot of formality or stamping and shouting or over-zealous saluting. It's all very British and understated. This tradition, which seems to have built up over centuries, first with horses and nowadays with tanks or armoured cars, may seem casual but it's really to allow individuals, while being corporate, to do things their own way. The officers in particular have inherited a socially confident style, such as befits those who historically used to be able to afford horses, expensive living and fine uniforms (paid for by the wearers). Their approach naturally affects the attitude of the soldiers and eventually the Regiment's psyche. The differences between the ranks are still there – this is the Army, after all – but no one relies on rank or the *Manual of Military Law* to get things done. (I'm proud of the fact that, in all my military service, I never put anyone on a charge.) Relationships are essentially easy-going, but respect is both given and taken and, in my experience, members of the QDG rarely took advantage of the apparently rather 'unmilitary' culture which prevailed in the Regiment.

Uniquely in the Army at the time we were, among the officers, all on first-name terms. The Colonel was known as 'Colonel Tom' or

'Colonel Peter' but everyone else, regardless of rank or age (and some were thirty years my senior), called me by my first name, and I was able to respond similarly. Another slightly eccentric but nonetheless pleasant custom was for us to be allowed to keep dogs in the Mess. Many a Labrador was seen walking round the camp during the day two or three paces behind the 'boss', carrying a swagger stick in its mouth. Most officers also cultivated a certain style, often reflected in 'modifications' to their uniform. One famous photograph of about a dozen Hussar officers shows them wearing a range of different military/sporting items of clothing. Not one garment or hat is the same and underneath the caption reads: 'and uniform will be worn'.

The people who surrounded me in these early, formative days were relaxed, confident, pleasant individuals who would have a go at anything. I would like to think that, in part, I have caught for myself a little of this essentially civilised approach to life and that it is now reflected in how I conduct myself. If so, my Army time was not a bad journey for someone who could easily take himself too seriously, and who was born with a propensity to be intense.

However, I have to say that I didn't completely buy into professional soldiering and rather played the part of the young officer. Fortunately in a cavalry regiment such reservations about military life were tolerated, although proper standards were expected and maintained. My friends were great characters and, after a short period of induction when I was the 'new boy' to be ignored, were mostly kind and supportive to me but, predictably, life in the Mess did have its downsides. By definition an Officers' Mess based in a foreign country is bound to be a bit insular and hedonistic. The average chat in the Mess didn't (at least during my time) include much about art, music, history, recent films or delve much into the pros and cons of the latest political and national news. It comprised mainly of pulling people's legs about slip-ups they had made (as a poor map reader I got my fair share of this), and chat about food, girls, parties, sport, clothes and other officers. Without in anyway denigrating this, I think most of us suffered from not completing our education at university. Besides, in those days the Army was bound to attract a number of people for whom a rather limited diet was perfectly OK.

The average time for armoured regiments to be stationed in Germany was about six years, and, although there was some rotation as officers went on postings and courses, long periods of institutional life in one place undoubtedly led to tension. With lots of young men cloistered together for long periods in a foreign country life in the Mess could become claustrophobic. This, among other things, predictably led to some people drinking too much. During my time we probably had one or two incipient alcoholics and there were plenty of officers who could consume considerable quantities with apparently no ill effect. A regular group of five or six people used to go on a spree every so often and this generally resulted in the bullying of unpopular or new officers. Thunderflashes would go off in the corridor at 3.00 a.m., the door would be flung open and the group would demand that you get dressed, sometimes with a bucket of water flung in as an incentive. Alternatively, the same group would trash the ante-room, which was the room we all used during the day. Although these officers had to pay for the damage, I think they probably got away with murder.

My attitude here may sound censorious, and it sums up a dichotomy in my nature that has never been entirely resolved and which the social side of life in the Army threw into sharp relief: in essence am I a 'Puritan' or a 'Cavalier'? I do rather agree with Noël Coward, who said 'Work is more fun than fun', and I also like to engage intensely with social, political and religious concerns. I guess my brother officers put their finger on this rather 'sharp' aspect of my personality when they nicknamed me 'Splinter', a sobriquet which stuck for a long time, as did my other nickname of 'Woody'.

Many of my memories of the Army are still very vivid. At one time we had a Colonel whose hallmark was his rather affected drawling voice. It was so distinctive that it was easy for the regimental 'jester', one Corporal Mackley, to imitate him, which he did often and to good effect. Mackley happened to be a Spurs supporter, and, while on exercise in a Saracen Command Vehicle, the adjutant decided to have a little of his own back on Mackley by setting the password for the day as 'Arsenal 4 Spurs 0'. Mackley, however, as befits an Army Court Jester, had the last laugh by deliberately giving the Colonel this password the wrong way round, so Spurs were the winners. In the middle of the night, when the Colonel wanted access to his command vehicle, he happily offered the locked Saracen doors the password 'Arsenal 0 Spurs 4', to which he received the somewhat surprising answer 'Go away, Mackley', and failed to gain entry to his own Headquarters! Needless to say, despite the Regiment being on exercise and camped over an area of many miles, this story had delighted everybody by the next day!

The best Squadron Leader I ever had was Tom Muir who was a brilliant trainer, but who had an uncontrollable temper. The story goes that when living in a hutted camp in Northern Ireland he got so cross with another officer that he rolled himself up in a carpet in his rage. That night, still seething, he took his sword and slammed it through the hardboard wall which separated his bedroom from the room of the officer he had fallen out with. It so happened that the officer in question was lying in his bed and was seriously upset when a sword zipped through the wall only a few inches above his nose. The best way to deal with Tom was to let his tirade run its course and then, if appropriate, stand up to him. Once, for example, he threw the telephone at Donald Swann, whereupon Donald calmly picked it up and threw it back at him!

During our stay in Wolfenbüttel, we had a number of regular special parades and parties. Waterloo Day was always a big event, as both the KDGs and the Bays had taken part in that famous battle. One year, several somewhat drunken officers finished up on the roof of the Sergeants' Mess, where one future general was seen pushing a wheelbarrow in which Sergeant Healey was sitting, rushing with it towards the edge of the building. Later he explained that he was trying to see if Healey could jump out of it before he was thrown off the roof.

Perhaps the maddest of our officers was also one of the nicest. Francis Chamberlain was a charming and kind person, and also a brilliant pilot. He oversaw the introduction of the first integrated flight of helicopters into any regiment and his personal flying skills were superb. However, after a few drinks he liked to go a bit crazy, blow things up, swing from chandeliers and generally cause mayhem. It was his idea, I think, to introduce 'Molo' to the Officers' Mess. After World War II, many Germans managed to get around their war-torn country either on motorbikes or using motorbike and side-car combinations. So, by the early 1960s, when the *Wirtschaftswunder* (economic miracle) had enabled most West Germans to become car owners, the dumps were full of these now redundant vehicles. Francis managed to scrounge some bikes at knockdown prices. And so, on the sports field behind the Officers' Mess, 'Molo' was born. Using cut-down polo sticks, a polo ball and redundant football goalposts, six or so of these assorted vehicles could be seen belching blue fumes as they roared from one end of the field to the other.

Normally a team consisted of seven players with three bikes. These included two ordinary motorbikes, each with a pillion passenger (who was able to switch hands to play on either side), plus a bike and side-car combination crewed by three people: one driver, one riding pillion and the third sitting low down in the side-car and generally able to give the ball a good, right-handed thwack. Silly hats and goggles were optional, and players with a good eye for a ball were much sought after. Often that year, on a balmy summer evening fourteen officers who would otherwise have been quite bored could be seen behaving not so much badly but more in the spirit of the great Victorian eccentrics who invented and played 'silly' outdoor games. Wonderful fun.

Some of this excess energy also got transmitted into preparation for elaborate summer balls. Regiments competed, especially in Germany where armoured regiments could find themselves stationed for seven or eight years, to produce the most lavish and theatrical dances. For example, Mike Parker, then of the Queen's Own Hussars, staged a ball using the defeat of Napoleon at Moscow as a theme. The regimental band provided appropriate music, while Mess waiters (augmented by volunteers) were dressed in Russian costume. The food reflected the period that had inspired Mike, and a cut-out of the Kremlin adorned the Mess lawn – though not for long. The *pièce de résistance* came at the end, and consisted of the burning down of Moscow, with all the scenery set on fire! We were living at the tail-end of another age and I suspect we all knew it.

The ball we gave that I remember most vividly had a Venetian theme. Once again all the downstairs rooms of the Mess were suitably decked out and appropriate food and music were on hand. The startling innovation on this occasion was that all guests were transported from the car park to the main doors of the Mess by boat via a temporary canal. For some weeks various officers and co-opted soldiers laboured with scaffolding poles and huge canvas sheets to construct a metre-high structure that ran for about 75 yards, containing thousands of gallons of water. On it were a couple of metal assault boats, normally used for river crossings, which were hauled up and down the 'canal' by 'gondoliers' pulling hand over hand on ropes. Needless to say, our first two versions collapsed, flooding the surrounding tennis court and lawn, with the second of these disasters happening only a couple of days before the big day. However, once we actually got it working, you can imagine the impact on our guests. One minute you are a bored captain's wife stuck in a unlovely married quarter on the outskirts of Bielefeld, and the next you are sitting in your best party dress being propelled by a (possibly) handsome gondolier down a replica of a Venetian canal. On arrival you are greeted by a fanfare from trumpeters in scarlet tunics, a banquet of sumptuous food and elaborate decorations. I may be wrong but I don't recall that tickets had to be bought as I think invitations just went out, and while the Army found the kit, the Regiment paid the bill.

After this particular dance I think things did in fact go a little too far. One of my contemporaries was a member of a titled family who had a sister, a blonde and feisty débutante called Annabel. The fun-loving Lady Annabel had flown out with others of a similar ilk to join our party which included two officers from The Royal Scots Dragoon Guards (Scots DG), on a short break between exercises. At some point in the early hours of the morning Lady Annabel and these two guys thought it would be fun for her to go for a ride in a tank and join the Scots DG out in the field. Somehow they spirited her away in their car, got her a pair of denim overalls and she spent the next two or three days riding around inside a Centurion tank – 'somewhere in Germany!'. The execution of this voluntary kidnapping may have been good, but the forward planning was awful as the press began to claim that she had been abducted. Maybe this was because no one remembered to let her parents know where she was; when her plane landed back in the UK after the party she wasn't on it and it was assumed that she had disappeared!

I must add that this sort of excess was extreme even by the tolerant standards of the 1960s. Most of the time we played lots of sport, socialised (almost exclusively with other members of the British military community), found things to do when boredom threatened and, from spring to early autumn, trained very hard. The nature and culture of a cavalry regiment in barracks appears somewhat relaxed, good-humoured and even laid-back but in military terms, especially on exercise, we were a very professional organisation. High standards were set and hard work expected: it is amazing how often the correct setting of standards and expectations leads to excellent results.

My first troop was 5th Troop C Squadron, which consisted of six soldiers, one sergeant, two corporals and myself: a total of ten men. To carry out our reconnaissance role we were equipped with two Saladin armoured cars (each with a crew of three) and two Ferret Scout cars (both with a crew of two) and with these four vehicles under my command we roamed the north German countryside. Every armoured car had two radio sets: an A set for us to speak to the rest of the Squadron and a B set which was for internal troop communication, and therefore the one most used on exercise. You could flick from one 'radio net' to the other by a switch on your handset and some people even organised their headphones so the A set was in one ear and the B set in the other.

Out in the field it would be almost impossible to be more comfortable. OK, we got very wet if it rained. but we carried spare kit on our vehicles and would eventually be able to change and dry our wet things over the engine decks. The infantry, on the other hand, would stay wet. The joy of an armoured car troop as your first command is that you are so self-sufficient. Out on the flat roads of the Hanoverian plain we could go pretty well where we wished. We had plenty of fuel, carried all our own food, fresh rations such as bread and vegetables were available from village shops and if we had any time to sleep at night we could make ourselves very comfortable. My bedding roll, for example, consisted of a large canvas cover inside of which were blankets, sheets, a camp bed plus pyjamas, all held securely with two leather straps.

The world of armoured cars suited my quick temperament. On a long exercise we would go for several days with very little sleep – maybe two or three hours a night. During these long days we would drive for miles, with sheets and sheets of maps held in large zip-up plastic cases. Because the whole Regiment was on wheels (not tracked like tanks), we could train anywhere in the British Sector, which effectively comprised all of northern Germany. Provided there were roads or tracks or fields and the ground was not too wet and boggy we could go cross-country, particularly in the huge woods that are a feature of middle Europe. All the time we were on exercise we were multi-tasking. During any given period on exercise a vehicle commander would have to map-read, give his driver instructions ('right here, slow down' etc), listen to two radio sets, control the other three vehicles in the troop, eat and drink and make tactical decisions in line with both his own situation and what the squadron was doing. Although initially I made lots of mistakes, after two or three training seasons I became quite good.

An important reason for my improving performance was increased personal confidence, much of which stemmed from the support I got from within my troop. After some months with 5th Troop I took over 4th Troop (from Charles 'Patchy' Bond, so named because he wore a black eye patch), which had a very good reputation.

Here I was looked after by the redoubtable and somewhat avuncular Sergeant Stones, who hailed from Liverpool.

One of the great strengths of the British Army, certainly in those days, was the acceptance by grizzled and experienced senior NCOs of the responsibility for looking after and advising often callow young officers – who nominally at least were their seniors. Jim Stones never let me down and helped me avoid numerous pitfalls out on exercise or in terms of handling my soldiers. His dry wit helped to keep everything in perspective. Once he told his driver to advance, but, because the forward/reverse lever was set wrongly, the Saladin went backwards. 'No, forward the other way', was the laconic response. Similarly, when discussing life in the Officers' Mess, I commented how some officers always seemed to have to 'borrow' someone else's shirt or Mess kit. 'Ah, yes', said Jim. 'That's always been the form in the Officers' Mess – first up best dressed!'

Where else in working life would a nineteen-year-old youth, promoted above those with more experience and who himself regularly slipped up, receive such loyal, friendly, practical and unstinting support? Certainly not in most of the offices and workshops of modern Britain, and I count myself lucky to have been part of the historic system of loyalty given by members of the Regiment, in particular the NCOs, to people like me.

In time I learnt ways of getting over my major mistakes, many of which involved map reading. I discovered that Corporal Marshall ('3-4 Bravo' was his radio call sign) had a wonderful sense of direction. So, if in doubt, I would often ask his advice and when we came to a large, unmapped wood with new tracks going all over the place I would call him up to the front and get him to lead us through, which he invariably did. Perhaps there's a leadership lesson here about trusting people and using their skills to the full.

However, sometimes even my excellent NCOs could not save me. For example one year our troop were constantly accused of not 'listening out'; that is, not hearing or responding to messages from other troops or Squadron Headquarters. Occasionally, tempers frayed due to tiredness, and once 'Mouse' Moreton, my then Squadron Leader, who was normally the mildest of men, snapped at me, 'Are you all deaf in your troop?' Taking this remark rather literally, I decided to have both my own ears and Trooper Rowe's checked. (Rowe was my gunner/wireless operator, whose job it was to 'listen out' on the Squadron net.) Sure enough, Rowe was found to be deaf in one ear and the mystery was solved.

Despite this constant help from my soldiers and NCOs things could still go badly wrong, and two incidents underline this. One night on exercise we were all given a long and complex set of routes to follow on the next day, including a verbal briefing involving a succession of complicated grid references. This information soon covered our map cases (which were made of 'talc', a sort of clear plastic you could write on) as the briefing included not only my lengthy route but those of the other four troops as well. Next day before setting out on patrol I was sitting on the turret hatch of my armoured car in the sun when a message came through about the day's route. 'No need to take these down,' I said rather lazily to Trooper Gobey, who was my radio operator. 'We were given all these last night.' How wrong I was. Either I missed it or we were never told, but the previous evening's information was now void and this latest message was not confirmation, as I had supposed, but brand new routes.

For the rest of the day I was on the receiving end of baffled requests from Squadron HQ as to my position, because to them I was nowhere near where I should have been. Eventually the Squadron

Leader lost patience with this new and inept young officer and, to my chagrin, came on the air himself, saying, '3-5, come and report personally to me. You are unfit to command.' He had been receiving angry messages from the Colonel and was being let down by a very junior officer, hence this message was born out of frustration. To this day I can remember my dismay at his comment.

About two years after the incident mentioned above, I found myself as a much more confident and capable troop leader, bogged down in some German forest. My Saladin was firmly stuck in the mud with the wheels virtually submerged. Eventually, a recovery vehicle found us and a cable was attached from its winch onto the stuck armoured car. Because of the nature of the ground and the general wetness, this cable needed to run at right angles, so a huge one-ton block and tackle was strapped onto a nearby tree by a chain with links some two inches (10 cm) thick. Without realising the danger, I stood at the corner of the right angle, where I could see both the recovery crew and my driver. This was both the right place and very much the wrong place to be.

Shortly after the rescue operation had started with a huge revving of engines and blue smoke, there came a loud bang and I felt something very heavy hit me on the back of the legs and knock me into the air. One of the massive links in the chain round the tree had snapped and I had been hit by the block and tackle, albeit landing completely unhurt. If the cable had hit me I would have lost both legs or been sliced in half. It was a truly miraculous escape, and I can only explain why I wasn't more seriously hurt by using the analogy of a hammer hitting a falling leaf. The leaf is so light and the hammer so heavy that the leaf gives and, at worst, falls lightly to the ground. In my case I picked myself up and carried on, with slight bruising to the back of my legs.

I close this chapter with a couple of recollections of the Cold War period. The coldest thing I ever did while in Germany was to escort a Russian general down the motorway. His name was Jakabovski and he was rumoured to have commanded over fifty Russian divisions during World War II. There was a temporary thaw in relations at the time between the Russians and the West and his was a goodwill visit. We had to take him down the motorway from Helmstedt (the border crossing point) to Bielefeld, about 150 miles away, which was then the 20th Armoured Corps HQ. It was a freezing late winter day and the cold was compounded not only by half of me being stuck out of the turret in the bitter air but by the fact that, for security reasons, we had to travel at over 60mph. Even with four or five layers on it was perishing.

The closeness of the border with its armed machine-gun towers and half-mile-wide minefields, together with the perennially tense international situation, meant the Russian threat was taken very seriously by all of us living near the border. At the time (1962) President Kennedy had had to deal with the Cuban missile crisis, which took the world closer to a nuclear war than at any time before or since. This brings me to my second Cold War story. In the light of the international situation and because of the threatening stance of the Russians and the East Germans, NATO liked to assert the right of the Western powers to use the autobahn connecting West Berlin with western Germany. This autobahn ran from Helmstedt, which lay about five miles from our camp, then across much of East Germany to West Berlin. An exercise was designed to test the Russian resolve should they attempt to close the crossing point. (It was called 'Gay Cavalier', a name which these days would not help the army with its image-building one bit!) An international convoy of French, American, German and British wheeled armoured vehicles would assemble about twice a year on the parade ground at Wolfenbüttel, and from there we would practise convoy drills in the surrounding countryside, ready to move down the autobahn if ordered to do so.

At this point the story moves from high strategy to good humour through a nice photo of me in my armoured car at the front of the convoy taken by some military 'snapper'. I'm pictured at the head of the international convoy looking down at Colonel Peter Body who was famous for over-using expressions such as 'Good show' and 'Well done' – sentiments of which the soldiers were always slightly suspicious. You can imagine my surprise and pleasure when I walked into the Corporals' Mess at a later date to find my 'Exercise Gay Cavalier' photo pinned up next to the dartboard. A bubble had been drawn in biro coming out of my mouth, 'And how would you like your steak done, Colonel?' it says. To which, of course, an answering bubble from the Colonel replies, 'Well done, Tony. Well done!'

To finish on a joyous note. It so happened that on 2 September 1962 the whole Regiment was out on exercise and the Squadron was leagued up, at rest and all together, in a large farmyard. This was, in fact, my twenty-first birthday at a time when people took such landmarks pretty seriously, so I was sad not to be back home on leave and with my family. However, when the Squadron formed up in front of its vehicles for First Parade before a day of routine maintenance and recuperation, I was summoned to the Squadron Leader's side. At which point Sergeant Stones marched up to me, saluted and gave me a large silver key made from our cardboard ration boxes and silver paper from cigarette packets. Then 130 soldiers broke into song with 'Happy birthday to you' and 'For he's a jolly good fellow'. A very special, moving and unique present for a young soldier far from home.

CHAPTER SIX

A Different Kind of Service

'Bliss was it in that dawn to be alive
But to be young was very Heaven!'

– William Wordsworth

A seminal moment in my Army days occurred not long after I arrived in Wolfenbüttel in the spring of 1960. I was coming down the stairs when I heard my Squadron Leader and another officer talking about me. The gist of it was that I was young and inexperienced and should stay in barracks during the coming winter to improve my skills, rather than go with the newly formed cross-country ski team to Austria. They also mentioned the problem that there was no officer to go with the team, as Colin Barclay (the first choice) wanted to go with the downhill skiing team, not the *Langlaufers* (German for cross-country skiers).

The common maxim among experienced soldiers, in those days at least, was 'never volunteer', but I rarely followed this precept and I believe I prospered as a result. In this instance, I whizzed round to the officer who was charged with all matters skiing to tell him I would like to go *Langlauf*ing and, guessing that this was some kind of stamina sport, gave him my credentials as a middle-distance runner and athlete.

I can't now remember who picked the soldiers to go with us that first winter but some of them were real rogues who were only too happy to take advantage of being away from camp from the end of November to late February, when the season ended. Nor can I remember how we got the necessary equipment – skis, boots, rucksacks, clothing – or the money and rations to keep a sports team operating 600 miles away from the rest of the British Army. I do know that Jeremy Railton and Tony Huddlestone taught me how to write military memos to quartermasters and nameless officials of the 20th Armoured Brigade in Bielefeld requesting authorisation for all this to happen. Lots of activities and outdoor adventures can be had in the Army, mostly out of uniform, but they tend to be administered via forms and systems that are similar to the ones that are used to send people on active service or on exercise. Just as with a modern corporation or institution, if you want to get the best out of the system you have to know how to operate it.

So, using money obtained via the 'system', we bought some pretty good wooden cross-country skis made locally by Fritz Schafer in the Hertz Mountains and we also bought proper *Laufing* boots. But our clothing was awful – and quite comical. We went off to the mountains and the ski slopes wearing blue rugger socks, baggy cotton knickerbockers, which were not waterproof, and an assortment of jumpers and sports tops. Gloves, ear bands and woolly hats we bought ourselves. It was a good job that these fearsome representatives of the British Army of the Rhine kept to the backwoods and the lonely trails which are the lot of the cross-country skier. Had that not been the case I suspect there would have been a further run on the pound, a common feature of the British post-war economy.

I ought to explain a bit about the nature of cross-country skiing, bearing in mind that at the time I knew nothing about it; had never been abroad; never seen a mountain over 500 metres high and had certainly never skied or skated. About this time Roland Huntford, now a well-known biographer of various Polar explorers such as Scott and Shackleton, wrote an article in *Soldier* magazine on the British Olympic cross-country ski team which, not surprisingly, was comprised entirely of Army personnel. He called this piece 'Every Breath Like Fire'; not a bad title, given that within the whole range of Olympic sports, both summer and winter, cross-country skiing is reckoned to require the greatest energy output.

The skis for *Langlaufing* are thin, perhaps half the width of a downhill ski, but of the same length. Rather than having the heavy safety bindings and boots associated with downhill skiing, the *Langlaufer's* boot is just clipped on by the toe so the heel can be lifted. The curious thing about these skis is that by applying the right wax the skier can glide downhill and on the flat but also move uphill if needed. The correct wax glides downhill but grips uphill, especially if the wax used is applied immediately under the foot. Cross-country skiing takes place generally over flat or gently undulating country and through woods. The recreational cross-country skier can go as slowly or as fast as they like, just like a walker or runner. However, we were training to take part in races over distances of 10, 15, and 20 kilometres, so we had to be able to go flat out in the cold and snow for up to thirteen miles. If we were doing biathlon, where you stop and shoot at targets every 5 kilometres, we carried a rifle as well. A race might last up to two hours.

In the skiing world Britain is known as a 'lowland' nation, because we don't have that much snow and consequently skiing is not really a major sport. For Scandinavians it is the national sport, with millions of people involved in clubs and races of all kinds or skiing for fun. Despite our background and the handicap of never having learnt to ski as children, I have to say the QDG team got pretty good at this rather esoteric activity. In a sense we were lucky, because as an armoured regiment we could rely on being in Germany for at least five years and hence our team (even in its in cotton knickerbockers) had the chance to develop over a decent period of time.

The man behind all our planning and preparation was Jeremy Railton, known as Bumble, who was a good downhill skier and eventually a member of the Army team. Jeremy was very conscientious and methodical and, although I didn't know it at the time, he had a long-term (five-year) plan for the Regiment to win the Princess Marina Cup. This was awarded to the team which did best overall in a combination of four races covering both skiing disciplines. The downhill element comprised a downhill race and slalom (zigzagging down a winding course marked out by poles), while the relay race (4 x 10 kilometres) and the patrol (20 kilometres) made up the cross-country section. To do well we would need good trainers for both types of skiing.

To start with Jeremy found us a trainer called Tony Maule who was an ex-army skier. Later, when Tony had to go off and do other things like earning his living, Jeremy hit on the brilliant idea of going to the German *Bundesgrenzschutz* (Customs and Border Police), who kindly lent us the services of one of their best skiers. I think a few bottles of whisky may have changed hands, and in return we got the nicest of men, Mortis (short for Timoteus) Scholl, who had recently been a member of the German Olympic cross-country skiing 'B' team. Over the years we did achieve success but this was only because we belonged to a regiment which believed in supporting these kinds of activities and let us go and train winter after winter. Once we had shown we had potential, the Regiment also backed us with money, but recognition and ultimate success were only achieved after a series of crises, and some tough and curious times.

I think the other thing that helped us succeed was that, over a period, we began to pick people for the training who were temperamentally and physically suitable to become *Langlaufers*. Being away from the normal disciplines and strictures of camp life meant that team members had to have self-discipline. Also, given the demanding physical nature of racing and the challenges of learning a completely new sport, they had to be resilient, intelligent and determined. Armoured regiments, like the QDG, generally recruit from the top level of entrants into the Army and in time we got some ideal people. Indeed, Peter Tancock and Tom Dakin eventually made it into the British Army team and represented their country in the Winter Olympics, held in Seefeld, Austria, in 1967.

So on a wonderful late autumn day in November 1960 I found myself in a little Austrian mountain railway carriage pulling up the hill to the small skiing village of Berwang. The snow had not yet fallen so the Alpine meadows were clearly visible, interspersed with small clumps of firs and the occasional ancient wooden hut. It was a wonderfully calm, rural scene that seemed just right for the brown Alpine cattle. With the window open all you could hear was the clank of the little train working hard to reach the summit and the sound of the occasional cowbell, as one of the huge beasts moved its head. You know how it is in life occasionally: time stops and you have a frisson of recognition, 'this is it, this is where I want to be'. For me it was to be in a foreign country, with the ski team, travelling in beautiful mountains towards a hidden village and new experiences.

Having arrived in the village of Berwang we found ourselves very comfortably housed in Pension Bergblick (Mountain View), run by Trudi, who was friendly and happy to have her little pension fully booked, as we and she supposed, for most of the winter. Indeed, to call Trudi merely friendly would be an understatement! Early on during our stay it was generally understood that she was 'a close friend' of a sergeant major in the German army stationed in Sonthofen, about thirty miles away. In terms of the team and our training, it was not helpful of her to become just as 'friendly' with the Brits, but that is what happened.

One of the first things we did after a few weeks in Berwang was to enter a local race, which meant the whole team leaving the pension early at about 6.00 a.m. We were already late leaving when I set off to find the team's 'woman-chaser-in-chief', one Corporal Franklin, who was, so I was told, still in the shower. I shouted for him to get a move on, and he rather shamefacedly joined us on the bus, which by now was very late. Only later did I overhear the boys discussing this incident and in doing so learnt that the real reason for the delay.

'Woody was hunting all over the place for Franco,' said one of them, 'but no wonder he couldn't find him. He was with Trudi in her bedroom fast asleep after a hard night!' The reality of what was going on was slightly lost on me but, in fact, Corporal Franklin was on borrowed time and not long after this we sent him back to barracks.

Trudi tended to serve up typical Austrian food, such as sauerkraut and meatballs, which didn't go down too well with our very British soldiers. Nor did it seem to go down too well with me, literally. After some intermittent stomach discomfort over a few days, I woke one night in severe pain. There was no doctor around so someone unselfishly drove me through the night to Garmisch Partenkirchen, which was some miles away but had an American army base. There, a kind female medic shoved a finger up my bottom and said I had a grumbling appendix. She prescribed some medicine, which worked, and I eventually had the offending appendix out the following summer back in Britain.

For the first two years I found skiing really hard. Not the physical graft; rather, it was the sheer difficulty of managing those long pieces of wood on my feet and the slippy-sliding feeling they created. I fell over an awful lot in my first two winters and didn't really get any good until well into our second season.

For our first season, as I've mentioned, our trainer was Tony Maule. He had been a cavalry officer for a short while and, I think, had raced cross-country in the 1956 Winter Olympics. Now out of the Army, he led a casual, almost bohemian existence, training soldiers to ski in the winter and relaxing in the summer. I think he was also in the Territorial Army SAS. He had a patient manner and tolerant half-smile, and I liked him a lot. It was therefore a nasty shock when he died young not many years later.

We spent hours each day flogging ourselves round a snowy two-kilometre circuit. In the afternoons we would practise techniques, step turns, skating turns, snowplough stops, double stick pushing and the like. There was frost on our eyebrows, our breath was like small patches of mist, our chests heaved and our limbs ached from the effort, all made worse, certainly in my case, by falling over many times. Curiously I enjoyed it all because I sensed that, once I could master my *Langlauf* planks, I could get good at this sport and I never forgot how lucky we were to be out there in the mountains.

Unfortunately, we then encountered a problem. The money we had applied for and had been granted ran out! Some staff officer must have found a problem with the BAOR Sports Budget and so, suddenly, we couldn't afford Trudi's Pension (or Tony Maule for that matter) and were skiing orphans – with nowhere to go. However, Jeremy worked his magic even in this crisis and did a deal where we were billeted initially with the German Army in their *Kaserne* (barracks) in Sonthofen, followed by a spell in Anton's hut in Oberjoch. Oberjoch is an amazing place as it has all the attributes of the classic skiing village including wooden chalets, good ski lifts and a rural population, which farmed in the old Tyrolean manner during the summer. However, it also has a darker element to its history. It lies conveniently close to the Austrian/German border, up the pass that Hitler built in the 1930s to enable the Anschluss – the annexation of Austria under German control – to be implemented. In later years I got to know that pass, with its hundreds of twists and turns and steep drops, very well.

The net effect of all this was that after the comforts of Trudi's pension and a two-week spell with the *Bundeswehr* (German Army) we found ourselves living very rough indeed. Anton's hut lay a third of the way up a ski slope just outside Oberjoch. As I recall we marched the twenty kilometres from Sonthofen to the hut while a German Army truck carried our kit. I had no snow boots, so I slipped a great deal as we climbed up the final snowy slopes to this most primitive of lodgings, no more or less than a cow barn, with an ancient kitchen and a couple of loos in an outhouse. In classic German country style we slept on straw above the animals, and washing was done from two cold taps splashing into a metal channel. The heating and toilet arrangements were equally prehistoric, especially when you remember that we were a team of twelve blokes. We did eat adequately, as someone thoughtfully sent down a field kitchen (called a hydro-burner) from Wolfenbüttel, together with plenty of tins of 'compo' – the composite rations British troops used to eat on exercise. But it was tough skiing combined with pretty rough living.

Things weren't made easier for me when I developed a nasty blister on my left foot. A blister may not sound much, but this lasted for three to four weeks. At its height this annoying wound was the size of a fifty pence piece and deep enough to embed the same coin. It hurt like hell just putting wet boots on in the morning, and during training it hurt even more. It produced a livid, angry, soggy wound that at one time I thought would threaten my ability to stay with the team. To avoid this outcome I just carried on skiing, which, of course, simply made my poorly foot worse. At this point I was helped by the arrival of the amiable Tony Huddlestone, who smoked smelly French cigarettes and had a Labrador called Kaffer, whom he brought with him. Tony was more sensible than I and sent me off to the doctor for some magic blister cream and advised me not to ski for a few days. Hardly Nobel prize-winning medicine but it worked.

Tony was never cut out for hearty sports but his experience as an officer helped me with the team and his very Gallic approach to things military, (he loved the French and spoke the language fluently), saw us through the Championships. Poor Kaffer suffered in the cause of duty, as the deep snow generally had a thin icy crust on it and the only way he could keep up with his master was by a series of leaps. Despite this method of bounding along, the crust still rasped at his hind quarters, especially in the mornings, and in quite short time Kaffer developed the reddest, sorest pair of 'dog's bollocks' in the history of Crufts.

At that time the Army Downhill Championships were held at St Moritz in mid-January, while the cross-country races were held at the same time in a rather gloomy, somewhat Gothic German ski resort called Winterberg, which is in the middle of the western part of Germany, in a region called Westphalia. Winterberg suffers in the winter from a lack of sun and, rather crucially, from our point of view, from a lack of snow, not being at a high altitude. After two years this problem got so bad that the Army sports board moved the venue to Oberjoch, which we already knew and which had the added benefit of plenty of snow.

For our first year in Winterberg, all the competing teams stayed in the German barracks while the officers holed up in the *Kurhaus*. This square, rather forbidding hotel had been built by Hitler as a rest and relaxation centre for Nazi officers, a place where they could take their blonde girlfriends and help to propagate the thousand-year Reich. In the sixteenth century it was at the centre of a region famous for witch hunts, and somehow this doesn't surprise me. Two quite unattractive incidents happened to me there, which may have biased me against the town.

Our first racing season was the winter of 1960–61. That year the snow was sparser than usual, even for Winterberg, and any snow which did fall thawed so quickly that much of the course was simply brown slush. In some parts soldiers with shovels were required to make artificial tracks. The effect of this was that there were a lot of falls onto the hard ground or even tarmac and, predictably, those new to skiing fell most of all. These conditions were at their worst for the 20-kilometre patrol race, where teams of four had to carry items of Army equipment, including the Army's standard issue SLR rifle. This was strapped onto your backpack with the butt behind your head; in later years we altered this so that only the barrel was uppermost. This first year, though, if you fell hard you had the added enjoyment of smacking the back of your head against the wooden butt of your rifle. I suspect that at the end of that three-hour race we were all mildly concussed as well as exhausted. Three weeks later, when all the racing was over, Colonel Jackie wrote a very kind of letter to my Father saying that the team's efforts 'were as thrilling and inspiring a display of courage and guts that I have seen since the war'.

So my first patrol race was Unpleasant Winterberg Experience Number One. The second occurred in the same race the following year. Once again, Winterberg was all slush and thaw, but to add to the difficulties it rained hard and became much colder during the race. Teams for the patrol race were required to wear a sort of British Army ski uniform, which involved military berets (with regimental cap badge), waist belts, Bergen rucksacks and some sort of white smocking and long socks. Our smocks, I kid you not, were made up by the Quartermaster's staff out of old sheets, and consequently had all the waterproof qualities of a sieve.

We got very cold and wet, and a few hundred yards before the finish I must have developed some form of hypothermia because I collapsed and was carried over the line by the ever helpful corporals Tancock and Dakin. We actually did quite well – finishing around fifth, I think – but all I remember is waking up in the *Kurhaus* with the Colonel's wife peering rather anxiously at me.

Long before that race, (that is at the start of our second season), we knew there would be no comfortable pension to stay in and no Trudi to cosset us; nor was Anton's spartan hut a runner. But money was still short and we only went up from zero star to one star in terms of accommodation – if that. It was decided that the QDG ski team would once again hire Tony Maule, plus his friend Harry Yeomans, and that we could prepare the Wettersteinwand Hutte near Ehrwald, in Austria. This would serve as the base from which several cavalry regiment teams would train, coached by Tony and Harry. In a sense we were the advance party, getting things ready for some sixty or seventy officers and men.

At this time, the issue of Austrian neutrality was very sensitive. The Austrians didn't want the Russians marching in (as they had done in lots of the European countries shortly after the war) on the pretext that the Austrians were 'training' British soldiers in the art of ski warfare. So our time in the Wettersteinwand Hutte, (which translates rather romantically as the 'Weatherstone Wall hut'; shades of Alfred Wainwright and the Cumbrian fells), was spent against this rather murky background and the need to be quite circumspect about the fact we were in the British Army. In the mist that swirled round these curious arrangements was the shadowy figure of one

Colonel Cross, who lived in the village, and who had fixed the lease of the hut with Tony Maule. I never met him and his chief claim to fame was that if he offered to buy you and your friend a beer he would get the waiter to produce a bottle (one bottle) and two glasses!

That November, we set off by train ahead of everyone else for another season's skiing courtesy of the taxpayer. On these overnight train journeys we always had to change at Ulm, where Albert Einstein was born. For the QDG ski team it is best remembered as being the place where we annually stood a good chance of both losing a team's worth of ski equipment and finding ourselves stranded. In the dead of the night we would grind into Ulm station knowing that we had about three minutes to unload our gear (twenty or thirty pairs of skis, rucksacks, endless suitcases, rifles, food and the rest). At my suggestion, we lowered the windows and relays of men would manhandle the stuff through the windows of one train through the windows of the next, waiting train. German railways wait for no one, middle of the night or not, so even if this technique owed its genesis to worthy eighteenth-century fire-fighters handing buckets to each other, we really had no option.

When we arrived, we found our hut was the base for twenty German construction workers who were putting up the big ski-lift which now runs from Ehrwald/Lermoos up the Austrian side of the Zugspitze. For a while we shared our limited accommodation with them, until the lift was complete and they left. We slept on camp beds and when the other teams arrived we all dried our wet skiing kit on various clotheslines draped round one of those big tiled German stoves, a sort of Widow Twankey meets Hansel and Gretel arrangement. There was a kitchen, which was fine as long as you enjoyed endless meals of tinned Scottish lamb (known by us as 'Mutton Jock Style') and corned beef. However, there was also only one loo, and our main task in the two weeks we were on our own was to dig out of the frozen ground a three-seater, 20-foot-drop communal outdoor toilet, suitable for sixty men to use for six weeks. So if, one day, you go up by cable car to the back of the Zugspitze, I hope you will look down on the large hut halfway up and recall one small piece of engineering designed to improve public health.

As part of preparing the hut for the impending invasion by several BAOR regiments we needed to get plenty of food in. That soldiers are hungry animals is a given, but it is even more the case if they have been flogging their young bodies round snowy training circuits and getting cold, wet and tired in the process. So Tony Maule, the mysterious Colonel Cross and a bevy of quartermasters had decided that sufficient tinned 'compo' rations should be supplied to start us all off. However, because of Austria's neutrality the Army truck carrying them could not be driven across the border. Therefore we all met up just inside Germany, where our food for the next two months was transferred clandestinely into Tony's old but spacious VW bus so it could then be manhandled by us up the mountain to the Wettersteinwand Hutte's kitchen. Of course the ideal time for such a covert mission is at night and so it was, with all of the QDG ski team sitting on several hundred tins of best quality army rations, that we crossed the Austrian border, pretending to be nocturnal tourists on a spot of leave from BAOR, keen just to see Austria's beautiful mountains. A story about as likely as English football fans on a trip abroad saying that they won't go in the pub before the game.

Thus one of my abiding memories is lugging a Bergen rucksack in the middle of the night, full of illicit food up the back of the Zugspitze, (which at 2,962 metres is Germany's highest mountain). I don't know precisely how much a rucksack filled with tins weighs but it is certainly a great deal. I recall a full moon set against the pine trees and the crunch of snow under foot while ten or twelve dark, sweating figures toiled up the mountainside. Eventually we got the stuff up the hill and decided to regard our night-time exertions as good training, in the knowledge that some of the food we had smuggled was at least for our own consumption.

In the event we managed the basic logistics of having about sixty men in so crowded a space, but only just. Luckily (or maybe not?) we had some entertainment. When recalling the past, people are often inclined to say 'we made our own music in them days'. Well, in our case we didn't, quite. We had a wind-up record player, owned by an easy-going South African called Hylton. Unfortunately, he only had one record, which he insisted on playing several times most nights. To this day, the strains of Johnny Mathis growling a worn version of 'Moon River' (Hylton never quite wound the thing up fully!) reminds me of the smell of soldiers' clothes drying, endless tinned meals and a freezing DIY loo, albeit one with a stunning view.

During this time in our overcrowded hut a curious episode took place which was to have reverberations later. As was the system for all officers, my pay was paid direct into my bank account. However, when in camp, all the soldiers collected theirs on a weekly basis, in cash. Because we were away from base, the plan was that the men's wages would be sent to the local bank so that I could withdraw the money and pay them. However, the money never arrived. As week followed week the men became more broke, and had to resort to borrowing from others in the hut. Stuck halfway up a mountain in a neutral country, they couldn't even buy their mates a beer, let alone afford soap or extra food.

This problem was my responsibility because, whatever else the British Army teaches, it instills in its junior officers the mantra that caring for the welfare of the soldiers in their charge is their primary task. My QDG soldiers were broke and I was required to help them. So, most afternoons, I put on my downhill skis and took on the deep snow on the virgin slopes running down to Ehrwald. My skiing improved massively as a result of this enforced activity, but there was no financial return, as our account in the local Ehrwald equivalent of NatWest remained stubbornly at zero.

Day after day I went down, and week after week the situation remained stubbornly the same. Having called in at the bank, I had to trudge the hour and a half back up the hill with my skis on my shoulder, often in the dark, aware that I hadn't achieved anything. There was some small solace in that on most of these journeys I was able to check out the quality of the local *Apfelkuchen mit Zahne* (apple cake and cream) and even bumped into the odd pretty downhill skier doing the same. But it was all a bad do. Eventually (and probably later than I should have done) I began to phone the camp, and was told by the Pay Office that the money was 'on its way', 'had been sent' or 'would be with you shortly'. Finally, I booked a call to the Adjutant (the Colonel's right-hand man) and the situation was fixed almost instantly.

Some light was thrown on the reason for our problem about a year later when the duty corporal doing his rounds of the Headquarter block in Wolfenbüttel checked the Pay Office to find the Paymaster slumped over his desk, having shot himself with a pistol. As I have explained, Mess life was not without its bullies, and the unhappy man had never really been able to fit in. He bought himself a large Mercedes and did other expensive things, probably in order to be accepted, but to no avail. In order to upgrade his lifestyle he had, it appeared, been forced to fiddle the books. This, I guess, included holding up my ski team's pay. He had a wife and two young daughters, so his behaviour, culminating in his suicide, was a tragedy for at least four people.

I hate bullying and hope that I have not ever bullied anyone myself. Nonetheless, doing nothing can be part of the process, as the following story involving the same unfortunate Paymaster underlines. We were on exercise in the south of Germany, which was unusual for the Brits as this was technically the American zone. On this occasion we finished up camping in the grounds of a famous German *Schloss* (castle). At a drinks party for the officers held in the garden, the Paymaster's hat was thrown into the empty swimming pool and he unwisely climbed in to retrieve it. It all seemed harmless enough but some people stood round cheering and cat-calling, preventing him from climbing out. During the five years we were in Wolfenbüttel, he and several others suffered this kind of behaviour and although most just quietly coped, or left the Regiment, for our poor Paymaster it was all too much.

While in the Wettersteinwand Hutte I shared a room with another officer who later memorably missed a race in Oberjoch because, it was said, he was in bed with a girl. Our room contained two camp beds and nothing else. The privations of the hut were unfortunately equalled when we eventually finished training and moved back to Germany for the championships (to Winterberg again). For some reason (probably lack of funds) we finished up living communally in a village hall some miles out from the race centre, so we got to and from the various events in a draughty three-ton truck; hardly ideal. In the hall we slept in rows of metal Army beds, and the place generally resembled a World War I field hospital. Most mornings we woke at five o'clock to the sound of Corporal Harrison getting the hydro-burner working to cook breakfast.

While in this rather dismal accommodation Corporal George Cox (whom I liked a lot) went a bit mad and discovered the metal trunks where the rifles for the patrol race were stored. For some archaic reason, someone had decided that if we needed rifles we must also require bayonets. I can still see the unhappy corporal standing naked on his bed with an equally naked bayonet threatening to 'do' anyone who approached him. In time he recovered fully, but sadly the story doesn't have a happy ending: George was shot a few years later by an IRA sniper in Belfast as he got out of his scout car to investigate an incident.

This was the season when I passed out in the rain and cold during the patrol race. I often wonder if our uncomfortable accommodation had something to do with my collapse. The Wettersteinwand Hutte was cramped and the food only fair. Sleeping rough and having to flog up and down the mountain to hunt for the team's pay was an extra demand on me physically, and, to cap it all, our accommodation during the racing was frankly inadequate.

Not surprisingly, given that I skied competitively for five seasons without break, the memories tend to blur, in the way that Dylan Thomas memorably describes when talking about Christmas in Wales in his childhood*. So I will summarise. We became, in British terms, a team of very competent cross-country skiers. Tancock and Dakin represented Britain in the Olympics, and in my last race I came seventh in the 15-kilometre individual race, competing against potential British team skiers. This success, plus the fact I was the only officer in the first ten, led to me being asked to manage the British team; however, the then Commanding Officer vetoed the idea, saying I was needed back at the Regiment. He may have been influenced in his decision by a caustic remark I made, in private I thought, about some alterations to the Mess. Had I been older, wiser and less duty bound, I should have contacted someone more senior to contest what was going on. But young officers didn't do that sort

---

* 'I can never remember whether it snowed for six days and six nights when I was twelve or whether it snowed for twelve days and twelve nights when I was six.' – from a Child's Christmas in Wales.

of thing in those days, nor, I suspect, would it be a career enhancing move to do so today.

So I picked myself up from this disappointment and resolved to learn to downhill ski, with a view to entering the competition for best all-round skier, which required you to take part in two downhill races and two cross-country events. This alternative plan worked out quite well and in my last seasons I twice won the Army All-Rounder – I have the pewter mugs and some press cuttings to prove it! Going off to downhill ski took me away from the constant slog of *Langlauf* training, and for two seasons I was able to enjoy the delights of such ski resorts as Lech, Zermatt and St Moritz.

In 1962 Oberjoch became the permanent location for the Army Championships, and this very much suited us. Our training base was not far away down in the valley, where we lived pretty comfortably in a pension in the village of Vorderhindelang. This was called Pension Zurblick and was run by a woman we referred to as Mutti (Mama), and her husband Herr Schoenacher, who was a survivor from the Russian Front in World War II. They had a teenage daughter whose name I have forgotten but I think my friend David Treasure would know! This family looked after us extremely well.

I should really have mentioned David earlier as he and I spent a lot of time together as part of both the athletics and the cross-country ski teams, and he has been a good friend for over fifty years now. Essentially David was a much better sportsman than I, as he was a good cricketer, a quick rugby full-back and a natural long-distance runner. However, he had one disadvantage: he didn't like training! Added to this he smoked a fair amount and drank a bit. As I was industrious and a non-smoker, this gave me an almost unfair advantage when it came to inter-squadron athletics and the demands of cross-country skiing.

David is well built and good-looking and spent a fair amount of leisure time in nightclubs and on various escapades until he settled down with the lovely Moni, who had lived in Wolfenbüttel during the time we were stationed there. He had the nous to pick the Beatles as world-beaters early in their career and this 'cool' approach even extended to having a cassette player fitted inside his pale blue Ford Taunus. I have an abiding memory of driving up the mountain pass to race in Oberjoch with David, and a recording playing of Brenda Lee singing 'Let's Jump the Broomstick'. David is a good pal.

During the Championships Oberjoch itself became rather a different place than usual, with hundreds of competitors milling about and a series of rather ugly British Army khaki marquees being used for eating, waxing skis and resting – rather as though someone had dumped some inflatable fast food restaurants on the village green. I managed to get us away from this rather heavy military presence by finding a small family hotel close to the start and, for a bottle of whisky, the owner happily let us use his cellar to prepare for the races. There, among the chopped logs, bottles of wine and drying bed linen, we spent two or three hours carefully waxing, polishing and testing our racing skis. The Scots DG ski team shared our underground haven and while we were preparing for the four by ten-kilometre relay race we were visited by their Commanding Officer. I next met him fifteen years later when he was lecturing at Sandhurst on a TA course, by which time he was in charge of the British Army. He told a story which I have never forgotten and have used often in my more recent role as a professional trainer.

'When I was a Major, just like most of you in this room,' he said, 'I was really disenchanted with my life in the Army and thought of leaving. However, before making a definite decision I wrote to an uncle of mine listing my grievances and saying how disillusioned I was. He wrote back a tolerant and understanding letter advising me to stay in but to try and get to the top, on the basis that if I did then one day I would be in a position to put things right. The years passed and on the day I took over my latest appointment I found a letter on my new desk. It was in an elderly, spidery hand, which I recognised as that of my uncle and simply said, "Dear Nephew. Congratulations! Now it's your turn!'

Over the years we had to race in some difficult conditions, but the worst weather I ever experienced in terms of skiing took place round the lake at Lermoos, a village a short distance from Ehrwald. I think it was a divisional competition because only the British, and indeed the British Army, would have been foolish enough to race when the temperature was −20 degrees Celsius. At this level of cold the breath can freeze in your lungs, so there is a real risk of medical damage. Almost half an hour before the start of the race I was testing my wax when I felt the end of my nose going hard; friends told me it was white, like a pencil rubber. This was my first (and only) experience of frostbite but using a degree of officer-like initiative I wrapped a black silk scarf round the bottom half of my face. I then proceeded to race quite successfully round the very frozen lake, looking somewhat like an Inuit version of Jesse James about to rob an Austrian bank. To this day I know when the weather has turned really cold because my nose begins to 'go'.

Of course, being away during winter meant that we often missed Christmas and New Year. But there were compensations. One year, feeling rather flat at missing the celebrations, we heard that the Scots DG (the Greys) were in a hut only a few miles away. So we drove over to see them and share a dram on the basis that only people from Scotland fully understand New Year celebrations. Sure enough, we were not disappointed.

The Greys told us that they had heard that some female German physical education teachers had booked in to a hut only an hour away. That year Ranulph Fiennes was flexing his exploring muscles via *Langlauf* skis, and I think it was he who suggested that we should take the regimental piper with us. So, David Treasure and I and the rest of the boys solemnly set off through the sparkling midnight snow in a quest to find our forty friendly German teachers. We were accompanied on this memorable journey up the mountain, as you would expect, by the haunting notes of the Scots Greys' Regimental March played on the bagpipes. We found our teachers, and did our bit to improve Anglo-German relations as well as mark New Year.

Overall, this happy period gave me wonderful opportunities to get fit, learn a rare skill and gain success for myself, the team and the Regiment. I would like to end on a high note by saying we won the Princess Marina (Duchess of Kent) Cup, and indeed, for an hour or so, we did, only to have it taken away from us by a rather foolish quirk of the rule book.

In our fourth or fifth season we entered the final race (the 20-kilometre patrol) needing only to come second (or better) to win the cup. We raced well and duly came second. However, not long after the race ended, we heard that another team had been disqualified from the patrol race, as their officer had lost a piece of equipment during the event. At the time, the rules said that any disqualification from the patrol race also applied to all other races, including the downhill ones that had been completed in St Moritz some ten days earlier. Removing this team from all race results had the effect of making another team the overall winners of the cup. I contested this arcane ruling straight after the race with the Race Committee (which was chaired by a general), but my protest was fairly quickly dismissed as they were keen not to delay the announcement of the final results. In the game L'Attaque, when a lieutenant confronts a general the four-star officer always wins, and this applies anywhere in the world.

So in the end I didn't quite manage the Olympic squad nor as a ski team did we achieve our five-year goal. It all mattered at the time because we put so much of ourselves into it, but I'm not sure it matters now. I knew then that I was privileged just to be there, enjoying the success, the sport, the mountains and being part of a happy team, despite the inevitable disappointments. Today I still think I was privileged.

CHAPTER SEVEN

Active Service

'Experience is not what happens to you; it's what you do with what happens to you'

– Aldous Huxley

My story now moves on from cold, snowy, mountainous places to those more redolent of the British Empire which, during my ten years in the Army, was, of course, in the process of quietly closing down. You could say that if the Empire was a classy restaurant, then I and my comrades in arms were collecting the glasses, turning the chairs onto the tables and sweeping the floor before closing.

Thus the locations I was about to find myself in would turn out to be quite dangerous, generally hot, and where you certainly couldn't assume that the locals were friendly. During the three years after leaving Germany I served in Northern Ireland, Borneo and Aden, with the last two being designated as active service stations. On these latter tours we represented the UK Government, and our job was to support the established order wherever we were stationed.

In the fact the reality was that we were largely in these places to assist Britain's exit, I can see now that for the first forty years or so of my life I was involved with institutions that were more or less in decline, but which have largely recovered – or at least not got worse. The Church was in a relatively poor way during the 1950s and 1960s and under almost permanent attack from powerful social and secular forces. The Empire, as I have indicated, is no more, and though our armed forces are now held in high esteem this was not universally the case during National Service days. When I eventually joined the UK's manufacturing sector in the 1970s it was in a bad way and, similarly, when I became involved with education too many of our schools were a disgrace. Both manufacturing and education are now in a much better state.

I can't remember much about my time in Northern Ireland. We were stationed in Lisanelly Barracks, Omagh, but I was sent away on a six-month detachment to Borneo not very long after arriving. At some point I was made Assistant Adjutant, positioned outside the Colonel's office; (this particular Colonel was my old friend Mad Tom). This post introduced me to the doubtful and certainly arcane delights of Army staff work, which at the time seemed to me to be a complicated way of making things clearer. During my short stay in this role I worked alongside the helpful and patient John Pocock.

A notable event that I certainly remember during our stay across the Irish Sea was a visit from Queen Elizabeth the Queen Mother, who had an honorary military position, as most of the Royal Family do; she was Colonel-in-Chief of the QDG. Given the long history of unforgiving violence between many of the Irish and the British, no member of the monarchy had been to either Northern or Southern Ireland for many years, so this was a seminal visit, fraught with political and social overtones. As part of the proceedings the Regiment put on a parade involving lots of drill, and therefore lots of drill parades, which I disliked. I was therefore very glad to be put in charge of the armoured car escort providing security for the

Queen Mother on her journey from the airport to Lisanelly Barracks. I hope the police were armed that day as we certainly weren't.

Somebody said they knew a good photographer in London, so this man was flown out to take some commemorative photos, including the standard picture of the Colonel-in-Chief with all her officers. This gentleman proved to be better at selling his services than taking photographs, as none of them ever appeared. In a fashion perhaps typical of Britain at this time, there was a cover-up, so nothing was said and the matter was quietly dropped. My only other memory of the historic visit was of the Queen Mother's eyes as she went along the line being introduced. I caught her gaze for a fleeting moment but the impression was everlasting and it made me glad I wasn't Edward VIII or some errant courtier.

About this time I learnt a skill which differentiates me from most other people and which has no practical value at all. I can drive a vehicle very fast backwards. It's not often that I am able to dazzle people with my prowess, so on the very few occasions I am required to reverse at high speed I am pathetically pleased. The reason I can do this is all to do with 'snake patrolling', a battle skill perfected by armoured car regiments during World War II and one which Colonel Tom Muir, quite rightly, insisted we should practise incessantly.

In Germany and Northern Ireland the role of the Regiment was armoured recce – short for reconnaissance. That is to say, using our armoured Saladins (the big ones with the gun) plus the smaller Ferret Scout car (equipped with just a Browning machine gun) we were required to be the eyes and ears of the Army, advancing to find the enemy or protect a flank. The snake patrol was the standard way of 'advancing to contact' to find out where the enemy was, and to do so with a degree of speed mixed with caution.

A troop, commanded by an officer or sergeant and comprising four armoured cars, would advance down the road with the lowest, smallest vehicle, a Ferret Scout car, acting as 'point', up front. In unthreatening situations we would do a 'green patrol', which meant moving quite fast one after the other, but what we trained for most were 'red patrols', when trouble was expected. Moving in unison so that we looked rather like a snake, one vehicle would draw up behind the other and both commanders would scan the countryside carefully. If clear, the first vehicle would move smartly forward to the next 'bound' or safe distance ahead, with the second, stationary armoured car in a position to give covering fire. When, and if, the leading vehicle 'bumped' the enemy, the driver would reverse rapidly back to safety

It was this manoeuvre of approaching a corner slowly, stopping, engaging the forward/reverse lever (which allows the vehicle to move backwards in any of its seven gears) and then reversing back down the road as fast as possible, that we tried to perfect in Northern Ireland. By simply slamming his foot on the clutch the driver could take his armoured car up through the gears and we happily reached speeds of 40 to 50mph, including going round bends, as we hurtled backwards down the Irish lanes. I always enjoyed my turn as the driver, to see what it was like.

Not surprisingly, the opportunities for me to display my mastery of reversing at speed are few and far between on the M25 or down Windsor High Street. Over the years I also honed another minor skill which does have some rather limited use. As a teenager, I taught myself to wolf-whistle using four fingers and my tongue curled inside my mouth like a bent sandwich. I thought, quite mistakenly, this would impress girls when I took them out (at least in my imaginings!) to smart places in London and needed to hail a taxi. I still employ my piercing whistle from time to time, for example to quell a noisy room or to attract a cab and, if Ursula is out in Windsor I delight now in being probably the only man in

Britain who regularly wolf-whistles his wife. She generally ignores the noise, but she knows full well who it is.

After a few months in Northern Ireland I was moved to B Squadron and we received orders to embark for Borneo, on a six-month operational tour. This little-known campaign was something of a success for the Brits, and we used jungle warfare techniques honed against the Communist guerrillas in the 1950s in Malaya. Although Borneo no longer belonged to Britain, the Malay Government asked for British military assistance to protect that part of Indonesia which now belonged to them. The Malay Government had hundreds of miles of land border, most of it thick jungle, to protect against the designs of the Indonesian army, led by President Sukarno, who wanted the Malays out.

After flying to Singapore, where we acclimatised for a month and listened to alarming medical lectures, my troop, together with another commanded by Gordon Ferguson, was dispatched on a small but smelly troopship to a border point called Sungai Tengang, where most of us would remain for the next five months.

There we lived, all forty of us, in and around an attap (a type of cane) bungalow previously belonging to a rubber planter, with some of the troops actually under canvas, due to a shortage of room. Fortunately Gordon and I got on well together as we were to live cheek by jowl for months on end in fairly spartan and claustrophobic conditions. Gordon was an energetic but thoughtful character and his generous spirit had extended to lending me his car in Germany when I needed to get to dates in Braunschweig. He went on to do great things in the Army, having had a major success during the troubles in Lebanon, and became a very young brigadier. He would surely have gone on to even greater things, but his health began to be a problem and eventually he died too young from the horrid motor neurone disease. I remember him well, and with fondness; and not only because he was an excellent sprinter, who filled a serious gap in our great little athletics team.

Gordon and I reached our new quarters by driving from the port of Kuching for a couple of hundred miles down the only metalled road in thousands of square miles of jungle. When I say metalled I don't mean tarmac. It was a narrow two-lane highway made of shingle and stone, rather of the kind you might bump down to reach a country farmhouse in England. This road ran parallel with a range of steep tree-covered hills, called the Kalimantan Range, along the top of which lay the border and across which the Indonesian army made its incursions. Our job was to patrol the road in both directions and every so often to stop at marked posts to turn the 76mm guns of our Saladin armoured cars to the sky and pound the jungle crossings up in the hills. This we would do a couple of times a day (and sometimes at night) in order to discourage the opposition and to remind them of the firepower we possessed.

We were one of a series of outposts dotted along the road and we never quite knew when an attack might come. Indeed, a month before we arrived 2 Para, who were based about forty miles away at Serian, had been attacked and lost six or seven men. Hence our compound was quite well fortified, and previous occupiers had placed sharpened bamboo stakes hidden in the undergrowth on the approaches. Add to this a series of barbed wire fences, some weapon pits and a couple of well-sighted machine guns and we had a fairly warlike appearance. But in truth I never felt very secure in the military sense at Sungai Tengang. For a start, we had any number of jerry cans full of petrol not far from the bungalow, and our best efforts to get it all stored underground never worked. In addition, our soldiers were inexperienced and not trained to defend a base as the infantry were. Despite practising many stand-to drills (where everyone takes up a defensive position, on the alert), I never thought we would survive a night attack, especially if the enemy got among us.

Fortunately this exigency never occurred and I believe this was for two reasons. First, the enemy knew we had armoured cars, and secondly, and most significantly, we had a company of Gurkhas up the hill only a hundred yards away. This was deeply comforting. The Gurkha soldier's reputation precedes him, and while we thought we were OK at mechanised warfare, no one surpasses the ferocity and skill of these Nepalese soldiers in the jungle or at close quarters.

Comforting as the closeness of these Gurkhas was, the disparity between us and them when out on patrol was sometimes embarrassing. Their speciality, like the SAS and Royal Marines, during this period of confrontation, was to set up ambushes for up to three or four weeks at a time. No washing, no shaving, no hot food and a minimum of movement, so even going to the loo had its own secretive procedures. At night, even though their base was right next to us, their compound was absolutely silent, with no lights and absolutely no drinking. This was not the case with us. Looking back now, I think that our way of operating, with alcohol allowed in camp, was quite wrong and rather dangerous. On the one occasion I did take our soldiers out on patrol Trooper Rees got lost and wandered back down the mountain. Had he stumbled into a Gurkha ambush they were quite clear he would have been shot.

Probably the most dangerous element in our quarters in Borneo was disease, especially that carried by rats, which came out in droves at night. Corporal Andrews made a speciality of using old domestic water pipes, purloined from nearby derelict bungalows, to build frames on which we could stretch our camp beds some three feet off the ground. I used to lie in the room, with Gordon Ferguson snoring gently, listening to the scurrying of rodent paws beneath me and the occasional trap springing shut. Taking the view that the rats were more of a threat than the Indonesians I had all the sandbags removed from inside the hut, and we destroyed nest after nest. To give you an idea of the size of the problem, when I went on to visit Semmangang (the Squadron HQ) I used to check the sentries at night. If you shone a torch on the cookhouse roof, literally hundreds of pairs of eyes gleamed back at you.

Life in Borneo was not all danger and disease and I made a good friend of the Gurkha Company Commander, Bruce Niven, a cousin of the actor David Niven. Although Bruce was quite aesthetic and serious-minded, he was very kind to me and we used to have long chats about soldiering and suchlike as the sun went down over the jungle canopy.

After about three months patrolling the road and living at Sungai Tengang six of us with our two Saladin armoured cars were moved nearer the frontline to join a company of New Zealand infantry at Batu Lintang. This was a well-defended hill-top enclave which nonetheless had been mortared on a number of previous occasions by the Indonesians. Consequently during the day we had the protection of armour plating, but at night we slept underground in bunks which had been built into cells holding five or six people. We had the ground over our heads, and walls lined with corrugated iron panels, behind which the friendly Borneo rats played happily. Living this close with soldiers really tests a young officer, for they see you exactly as you are and they can challenge your views and, in a sense, your authority. The upside of this is that you get to know how the enlisted man thinks and, if you survive with your self-worth intact, you become a better officer and leader.

Soldiering in this fairly tense situation in the Far East, with all its strange scents and sounds, left a strong impression on me. However, the memories as such are fleeting: watching a cockfight in Borneo in a compound, visiting a Dyak longhouse (no shrivelled skulls as far as I could see), cruising some of the huge rivers of the archipelago in Army-issue assault boats, taking Communion in a dug-out with the Para's boxing-champion Chaplain, just me and two others, and, finally, experiencing the delights of an Army Mobile Bath Unit. This strange sounding organisation is a godsend if you've been living rough for weeks. The unit arrives with large canvas tents into which they put duckboards and shower units. Using portable pumps and heaters they find a water supply to provide hot showers, and to top this wonderful service they then issue everyone with a clean set of uniform, including underclothes. It was, as you can tell, a strangely memorable experience, and I recall coming out of the Unit just as it was dusk to see a deep red sun slowly sinking down behind jungle of the darkest green – foreign, somewhat alien and in every sense impenetrable.

There is a World War II story, which I believe is true, about someone who used a Mobile Bath Unit somewhere in Italy. The guy in question had a shower and a change of uniform during the early part of the war and duly left all his very dirty clothing to be washed and then issued elsewhere. About a year later, having been posted hundreds of miles away, he again went to have a shower – and you can imagine his surprise when he was provided with newly washed underclothes that had his name in them and were precisely the ones he had handed in some twelve months before!

Reading this you may think there are hardly any links between being hearty on skis in Germany and Austria and active service in Asia, but without going in depth into the military virtues of physical fitness, endurance and leading teams, there was one particular, rather strange, incident that did indeed link these divergent worlds.

In the middle of our Borneo tour I was sitting one day on the veranda outside Squadron HQ when a large helicopter landed close by. Shortly after this a smart young man wearing white shorts and a white uniform shirt and carrying a briefcase came up the steps asking to see Lieutenant Wood. Having introduced himself, he said he was from Special Branch (SIB) of the Military Police looking into a case of fraud. This, as you may guess, was somewhat alarming. He then produced from his briefcase copies of some BAOR petrol coupons, signed by me, some eighteen months before when I was competing in cross-country races in Germany. I confirmed my signature and he then indicated that the coupons in question had been 'lifted' from the Motor Transport Section of 40th Field Regiment. By 'lifted', he meant these coupons were designated only for use by official military transport (such as Army lorries and Land Rovers) and were not for civilian cars.

He then proceeded to interview me as to how I had got them, who from, when and so on. As it was such a long time ago I genuinely couldn't remember much about their origin or how I got them. Certainly I hadn't noticed the unit stamp on the back, though I suspect I could have guessed who the original owner might have been. Anyway, suffice to say after about half an hour of all this he went on his way back to Singapore. Quite an expensive outing for the taxpayer to fund and I doubt they ever found the culprit.

Soon my Borneo days came to an end and we flew home for some leave, to await either a cushy two-year posting in the UK or maybe somewhere more adventurous. As it happened, in military terms I was about to embark on the most challenging posting of my Army career. We were off on our travels again to another active service station, this time Aden, a port in the southern part of what is now the Yemen. The omens were hardly encouraging. Aden was then known within the Army as 'the backside of the Empire' as it is made up of a wasteland of arid desert in which are set jebels (hills composed of volcanic type rock). The weather is very hot, and it is one of the most humid places in the world, so during the first few weeks we all found it quite difficult to breathe because the air was so cloying. Added to these inhospitable characteristics was the fact that the British Government had recently announced we would be leaving, thus encouraging the various terrorist gangs (FLOSIE, NLF etc) to see how many of the British military they could murder – that is, when they weren't shooting each other. Aden itself, although quite a busy port, was essentially a shanty town peopled by urban Arabs who had few of the fine characteristics of their desert cousins.

We were quartered in Little Aden, which was a proper camp but which had only a limited amount of air-conditioned accommodation and which lay close to the BP refinery. As Signals Officer I needed to be near the operations room so I took the door off a nearby stationery cupboard and thus finished up with what I could describe as the world's smallest office. There was so little room that even with a cut-down table and a tiny chair half of me was still stuck out in the corridor, but at least it was cool and you could think and write.

There was a similar problem with the Officers' Mess, because, being a junior officer, I had to spend much of the year moving between the main building, which was air-conditioned, and a series of tin huts which formed the Mess annex and were consequently boiling. Every time some more senior officer arrived I vacated my cool room in the main building and went into the annex until a room became vacant. I suppose the heat and the generally tense situation sent us all slightly mad. I recall setting out to read the dictionary (yes, all the words from A to Z!) and sitting for hours in my room typing out Shakespeare soliloquies, as well as the lyrics of Flanders and Swann songs. This I did on an old portable Olivetti typewriter that I had bought from Francis Chamberlain in a rather forlorn attempt to teach myself touch-typing.

My involvement with Shakespeare must have rubbed off. Not only in terms of quotations (saving, storing and using good quotes is a great love) but also in terms of positioning myself as one of the 'liberal', 'arty' members of the Mess. For example, in line with the 'Swinging Sixties' image of Britain then in vogue I made my own statement by being one of the first QDG Officers to buy a coloured shirt to wear with my suit at dinner. These were the days when the dress code every night would be either a country suit or dark suit, white shirt, tie and leather shoes. So my yellow shirt caused some commotion that evening with whoops and mild criticism. Turning from the sideboard I defended my modernism with a quote from *King Lear*: 'I am a man more sinned against than sinning.' Nobody really minded, and I could well defend myself since it was just horseplay by all concerned – I'm sure people subconsciously knew I was merely conforming to my image.

Sometimes I used to go up-country to live in one of the defended outposts we had created in the interior. For example, I travelled by helicopter to Habelain, which was actually a series of sandbagged defensive points on top of an outcrop of rock. We landed just as the sun was setting on the hills around, which created huge shadows and gave me a sense of the mystery of this ancient land. It was useful to do these trips since not only did my signals team communicate with these outposts on a daily and nightly basis but we also ran convoys to them. These were constantly in danger of being mined or ambushed.

I remember going on patrol into Aden town itself. This we normally did in Land Rovers but when there was the possibility of riots or serious trouble we used our armoured vehicles. I always took a rifle on our Land Rover patrols as the small Sterling sub-machine gun was not much use in a fire fight. Standing in the front passenger seat it was easy to keep a rifle pointed at the regulation angle of 45 degrees towards the sky, and it was lucky I did so as a matter of routine and good training.

On one patrol I was fiddling with the safety catch on my rifle with the intention of being fully prepared for trouble when it went off and I accidentally fired two shots in the air. Such behaviour was dangerous and therefore, technically, a chargeable offence. Fortunately my loyal team said nothing and I breathed a sigh of relief that no one had been hurt by my ill discipline. But the boys did have the last laugh and made a point. About four days later on the British Forces Broadcasting Service there was a request for Lieutenant Tony Wood from his troop. It was Sonny and Cher singing 'Bang, Bang'.

Another illegal incident was in fact the responsibility of my Troop Sergeant, the irrepressible Sergeant Barry. Small, tough, curly-haired and with the wickedest grin, he used to regale our signal troop soldiers with lengthy stories of his escapades in Cardiff and Swansea. No detail was spared as he related, to the soldiers' never-failing delight, his inexhaustible pursuit and conquest of the girls of South Wales.

About halfway through our stay in Aden, Sergeant Barry took a couple of Land Rovers out for what was euphemistically called 'a two-day patrol'. At some point he went off the approved route and finished up on the beach, whereupon everyone went for a swim. Needless to say, as the tide came in one of the vehicles got bogged down. Overnight it became completely submerged by sea water; not good news for an unprotected engine. The next day the poorly Land Rover was rescued from the waves but was, of course, a complete write-off and Sergeant Barry was in line for being charged and demoted for wasting thousands of pounds of taxpayers' money. Those in charge set out to invoke Army rules and regulations and to 'get' my Troop Sergeant. However, loyalty works two ways. If my men were in trouble I saw it as my job, as far as was both reasonable and possible, to fight for them. I did all I could, short of lying, to hold up the process and to obfuscate the issue. This seemed to work and ultimately charges were not pressed. I'm afraid that if it comes to a choice between the system and a member of my team then my instinct, assuming the issue is not a major one, will always be to side with the individual.

It's always odd for those outside the military to appreciate that, in modern insurgency conflicts or terrorist situations, troops tend to be on the highest alert 24/7 in the sensitive areas but, in the more secure base camps, life goes on in a fairly normal way. In Fallaise Camp, Little Aden, we played sport, held parties, listened to music, drank, wrote letters and each night sat down to dinner served by the Mess waiters. A really quite civilised existence continued even though the officer opposite you at lunch might just have returned two hours earlier from an ambush in which he and his soldiers had killed three terrorists. You just had to accept this was the norm and adjust to it. Army life in such situations is not all about kneeling behind sandbags clutching a rifle with your teeth gritted.

For example one of my roles in Aden was 'Office in Charge of Films'. 'Films' meant full-length feature films provided by the Army Kinema Corporation (AKC) for social and recreational use, rather than gritty training documentaries on how to throw a grenade or live on one cup of water a day in the desert. Someone had to be Films Officer, because Colonel Tom had decided that the Mess would hold film nights every Sunday evening to which he could invite the officers, their wives and any guests. Out in the open air, under the wide and open desert sky, we sat in our cane chairs while waiters served food and drinks, watching what passed for the latest movies. The choice of what we saw was down to me, and every week I used to drive the communal Mess Mini into Aden to choose from the AKC's somewhat dated stock.

Not that my role was one of unalloyed success and pleasure, for being Films Officer came at a price. Having only one projector meant that Corporal Russell, our AKC-trained projectionist, had to change reels at least once during the evening but, in the languid atmosphere we were temporarily enjoying, this was merely a good opportunity to charge your glass, chat or go to the loo. It's true, too, that my choices weren't always appreciated by the more hearty of my colleagues, but endless car chases and confrontations with silent girls in small bikinis do pall after a bit, and films requiring a little more application from the audience were in fact quite welcome. No, my problem was a technical one and to do with Cinemascope.

To show a Cinemascope film you require a wide screen which is curved slightly in towards the audience at the sides. We had a wide screen all right, but, since it was made of plywood painted white, curves of any kind were difficult to create. Thus, whenever a Cinemascope film was on, the audience would be treated to moving images, albeit ones which were blurred at the edges. This, together with the occasional breakdown, used to incense Colonel Tom who was busy (quite properly) trying to entertain regimental guests and, less properly perhaps, impress the latest lady to catch his eye. So when things went wrong he would shout out in the middle of the film, 'Where's the Films Officer?' and I would have to report to him and crouch by his chair in the half-light to tell him what was happening and the action being taken.

Such events became quite regular and therefore both an expected delight and a small piece of sport for my fellow officers, who would cheerfully join in with choruses of, 'Woody, where's Woody?' when the Colonel lost his temper. Twenty years later Georgie Powell was able to record that he was sitting in the Odeon Leicester Square when the film broke down, and immediately two voices called out in the darkness, 'Woody, where's Woody?'.

So we did enjoy a social life and we also played sport when possible. Exhausting games of hockey played in the heat of the day on the drill square come to mind. So does the time I captained the Army (well, Aden Garrison) athletics team in a match against the Navy and the Air Force when Sergeant Healey and I crossed the winning line together in the 3,000 metres. One time after a hockey match against RAF Khormaksar I found myself talking to an RAF fighter pilot. He took my polite interest in what he did rather further than I intended, and half an hour later I was being fitted into a G suit and pilot's helmet preparatory for a quick spin up country in a Hunter jet. He said he liked low-level flying and the desert was the best place to do this. So, one metre above the desert floor, we whizzed along at 600mph while I, securely strapped into a seat behind him, looked at the back of his helmet and hoped he knew where the sticking up bits were. Actually it was a thrilling and totally enjoyable experience.

Before leaving enjoyable experiences, I ought to mention that because service families were still stationed in the area and because both Aden and Little Aden had officers' clubs, it was possible to take out girls. Indeed, during one rather pompous and possibly alcohol-fuelled moment I foolishly ventured the comment during dinner that, 'There are a dozen girls in Aden and I know ten of them'. Not my finest moment, especially since someone else could have added, 'Maybe. But that's because you spend your time sitting in HQ and are able to get to the Officers' Club three times a week!' But there's no doubt that dating was possible.

One evening I went for a meal in town with Avril Hancock, the daughter of a local engineer officer, and afterwards we took a stroll along the beach in the moonlight. Sitting on the shingle with the waves splashing in under a starlit sky with a pretty (well, actually very pretty girl) next to you was indeed the essence of romance. The only disturbing note was the Sterling sub-machine gun I insisted on carrying, with eighteen rounds in the magazine.

Perhaps as a young man in these far-off stations it is possible to go too far. One of the more senior naval officers had an ADC who had invited his sister Catherine to stay with him in Admiralty House for a month. We met at a party on a boat and it was all very passionate. We did dangerous things like discussing poetry, planning dates for when we were both back in England and chatting about what she was going to read at university. At another party only a few days later, this time with her brother present, I fear we danced too close and kissed a mite too publicly, for the next thing I knew she had been whisked off to England without a word. Still, I suppose it was the 1960s and, as I belonged to the very conservative world of the forces, I should perhaps have been a little more judicious with my where and when and what!

One of my favourite Aden stories throws a little light on the art of leadership. The Commander-in-Chief of all Aden Forces (including the RAF and up-country elements) was one Admiral Sir Michael Le Fanu. He had a fierce intellect, a commanding presence, a great rapport with ordinary servicemen and, although balding, also had tufts of ginger hair. One day, when he was inspecting RAF Khormaksar, he got detached from his escorting party and found himself standing alone at the back of a Hercules transport aircraft, full of freight and packing cases. Suddenly out of the gloom at the front of the plane a voice shouted 'Oy'. Peering into the dim recesses he saw a solitary soldier dressed for work in hot climes (army boots, rolled-down socks, short shorts, with hairy legs and sweaty chest, topped off with a beret of some sort). 'Oy,' said the soldier again, 'Don't just stand there, Ginger, give us a hand.' At this point the Admiral would pause, and someone would say, 'Well, what did you do?' 'Why, I gave him a hand, of course.' That is until the accompanying party recovered their lost leader and instead of unloading boxes he was given things to do which were more appropriate for the Commander-in-Chief, Middle East Land Forces.

The rather humdrum job of Signals Officer was turned into something more interesting when General Tower, then the Army Commander, had to send his ex-Parachute Regiment ADC on leave to the UK for medical treatment. He asked our CO, Georgie Powell, to find a temporary replacement and I was asked to stand in for a few months. This time, instead of moving my kit into the fetid environs of the huts in Little Aden, I moved distinctly upmarket into the very comfortable environment of Government House, with gardeners and bearers and dinner parties and an air of hushed importance. There is a picture of a very slim me, aged twenty-five, standing outside the front entrance with palm trees in the background, Union Jack flying and the General's staff car in the foreground.

General Philip Tower was not a conventional Army officer, far from it. He went to Harrow and had fought at Arnhem as part of the Parachute Regiment. He had an urbane and charming manner and was very sociable. For example, he made a point of writing his thank-you letters immediately on returning home from a party, before going to bed. He reminded me regularly of the importance of looking after people in your team and he was punctilious in his genuine concern for soldiers and those of junior rank including myself; as a result I was often the beneficiary of his kindness and encouragement.

He was quite a political general, in the sense that he was well attuned to the needs of Whitehall, and this didn't always go down well with the rank and file. If asked for their solution to the Aden problem they would probably have said, 'Shoot any Arab that moves and if you can't do that then lock him up.' Subtle and designed to reduce tension this attitude was not, but at the time I fear this would have been a general view, officers included. It was not, however, one shared by General Tower.

My aide-de-camp duties at Government House essentially meant looking after the General, carrying his bag and standing 'one pace, right rear' on any official occasion. I remember once we flew in an RAF Hercules to visit some offshore islands which were used, I think, as a signal station. There I discovered that another of the General's idiosyncrasies was to enjoy nude bathing. Stripping off, we enjoyed a swim in the cool waters of the Red Sea in a sheltered cove. This penchant of his, of course, got talked about as did his tendency to touch people, an arm here or a slightly too hearty handshake there; inevitably he became known as 'Toucher Tower'. There was a feeling that he was too soft on the Arabs and this, as well as the characteristics described above, hardly helped his reputation among the troops. This was a pity as he was in many ways a very modern and wise commander.

On one occasion we visited the Parachute Regiment on patrol in the middle of the night in Sheikh Othman, which was a very run-down area close to the docks. I was asked to make sure that the General's parachute beret (with its famous parachute badge) and his shirt with 'wings' on it were in the car for him to change into. I forgot and was pretty cross with myself at the time for letting him down.

There was one incident during my three to four months as General Tower's stand-in ADC which produced the most dangerous moment of my time in the Army. The British plan was the usual one for when we were about to withdraw from a colony. In this case it had been updated by the Governor Sir Humphrey Trevelyan and it hinged on us being able to build up the local administration during the course of a two-year handover. The intention was to train, equip and support the indigenous politicians, police force, health service, Army and other officials so that they could take over from us bit by bit as we prepared to leave. In the Yemen (or the Aden Protectorate as it then was) this was a very fond hope indeed. But there really was no other feasible option and we had to maintain the pretence that this policy was going to work, right up to the point when the last Royal Marine was helicoptered off to a waiting aircraft carrier.

Shortly after I joined the General's team the Argyll and Sutherland Highlanders arrived for a six-month tour to relieve the Northumberland Fusiliers, who were due home. The base for the two-week handover from one battalion to the other was the police station in a quarter of Aden called Crater. The police were largely composed of local people, some of whom were almost certainly secret members of the terrorist movement. At some point into the handover a very ugly incident occurred, which became known as the Crater Massacre. Two or three Land Rovers comprising troops from both battalions were approaching the doors of the police station when they were ambushed and nearly everyone was killed. As I remember it, the dead numbered ten or twelve soldiers, including several officers. One from the Yorkshire Regiment was last seen being dragged alive by locals from the wreckage and his body was never found.

For the Argylls this was an insult as well as a terrible start to their tour. They were angry, hell bent on revenge and also extremely trigger happy. Despite this, they continued to occupy the police station as their base and follow the policy that 'we will hand over policing, in due course, to the relevant local forces'. So, in complete denial of the self-evident truth that the police themselves took part in the ambush, we all continued to pretend that they were an important and loyal part of the British administration.

In pursuit of this policy only a week after our comrades had been shot dead, I found myself escorting the General on a tour of inspection of the Crater police in the very compound from which the ambush had been launched. We walked up and down lines of native police, looking at their gleaming boots and shining cap badges. Watching us were a considerable number of the Argylls, whose body language showed how they despised this charade. No doubt inside the police station itself there were also numbers of the men who had mutinied the week before (and presumably would happily do so again), while in the buildings surrounding us there were certainly plenty of putative terrorists, just waiting for the chance to cause mayhem. My view now is the same as my view then: namely that had a car backfired or any one of these groups opened fire, the General and I would have been the target of many people and at the heart of a murderous crossfire. Without doubt we would not have survived.

Over the next weeks I watched the relationship between General Tower and the commanding officer of the Argylls deteriorate to the point where they were hardly on speaking terms. Colonel 'Mad Mitch' Mitchell was a tough, fighting officer who believed in British rule and that the natives should be put in their place. Although he was modern in his style and clever in his use of the media, his mindset was essentially late Victorian He thought General Tower and the politicians were 'wet' and they gradually began to see him as disloyal, egotistical and dangerously gung-ho.

Things came to a head about a month after the attack. As a placatory gesture and a tactical adjustment the Argylls had been ordered out of Crater shortly after we had inspected the police. This move was much resented by them, as it looked as though they had been defeated and that we had given in. Mad Mitch was not prepared to put up with such craven and, in his view, mistaken behaviour.

Without any consultation or pre-warning, he moved in overnight and reoccupied Crater, telling the *Daily Express* (then the most pro-Empire of the newspapers) what he had done. Indeed, I think he even took one of their reporters with him to watch as Crater was occupied to the accompanying skirl of the Argylls' pipe band, with QDG armoured cars in the van. It was a smart, professional manoeuvre and through its daring and surprise a complete success.

Mitchell's actions, though not actually mutinous, were a flagrant breach of British policy and the spirit of his instructions. He knew he would never be given permission had he asked for it, so he went in secretly. Commanders in the field in these situations are given explicit orders as to their task and it isn't practical to accompany them with a whole list of 'don'ts' – many of which will be political. This senior officer who expected complete obedience from those under him was, it appeared, not prepared to accept the same discipline for himself. Providing it succeeded it was a sort of blackmail of General Tower, Sir Humphrey Trevelyan and the elected politicians, challenging them to undo his achievement. However, rightly or wrongly, the standard response to this illicit action, putting Colin Mitchell on the next plane home, was not taken. The Brits accepted a temporary success in the knowledge we would be gone in a year and Lieutenant Colonel Mitchell stayed on as CO of the Argylls.

However, the system and the establishment won in the end. Colonel Mitchell was a brilliant, talented soldier but he was never promoted and, sufficiently disillusioned, he left the army to become a right-wing Tory MP. Britain left Aden on schedule and in some sort of order and the General was effectively promoted by being given the job he most wanted for his final posting: Commandant at Sandhurst. I think in this case the establishment played their cards right. At the heart of Mitchell's behaviour was an ego which could not ultimately accept restraint as well as a set of beliefs about

Britain and how it should behave abroad. He thought he knew best and paid a heavy price.

My time as the General's ADC was demanding but I guess when you join the military that's what you expect. General Tower rose early, worked hard and attended many social events, including Mess dinners. Once, at a dinner party, he fell asleep during the main course and the hostess and I had a discreet and whispered conversation about the duties and role of an ADC if the boss drops off to sleep. I think we disagreed about what to do, for I ignored her advice to wake him up and did nothing.

Towards the end of my year in Aden the phone rang in my tiny office and the caller was our relatively new Colonel, George Powell. 'There's an officer in HQ Aden whose family, including his daughters, has joined him for Christmas and they're inviting two officers from the QDG for Christmas lunch.' Tim Holmes and I duly booked the Mess Mini and drove over to the area where the 'married pads' were. Everything seemed fairly normal – Christmas decorations round the bungalow, table laid for lunch, drinks on a side table, though I did notice the villa had rather large quantities of razor wire round it and, unusually, a native soldier with rifle patrolling the veranda. The biggest surprise was reserved for when our host joined us for dinner. Slipping his jacket off, he revealed a shoulder holster from which he extracted a revolver and laid it carefully next to his knife and fork. We were having turkey and all the trimmings in the glare of the Middle Eastern day with Mr and Mrs James Bond and family. As part of the fun we each had a little present by our plate and mine was a small paper knife in a bamboo case, which I've still got and rather exaggeratedly refer to as my 'MI5 knife'.

Overall, apart from my few weeks as an ADC, Aden was both tense and monotonous which is often the way with such foreign postings and with active service in particular. Although we had had a memorable time there, my fellow soldiers and I understandably began to look forward to getting back to England.

I didn't know it at the time but on leaving Aden I was also effectively leaving the Regiment, which had been my home since the difficult and testing days at Mons. I am quite clear about the debt I owe the Queen's Dragoon Guards and the regimental family while the Army and its system of training gave me a degree of confidence and self-belief which have been invaluable. It taught me the value of personal discipline and also gave structure to my life. I lived 24/7 with a like-minded body of friends and people who thought as I did and with whom I shared many different experiences. In a real sense we were never off duty and this vocational way of life suited my temperament.

My work in the Army allowed me to travel in Europe and the wider world, including both the Far East and the Middle East. I had a go at all sorts of activities such as sailing, skiing, athletics, climbing and canoeing, learnt how to survive in wild country and how to keep going even when short of sleep, hungry, cold and frightened. At an impressionable age I learnt the basics of leadership and how to be part of a team. In particular, I learnt a lesson that has stayed with me through the years, which is that leaders (and managers) have a duty of care to those in their charge. Only the boss can protect individuals against the unfairness of the system and only the boss can encourage them to go the extra mile. People know if you care about them and they respond in kind.

Above all, the Regiment cared for me. I belonged to a unique organisation that made a speciality of looking after its own, and that allowed me to grow and be myself. This is all the more extraordinary when you consider that essentially the military approach requires people to conform and to be under command, but then the British have always been good at paradox!

So I acknowledge my debt to 1st The Queen's Dragoon Guards and all those with whom I served. I like to think I did my bit and gave something back during my ten years in uniform, but the Regiment gave me more, much more and I'm grateful.

CHAPTER EIGHT

Making the Break

'The world is too much with us
Late and soon, getting and spending
We lay waste our powers'

- William Wordsworth

My final two years 'earning the Queen's shilling' were spent in Dorset at the Junior Leaders' Regiment, Bovington, which was both in military and personal terms a very happy time. I can't quite remember the sequence of events, but for some reason I left Aden early and therefore had time to spare before starting my new posting. I decided to improve the schoolboy German I had picked up at Aldenham by attending a three-month language course in Germany. With the CO's permission I enrolled at Collegium Palatinum in Heidelberg and wrote a somewhat lyrical account for the Regimental Journal covering that period.

As a prelude I went to Wolfsburg, which was then and for many years continued to be the home of the Volkswagen Beetle. I picked up a brand new dark blue VW from an export agent outside the factory gates, thus avoiding both UK and German taxes. It cost me about £430 and I felt very pleased at the age of 26 to be the owner of a brand new car. This was only possible because being stationed in Aden meant you got extra 'hardship' pay with nothing to spend it on. Desert landscapes are very good for the pocket!

While I was in Heidelberg General Tower and I kept in touch, and our correspondence resulted in two contrasting visits, both of which he set up for me. He was keen for me to visit a titled German lady who lived in a big castle near my old haunt of Winterberg. My visit turned into an odd, indeed almost surreal, weekend. Winterberg was its usual grey, moribund self when I trundled down the long drive to the *Schloss*. The first unnerving experience was when I had to explain to the butler that, 'No, I didn't need him to unpack my suitcase!' (Surely butlers are taught that the inside of an army officer's suitcase is but a distant cousin to the inside of a tram-driver's glove!). That evening, this German aristocrat and I sat in a baronial dining hall making spasmodic conversation about the British economy, the Cold War and the joys of shooting (which I don't do and rather dislike in principle). I'm not sure she entirely approved of me, as undoubtedly my liberal view of the world must have clashed with her aristocratic, somewhat Prussian attitudes. However, we were stuck with each other for the duration of a long winter's evening and during my stay I did give her a bottle of whiskey as a thank you.

We seemed to have travelled back to the Middle Ages when she and I attended church, singing German hymns in the ecclesiastical equivalent of the royal box. Our four-sided wooden pew was set high up at the front of the church by the choir, so all the locals had something to look at. The Duchess was all in black and wore a small hat with a veil. The afternoon was a little easier, as her son Klaus, who spoke very good English and was about my age, appeared and took me for a walk. I remember that I had to grasp the finer points of wild boar hunting as we tramped through the wet and leafless beech woods. He was a nice guy, and from his conversation it was clear he genuinely moved in fairly exalted circles. The whole experience was very odd, and in film terms rather like a cross between *Babette's Feast* and *The Shooting Party*.

The other visit General Tower arranged for me up took place when I returned to England from Heidelberg. By then the General was Commandant at the RMA Sandhurst, and I stayed there overnight for a Sergeant's Mess dinner night. The General had caused some shock waves by his liberal regime at the RMA, symbolised by his proposal that Officer Cadets could wear their hair a little longer.

The Warrant Officers' Mess at Camberley has generally been the preserve of NCOs from the Guards' Regiments and although it is an exaggeration to say that they objected to the General's suggestion, even after a compromise was reached they were still pretty disgruntled. So it was into this atmosphere that I was propelled as a guest. The next morning the General maintained his habit of inviting two Officer Cadets to breakfast and on that day he chose two putative QDGs: Mark Phillips and Philip Mann, whose Army careers turned out very differently.

Mark, as the world knows, went on to marry and then divorce Princess Anne, while sadly Philip was killed on extra Regimental service in the Yemen (formerly the Aden Protectorate). He was the only son of the Right Reverend Michael Mann, who had been a KDG during the War, and who became Dean of Windsor shortly after we moved there. Michael Mann was very kind to us and as Chairman of the Governors of St George's Choir School helped us by providing James with a bursary when times were hard.

Work at the Junior Leaders' Regiment (JLR) was very satisfying. Young men aged 16 would arrive and through a combination of military training, outdoor activities (such as canoeing and trekking) and education we would prepare them to be the future NCOs of the British Army. The essential ingredient in this cocktail was their education and they could not be promoted (which meant more pay) without getting various levels of Army Certificate. Many of them had been failures at school, and all I can say is that this mix of stick and carrot worked and the transformation was wonderful. For myself the job suited my temperament (putative teacher/trainer) and the combination of long hours seven days a week in term time, followed by holidays, was ideal. There was also lots of sport, including hockey, which I enjoyed hugely and at which the JLR staff team did very well, winning several trophies.

While I was still at the JLR, John Lidsey came to visit us and he and I went out to supper at a pub deep in the Dorset countryside. John had just taken over command of the Regiment. In modern terms he would be the equivalent of Chief Executive of a sizeable company with me as a relatively junior manager. We enjoyed chatting happily over our meal. and at the end of the evening we climbed into my VW and started for home. Now, the VW Beetle in its day was both innovative and startlingly successful but it did lack a petrol gauge, so you needed to keep an eye on the mileometer and to know your car's average mpg. This allowed you to calculate when more fuel was needed. I'm not sure I was very good at this, as several times I found myself stranded, out of fuel. Unforgivably I didn't carry a spare can. On this occasion, halfway home the trusty VW gurgled to a halt with no remedy to hand, and only the dark space of Hardy's Egdon Heath to keep us company. There was nothing for it but to step out along the road, at that time of night completely deserted. I had a very embarrassing two hours of tramping silently under the stars while my boss made the occasional pleasant remark. If he blamed me, as he could have done, he never showed it and that just underlines what a good bloke he was and the kind of lovely people the Army, and more particularly the Regiment, could produce.

In those days if a woman wanted to visit the Mess an officer would normally be expected to inform the Mess Sergeant, so she could be escorted to a drab little room at the end of a corridor, called the Ladies' Room. This would be sparsely furnished with lino on the floor, a lamp stand and a couple of uninviting high backed chairs. The message was clear: 'We are just being polite here and we'd rather you didn't invade this male bastion.' I thought this was all nonsense, and happily enjoyed a modicum of unpopularity by saying so and by predicting that in due course women would serve alongside men.

The Ladies' Room convention was regularly flouted by Ursula and me as we got to know each other. I will talk about how we met and the significance of that special time later, but suffice to say we were increasingly an item during my time at the JLR. On Friday afternoons the good and lovely Ursie used to regularly tear herself away from the Notting Hill Junior Mixed Infants' School, where she taught, and catch the train to Dorset. Spending the weekend together depended on my duties and also the tolerance of some of the married officer's wives, as Ursie needed somewhere to stay on Friday and Saturday nights. There was, of course, was no possibility of her coming to my room or visiting the Mess unannounced. Nor was it considered acceptable in those days, certainly in the Army, for couples to sleep together before marriage. Of course, many did and the arrival of the contraceptive pill in the mid-sixties changed sexual dynamics forever, but at the time the Army and polite society certainly didn't want to go there. Luckily for me this pretty and laughing girl was happy to come to the Ladies' Room and then nip up the back stairs to my room, where we increasingly discovered how much we liked each other. To maintain appearances Ursie, rather like Cinderella, needed to get back to whichever family was hosting her before midnight.

On one occasion, she took off her shoes and, holding them in one hand, set off quietly along the first floor corridor, which was lit by a strip light down to the back door. Suddenly there was the sound of footsteps in an adjoining passage, so Ursie grabbed the nearest door, stepped in and found herself in the small cupboard that served as a drying room. Surrounded by wet rugger shirts and drying socks she stood next to the wooden racks in the darkness. The footsteps came nearer... and.... help.... stopped by the drying room door. I don't know what Bill Le Blanc-Smith felt but it certainly must have been a surprise for him, when turning on the drying room light, he was confronted at a distance of three feet by a charming girl wearing a coat and a smile and carrying her shoes. However, in the circumstances, he did the only thing possible. 'Good evening', he said, as though this was absolutely the norm. 'Good evening', said Ursula, not sure what happened next. And with that Bill hung up his newly washed shirt, turned off the light and closed the door. The next day he rounded off this piece of accomplished behaviour by giving us a huge wink during church service.

My time at the Junior Leaders' was a very satisfying and happy end to my Army days, for quite early into my tour I began to realise that I didn't want to be in the military all my working life. I was now living permanently in England for the first time since I was 18 and at the back of my mind was the thought (or hope) that I might now have the chance to find a job and possibly a partner. Since I didn't know many people and had never had a settled relationship this was a bit of a fond hope.

Each term at the Junior Leaders' included two weeks adventure training at Renney Rocks Camp, which overlooked the sea in Devon. I've never been a great fan of Dartmoor finding it bleak, damp and barren, but the activities we did there were fun – map reading, climbing, canoeing, trekking and night exercises. Also, although term time was very busy, we did manage, as I said, to put together an excellent hockey team which got into the finals of the divisional competition. On the strength of my contribution as a midfielder I got asked to tour the Channel Islands with an Army (South-West District) team, so I was probably playing quite well at that time.

During my ten years in the Army I remained a keen athlete. I left school able to run the mile at around county standard, and rather hoped that the Army would give me time to train full-time so I could fulfil my potential. But although I continued to train and run competitively, I wasn't absolutely single-minded about my running, nor did I work out what I really wanted to do in terms of athletics. I had not yet learned that if you want something you must both ask for it and push for it. So athletics got subsumed into all the other things like learning to be a troop leader; cross-country skiing; squash; courses; Mess life and so on. During our four years in Wolfenbüttel I ran for both the Regimental and the squadron athletics teams. I tended (but not always) to win the regimental mile, three miles and cross-country – though David Treasure and Alan Healey will tell you different! One of the delights of Wolfenbüttel was to jog out through the back gate of the camp at about teatime and go for a run in the beautiful German beech woods, which lay directly behind the camp. But I didn't really use the acres of time available to me or train hard enough to reach Army team standard.

Nonetheless there were some successes. Twice during these years I captained our athletics team when we won the brigade and divisional championships and on the second occasion we got to the Army finals in Aldershot where, out of eight teams, I think we came fourth or fifth. This may not seem all that good but you have to remember the context in which we competed. We were a front line (sabre) regiment and our training in terms of sport was limited. As a cavalry regiment we were only 450 men, while Gunner Regiments

Dad in uniform – 1942

Mum as a young woman
in her early 20's

Mike and me – Bowden,
Cheshire – 1943

1950 in the garden –
Elstree Rectory

**First term at Aldenham
– 1954**

**Aldenham: Running the mile
– 1959**

Visit of Arsenal – December 1958
Ron Greenwood – back row 2nd left. ASW front row 2nd right

Hand-over during a 4 x 10 km relay race.
Oberjock – 1961

1962 – On exercise in Northern Germany

Final year in the Army. Junior Leaders' Regt.
Dorset. 1969

and Infantry Battalions had nearer 1000 men. All the main corps, including the infantry, were able to pack certain regiments with talent according to the sport. Thus the Cheshires majored in athletics; the Duke of Wellingtons specialised in rugby and 40th Field Regiment Royal Artillery concentrated on skiing. The QDG could not hand-pick or rotate individuals, nor did we recruit especially fit soldiers, such as might be attracted to the Infantry. Thus, in effect, at Aldershot we were up against units specialising in athletics, which generally had time to train and who had double our numbers. We did amazingly well coming in the top five and it is worth noting that out of our small team of twenty-four athletes nine were officers, – most of whom took part in more than one event.

I did do some competitive races in Aden, and these turned out to be my swan-song apart from a marathon 20 years later and in more recent years quite a few half marathons with a best time of 1 hour 42 minutes in the late 1980s. I still run for fun and fitness and like to be able to keep going for an hour as my annual target. But these days I am a fair weather runner.

The other over-arching activity (apart from sport) that I kept going from Aldenham days was drama. Although many of my drama experiences after school took place while I was working in Banbury, I did do some acting in the Army. In 1963, a year before we left Germany, I took on the task of producing the regimental pantomime. We had among us officers like Max Browning and Tony Benda, who had put on such shows before and went onto make a name for themselves doing similar productions at Staff College. The whole event proved to be a tremendous strain, partly because I didn't share the load enough by getting people to help with the script, administration or stage management, so Lieutenant Wood finished up as scriptwriter, producer and director. We had the use of the lovely little Lessing Theatre in Wolfenbüttel, and I think we put the show on early in December, so I could go off to Southern Germany with the ski team.

One advantage we had in those days was that each cavalry regiment had its own band, so I only had to choose the music, and then the band would turn up and do a professional job. In the event actually providing the music proved to be less straightforward than I have just made it sound. I admit that my relaxed attitude to the script meant the Bandmaster's 'cues' were never that clear on paper. But he appeared slow on the uptake and also a nit-picker so, harassed as I was, his need to be told most things at least three times and to look aggrieved at pretty well everything I suggested added to my stress. I think he felt I rather disliked his egregious manner with senior officers (which I'm afraid I did) and the net result was that during one rehearsal the Bandmaster and I fell out big time.

A bit of shouting during the preparation of a show would normally be water under the bridge. But we have to remember that this was the narrow world of the British Military and it wasn't 'on' for Lieutenant Wood to be ticking off the Bandmaster with his irritation echoing round the Lessing Theatre, especially in front of said Bandmaster's trumpeters and drummers. The second–in–command's wife was at this particular rehearsal helping with the costumes, and she felt the incident needed reporting to the Adjutant, who perforce had to tick me off. I have the feeling, looking back, that the Adjutant was in fact rather envious of me and would quite like to have been able to shout at the Bandmaster himself.

Notwithstanding these and many other difficulties, the show was all right on the night. Indeed, despite my limitations as a producer it turned out to be a big success and much enjoyed. The whole idea behind *Mother Goose* was to link a series of 'sketches', stand-up comedy, songs and dance using the platform of a conventional pantomime story, with the result that our one night panto had everything. Donald Swann as Mother Goose did a Charleston routine that not only stopped the show but subsequently was performed by Donald with great success in nightclubs and parties all over the place; Corporal Mackley did some fabulous impersonations of regimental personalities and UK celebrities by the simple device of wearing a series of hats; Corporal Chapman came on (slightly drunk, which caused some nervousness) to do a stand-up routine; the LAD (Light Aid Detachment) built a machine which made smoke, flashed lights, blew hooters and eventually exploded; while Lance-Corporal Jones, with his fine Welsh tenor voice, left us all reeling with a wonderfully sentimental version of 'There's a long, long trail a-winding.' Amid all this the band played on – rather well as it happens and, with everybody's help, it turned out to be a 'jolly good show', as Colonel Peter Body might well have said and indeed did.

I did two other shows during my time with the Regiment. One was a revue which took place in Omagh Town Hall in Northern Ireland and ran for a couple of nights. I don't recall much about it except that it was cleverly called *The Dragoon Show* and Mackley did his 'hat' routine again. Sergeant Peter Billson and I wrote the script, including a pastiche on Jewell and Warriss, who were the Morecambe and Wise of the time. It seemed to go OK. I still have the programme, plus a letter requesting £30 of Army funds to help with the costs – Hollywood it definitely wasn't.!

Two years later, in Aden (1966) I put together a 30-minute radio show for Christmas, which raised funds for the Army Benevolent Fund and which went out on the British Forces Broadcasting Service. It included an excerpt from Elgar's *Enigma Variations* ('Nimrod'), a reading by me of Walter de la Mare's *The Listeners* and a comedy routine, using the novel idea that the BBC's sports commentators had to cover the state wedding of Princess Anne. Charles Bond was able to do a very good 'cover' of Peter O'Sullivan (a BBC racing commentator) describing all the horse-drawn carriages charging round London, while I, masquerading as the cricket commentator John Arlott, did a 'take-off' on the service itself − including my favourite line: 'The Archbishop moves slowly towards the East Window, turns on his mark and starts to deliver the service.' There's a recording of this broadcast in the bookcase behind me, on one of those enormous 1960s tapes, like the ones the Stasi used to eavesdrop on people in East Germany.

By the time I joined the Junior Leaders' in 1968, I should have been thinking about taking the Staff College Exam. Among officers at Regimental duty (as opposed to those away on Staff Appointments) this was positioned as the great 'make or break' for those bent on doing well in the Army. For most of my career I considered myself to be in this group and certainly I took soldiering pretty seriously. However in this I was not typical and only a minority of officers wanted a full Army career or to do anything more than command the Regiment.

When I returned to England, I realised that even though I was loving my two years in Bovington, a career in the Army stretching ahead for the next 20 or 30 years seemed to pall. I must also admit that I fell into the trap of not wanting to take the exam because I feared failing. I felt I was capable, at my best, of being energetic and articulate and was the sort of person who enjoyed reading books, which ought to have made me a reasonable candidate. But, at heart, I was not all that confident and in effect not much good at coping with risk, as I feared exposing myself to failure. At that time I could have done with a coach or mentor to talk things through; it just confirms that under an outwardly confident manner old insecurities can continue to lurk.

Although things were now fine at home, I knew that my Father would think it was best for me to 'stay in.' I was doing well in the

Army, with the prospect of a good and secure career ahead. A home would always be provided until I was 55; children's school fees would be mostly taken care of and a pay cheque would arrive monthly. Also there was the fact that at the time, as indeed now, being an Army Officer was regarded as prestigious and worthwhile.

When I wrote to General Tower saying I planned to leave, he gently encouraged me to stay, adding that I would have more 'fun' in the Army. He may have been right, but it is a comment on some aspects of my personality that this consideration, though likely to be true, was not influential. Not for the first time reflecting on these things causes me to wonder whether my DNA is more Puritan than Cavalier.

Given all the obvious advantages of sticking rather than twisting, I have tried to set out in some detail why I made such a big change when I did. Let me say straight away that, with hindsight, it was absolutely the right thing to do. The decision provided me with a pretty tough five or so years hacking out a new career (or rather, careers) but I have no regrets about the two major employment choices I have made. I thank God (literally) that I didn't go into the Church and I know it was right both to join the Army at 18 and equally right to leave it ten years later.

In 1968/69, as I thought about what to do next, my reasoning was as follows: 'You've have had a great time but this is mainly because of the sport, and you can't go on running your life on the basis of athletics and cross-country skiing, with the occasional sailing expedition, hockey tour or mountaineering course thrown in!' I was conscious that in career terms there was another world out there which I wanted to explore. I was tempted to try out non-military activities such as management or even self-employment. As for the Army, I'm not sure I wanted to enter the rat race which develops when a dwindling number of people seek fewer and fewer promotions in an already narrow world. In addition I had a sense that 'home' was an important concept to me and I knew that in the Army (without meaning it to be so) wives, children and family are not just second choice but sadly sometimes third or fourth. I didn't want to be holed up in some rather grim Army quarter, with children who had to go away to boarding school and a partner who wasn't expected to be anything other than an Army wife.

I saw a future in which my somewhat idiosyncratic streak would be less and less tolerated by the rest of the Army and I would be penalised for not 'conforming'. The British military system is pretty good at tolerating eccentricity in wartime, but you have to be genuinely talented to get away with it in times of peace. Those who wanted a safe, relatively comfortable and possibly successful career path could stay in and take the spoils. With the benefit of time, I now wonder when I meet some contemporaries who stayed in (though not all) whether they have grown and developed as much as they might have done. The military system has embraced them for so long that their capacity to learn, to grow new skills or adopt liberal attitudes seems frozen and in many ways their mind set appears to be pretty well where it was when I lived with them.

My original misgivings about the impact that constant postings, courses and active service stations would have on building a home and nurturing children have been well born out. I realise now that I wanted to build a nest, not fight small wars or live in 23 houses in 30 years. To an extent I now also wonder about my capacity to issue orders which would send men (and women) out on missions which might lead to their death or wounding. I would have done this when younger and would probably do so again faced with a Nazi-type threat but for the Falklands, Bosnia, Iraq or Afghanistan? I respect those who will command in these cases and admire those who will carry out such orders but I'm not sure it is any longer for me. These days I'm afraid I'm in camp with the Royal Marine Captain who said, during the Falklands conflict: 'Right, I'll fight this war for these people, then I'm off.'

And so when Colonel Churnside, then in charge of the JLR, asked me for a decision about what I wanted to do when my posting came to an end I told him ten years was enough and began to go on courses to teach me how to be a 'civvy' and how to look for jobs. The latter was rather difficult since I had really no idea who I was and therefore what I wanted to do. I know now that I am by nature a trainer, communicator and campaigner, but unfortunately I hadn't worked that out then and it was to be a number of years and some false starts, before I discovered the truth about myself.

CHAPTER NINE

Dorset Romance

'Very wonderful and beautiful things do happen, don't they? And we live most of our lives in the hope of them.'

– Old Gentleman, E. Nesbit's *The Railway Children*

While pondering whether to continue wearing khaki I still had to 'Carry on Soldiering'. This included dashing off to adventure camp for two weeks each term, hockey tournaments, dinner nights and days spent as Orderly Officer. Meanwhile the domestic front was hotting up and I, had I but known it, was moving towards both the most important and the best decision of my life.

While skiing in St Moritz I had met a nurse on the train going up to the resort who turned out to be a very good skier. Her name was Jimmy (don't ask me why) and we got on well, doing all the happy things that are possible in the mountains in winter. The family was Scottish and her Father had been something senior in ICI, which at that time was just about the UK's biggest company. The family had a big home in Dunblane as well as their own chalet in St Moritz. I admit that being involved with a girl whose family was well off did influence me in continuing the relationship.

I went to see Jimmy when my first UK leave came round and things got sufficiently serious for me to propose to her on a ferry going across one of those countless Scottish lakes. This was in fact a deeply foolish thing to do as we were spectacularly unsuited and it was lucky she didn't take me seriously! Things came to a head one evening, over a disagreement about whether to watch an RSC production of *Hamlet* or something in a lighter vein on TV. I knew Jimmy had many good qualities, including terrific energy and *joie de vivre*, but books, films, theatre and poetry, were not especially her line.

The denouement came at a party in Surrey where she spent a lot of time with a trainee helicopter pilot. This oh so feminine wile, designed to egg me on, completely backfired and I told her quite strongly to forget it. This in turn had the opposite effect and suddenly I was the best thing ever. We all know the turmoil and upset caused by these affairs of the heart and how, in the midst of them, you can't think of anything else. So it was. Someone in the Regiment tried to 'match make' by getting us back together but it was really Annie who helped me make the break and stick to it. After Jimmy had been to supper at the Rectory, Anne picked up that I was being manipulated by Jimmy, who was quite a strong character. Without saying so and thus making me feel inadequate she asked me whether Jimmy ever put my needs first – which was a good and perceptive questioin. This got to the heart of the matter and soon after Jimmy and I broke up for good.

At this time I was also seeing something of Catherine the girl who had been sent home hurriedly from Aden. Her parents liked me but thought it was crazy for their 18-year-old daughter, poised to go up to Oxford, to be knocking around with a 27-year-old Army captain. Dad and Anne thought the same, but I ignored everybody and any consideration about our different ages. To tell the truth, and I blush to admit it, I secretly thought myself a very clever fellow to have at one stage two girlfriends on the go, one of them an adoring Oxbridge student.

That summer going up to meet Catherine in Oxford I had one of those photographic moments that remain in the memory forever. It was a summer evening, and I was outside the college gates and waiting beneath a nearby chestnut tree when I saw a solitary figure, also waiting, whom I thought I recognised. As I looked more closely, I realised that it was King Hussain of Jordan, with no bodyguard or retainers. Shortly afterwards I learnt that his sister was, like Catherine, a student at Lady Margaret Hall. That very still, slightly shadowy figure under the tree exuded such charisma that my mind has retained the image these 40 years.

Later that evening Catherine and I met up in the library at Lady Margaret Hall where I discovered she had invited another bloke to join us, so I walked away. This was a pity (as well as quite immature on my part) because Catherine was a very nice girl, with a terrific sense of humour and we liked lots of the same things, but it was right that it ended as she needed to be free to enjoy university. By the same token, I needed to stop seeing women as items to be pursued and collected just to meet some rather immature fantasy. What I needed and deeply wanted was a soul mate.

By the end of 1968, instead of having two girlfriends I found myself fairly bereft, at a time when I was contemplating leaving the Army for a totally unknown future. It was a tough time, and after a demanding hockey match, in which I had run myself into the ground, I remember a great sense of depression coming over me, and saying, 'Oh God, please let me be loved.' We've all had such moments and although we could do without them they serve to throw the good bits of life into context.

Fortunately, everything was about to change. One of the people I knew in the Regiment was Tim Holmes, whose parents, Douglas and Trixie Holmes, ran a nursing home out of Brecon House, the family's large and rather gracious home in Sherborne, Dorset. Tim was in

England on a course, and kindly invited me over for Sunday lunch. Tim's sister, Cherry, was a trainee nurse at Guy's, and she decided to come home the same weekend with a friend and fellow trainee called Ursula. I think they both fancied some home comforts and the chance to take back a box of food from Trixie's well-stocked larder.

'Oh, by the way', said Cherry, 'Tim's bringing another QDG officer over with him.'

Ursula's reply, as recounted, was classic, 'Oh God, not an Army Officer. I can't stand them.'

Cherry's reply was equally crushing, 'Oh don't worry. He's called Woody and he talks a lot, but he's OK!'

Fortunately I was unaware of having been damned with such faint praise and set off for Brecon House in happy ignorance.

My first meeting with Ursula took place in the area fronting the cottage part of Brecon House, where cars could park. Trixie, Douglas and I were inside, chatting in the kitchen, and when the two girls arrived back from a visit to Lyme Regis we all piled out of the front door to greet them. At this point Kelpie, the Holmes's snappy little Scots terrier, decided to nip Ursula in the leg. My first impression was of a pretty girl, wearing a short skirt (then the fashion), with a cheerful disdain for something as trifling as being bitten by a dog. This lady was clearly a person of character, and so it proved.

Later that evening, I went down to the Holmes's sitting room to join everyone for drinks. Trixie had created a truly beautiful room, one of those rooms where you instantly feel at home. It was comfy but classy, with button-back chairs, polished antiques, fine pictures, soft, squashy sofas and lots of flowers. Ursula was standing up reading *The Sunday Times*, with her elbow on the mantelpiece.

Up to this time I had met both attractive and intelligent girls, but I don't recall meeting many who were both. As we talked I'm sure the inner me must have clocked the fact that here was a person who combined these qualities, and that I was going to have to adopt an improved persona if I wanted to be taken seriously. However, my subconscious must have been rather slow in processing this, because my opening remarks can only be called crass.

'What are you reading', I began.

'An article about Lawrence of Arabia.'

'Ah', said the foolish boy, wishing to impress, 'I know a lot about him.'

After that I presume the conversation got better. Indeed, it must have improved considerably for, by the time we went down after dinner to the 'snug' to watch TV and chat, Ursula was admiring my hairy arms and wondering if I was mostly like that (I'm not and I wasn't) and I was working out in my mind what my next move should be. In fact nothing happened at that stage, but you could say that we 'fancied' each other right from day one.

If the first phase of this romance was pure Barbara Cartland, then the next was pretty good Whitehall farce. I followed up our first meeting with a phone call to the flat which Cherry and Ursula shared with two other girls. (History now relates that life at 11 Stanwick Mansions was pretty squalid and because of a shortage of money the girls practised 'hot bedding'. This meant that those on night-shift slept in the beds recently vacated by those flatmates who had just roused themselves for a day's work). I badly wanted to speak to Ursula and to invite her out but, by chance, Cherry answered the phone. Total ineptness on my part then ensued, because I didn't want to hurt Cherry's feelings by saying it was Ursula I wanted to ask out. So I engaged Cherry in five minutes of pointless, rambling, conversation about nothing at all before ringing off. Fortunately, Cherry, though puzzled, was a sensible woman. Putting the phone down she said to Ursula.

'That was Woody. He chatted happily with me but I think he really wanted to talk to you.'

Despite my gaucheness, communication was eventually established and a date arranged. Our first outing together was tea at the Cavalry and Guards Club, Piccadilly, in the Ladies' Room, of course, followed by a surprise trip to the theatre. Again this wasn't absolutely straightforward, at least not in Ursula's mind. Having got over the problem of what to wear to the Cavalry Club and got used to the idea of an evening out with one of the dreaded clan of Army officers, she rather feared that I would behave true to her view of the type and choose some awful play. Because of Ursie's pre-conceived view of the military she was convinced we were about to go and see the 900th performance of *Whoops, There Go My Trousers*, and a promising romance would end before it had started. However, on this occasion at least, I managed to rise above the stereotype. We went to see one of the first productions of *Forty Years On* by Alan Bennett, which was wonderful fun and, dare I say it, just the right choice. The cast included Alan Bennett himself, with John Gielgud as the Headmaster, and Paul Eddington also taking part.[*]

Three or four months later (in May, I think), I proposed to Ursie overlooking the sea at Renney Rocks, near Renney Point, a lovely spot in Devon. It was a great and important moment in both our lives and one of the consequencies was that I also I got to know the rest of Ursie's family.

When I first met Ursie's Mum, Mary, she was in her early fifties, with a cosy, comfortable figure, eyes that twinkled easily and a ready laugh. I could see that as a young girl she must have been very pretty, with lovely hair. Also she had beautiful soft skin that stayed

---

[*]   Incidentally, I was to produce the same play a few years later when we were in Banbury and, even further ahead, James both acted in it and produced it at St Edward's School, Oxford.

that way all her life. Mary was so kind to me, and indeed 'kindness' was metaphorically her second name: she was the nicest and most generous Mother-in-law you could ask for. She had inherited this generous streak from her Dad, 'Grampy' (Frederick Lee), who with his four brothers had fought all through World War I. It used to amuse her when I serenaded her with lines from the old music hall song, 'How I love her, How I love her, How I love my Mother-in-law'. Giving presents, writing supportive letters, sending postcards and making nice food were very important to her and indeed were writ large in her DNA.

Mary was very artistic both in terms of talent and temperament. As a girl she had a lovely singing voice and should have gone on to take up singing professionally. Similarly, she could also draw and paint well and we have some very pleasant watercolours of hers dotted round the house. She would always deny it, but we all sensed there was perhaps an unfulfilled, even frustrated, element in her life. As is sometimes the way, her artistic legacy lives on through her two daughters, their partners and her grand-children, who are all either musical, or artistic or work in the creative arts.

Mary met Reg Nicklin in 1936 when he was a teacher at Marling Grammar school and they married in 1937. Reg was the gentlest, calmest and most considerate of men. He and Mary lived at 'Firwood' (just outside Stroud) the whole of their married life, where they were wonderfully happy together. Reg loved his cricket and in his youth had been a useful fast bowler, playing to a good standard in one of the many league sides round Birmingham. Indeed the 'hat trick' ball he won in September 1933, playing for Walsall First XI, is on the mantelpiece as I write. At social events he would be quite quiet but there was more to him than you might think – after all, he swept Mary off her feet when she was an 18-year-old school girl and he was nearly 30! However despite this bold flurry Reg was by nature a cautious man and tended, in particular, to be careful with money. He was lightly built with a strong constitution and he lived into his nineties. His hair was very black and his skin was a rather lovely olive colour. Poor eyesight meant that he always wore strong glasses. Although Reg was definitely not an extrovert, he could be quite firm and at school he had a reputation as a strong disciplinarian. Without him really saying or doing much, pupils at Marling school knew that they couldn't mess about in 'Jimmy' Nicklin's English classes.

Between them Mary and Reg gave us lots of support, particularly during the early years of our marriage and, given my curious start in life, followed by ten years racketing around in Officers' Messes, it's not surprising that 'Firwood' came to feel like my first proper experience of home.

Ursie and I were deeply in love from the start and used to see each other as much as possible, particularly at weekends. She was doing her probationary year as a teacher at a primary school in a challenging part of Notting Hill. However she dutifully and regularly leapt on a train on Friday evenings, bound for Dorset, still with poster-paint in her finger nails and chalk dust in her hair. To my shame, on one occasion I forgot the time of her arrival and she, poor girl, was left shivering on the platform at Wool station for nearly an hour. It was bad, and what made it worse was that she was so nice about it!

Perhaps I redeemed myself a bit when we went visiting Athelhampton Manor, which wasn't far from Bovington Camp. I remember a bright, calm, sunny day, ideal for wandering round a garden that had been carefully tended for a couple of hundred years, and perfect for a young couple in love. After touring the house in the obligatory way we went to have tea. As we both felt cash was in short supply there was an unspoken agreement that a cuppa each was all we could really afford. At the nearest table, however, we found the detritus of the previous customers, including a plate of cakes that had hardly been touched. Quicker than you can say 'iced buns' I opened the 18th-century wall cupboard right by us, popped the plate of cakes inside and closed the door. Thus when our pot of tea came I was able to supply the future Mrs Wood with both the quality and number of cakes she might reasonably expect, and all paid for of course, though not by me.

I fear in many ways I was not much good as a fiancé and didn't really understand the niceties of courtship. Looking back, I can see that I was pretty untutored in the gentle art of taking a girl out and making her feel how girls should feel on such an occasion. I'd plead in mitigation that Ursie was, in fact, my first *proper* girlfriend. You may not believe it but, despite being 27 years old (with all my own teeth), she was the first girl I went out with on a regular basis. Anyone who is serious about a girl has to learn the lessons, particularly someone with my background and relative immaturity. The whole important business of cards, gifts and nice meals rather passed me by; or rather, they passed Ursula by! For example we twice ran out of petrol (and had to walk back in the dark) and a candlelit dinner for two was often more a case of fish and chips in the car. I still shudder to think of the cheap and tawdry present I gave my dear bride on our wedding day, when she in truth spent all her cash on a fine pair of engraved silver cufflinks for me.

But maybe I got some things right, for our relationship was happy and physical and we laughed a lot. As well as constant phone calls I wrote Ursie lots of letters and she, dear girl, wrote every day from the time we became engaged. I had to argue my case with my parents, who were anxious about the speed of things, and there was an unfortunate mix-up about the wedding date itself. However, I loved Ursie and she loved me and our mutual love helped enormously in terms of our being strong about our wish to be together as soon as possible. I followed the maxim of the great Bertrand Russell: 'Of all forms of caution, caution in love is perhaps the most fatal to true happiness.'

We passed the spring and summer of 1969 making plans, thinking about jobs, money, and organising our wedding. Although we had a lot of hard work to do, I remember this period as a happy time. and it was really wonderful to discover that my wife-to-be was also my best friend. I was aware of learning so much about things that had passed me by such as music (at Easter we heard the *St Matthew Passion* at the Royal Festival Hall), art, good novels, cooking, nice furniture and all the kinds of things that go towards making a civilised home life. In particular I learnt the importance of giving and being generous. In this respect my DNA is inferior to Ursie's, as she is a natural giver, but over the years I have got better.

Gradually, everything fell into place. The most important need was for me to get a job, so I did various Army pre-release courses and replied to newspaper advertisements in the usual way. This process was helped by there being lots of jobs around, for at that time both the manufacturing and service industries were labour-intensive. It was also still the case that few women were in employment, so work was plentiful.

Some time in the summer of 1969 I got selected to be a Production Planner with General Foods (GF) in Banbury, starting in November, on a salary of £1,400 a year. In truth I had no idea whether the pay was good or bad, because, such was the world I inhabited, I didn't know what the cost of living was for a civilian or, indeed, what my Army salary was. You must (rightly!) be thinking there was a degree or two of innocence here about the wicked outside world, and indeed getting this job at GF was both good and bad. It was good in the sense that it was a job; there would be money coming in, and also

Ursula and I now knew where we were going to live. It was good too that GF was a successful, well-run international firm which would teach me the rudiments of business. It was a sensible place to start my managerial apprenticeship because it was not going to go bust and in addition the Banbury area would not be expensive as regards housing. However, with hindsight, I almost certainly sold myself short and started too low down the managerial tree, as reflected by the modest salary. I also never considered other options, including working for the BBC, or journalism. In terms of earning my living I was still trapped in the careful, uncommercial, middle-class mindset that had shaped my upbringing. In those days it was felt a job should be respectable, safe and long term, while nowadays these criteria are far less relevant to many young people looking for work. I was hampered too by not knowing what I wanted to do or how my ability compared with others in the same field.

With my job decided, we started house hunting and found a delightful little two-up and two-down cottage called 'Roseneath' in the village of Weston by Weedon, six miles from Banbury. It cost £4,200 and our mortgage was going to be £23 per month, which seemed a lot. Indeed such a lot that I was not certain we could afford it out of my net income of about £100 a month, and very nearly cancelled the deal. Fortunately I didn't, because not long after, Ursie landed a full-time teaching job in the nearby village of Culworth.

The way this worked out is instructive and typical of those days. We learned later that numerous applications for teaching jobs were being rejected by Northamptonshire LEA (Local Education Authority) on account of there being no vacancies. However, about this time Stan Ruddlesden the headmaster of Culworth Village Primary School was chatting to a pal, while they watched a Saturday football match, about how he needed a new teacher after Christmas and that he couldn't find anyone. By pure chance Stan's friend had seen Ursula's application and suggested Stan contacted us over the weekend. Forty-eight hours later, following a brief chat over Stan Ruddlesden's garden wall, (nowadays this would be logged as an interview) Mrs Wood had the job, starting in the New Year! In the mornings we would put her bike on the roof of our VW Beetle and then I would drive to Banbury via Culworth, so that Ursie could cycle home along the country lanes after school.

So we had a home, jobs for each of us and a date for the wedding all settled and fixed before the wedding itself. And with the help of Reg and Mary we returned home from honeymoon to a fully equipped and furnished cottage. In particular, Joy Finzi (wife of the composer Gerald Finzi), an artistic and well grounded friend of Ursie's, greatly assisted this process by very kindly giving us a king-sized double bed, which we still use. This was a lovely and important gift, so it was well worth sawing through the banisters in our tiny house to get it up the stairs!

The date of the wedding rather decided itself. As I had joined the Army on 18 October 1959, I couldn't leave before 18 October 1969, if I was to do my full ten years and collect a gratuity of £1,000. (This lump sum went straight in as a deposit on the house, and as you might guess has accrued mightily over the years. It was well invested.) We wanted my Dad to take the service and his schedule combined with the availability of Ursie's home church meant that Saturday 18 October fell into place as the best date. So it came about that I left the Army in the morning and got married in the afternoon.

No engagement/wedding takes place without some degree of hiatus and in a relatively small way ours was no different. Often the guest list is the challenge but for us it was the wedding date. Having provisionally fixed up 18 October, I still had a couple of things to check. However, by chance Mary Nicklin (my Mother-in-law to be) met Anne's Mother Mrs Hancock in Stroud, and told her that 18 October was the agreed date. Mrs H, who was not always easy, probably took great delight in being first with the news but, of course, Anne and Dad felt very left out and said so. This was a tricky and anxious time. But, as with all these things, we got over it.

And so, a mere ten months after our first meeting, on 18 October 1969, Ursie and I were married. Quite simply, meeting Ursie was the best thing in my life and that Saturday in October was the best day of my life. As Hugh Grant says in the film *Notting Hill* to his married friends Max and Bella: 'I don't think you realize what an unusual situation you have – to find someone you actually love who'll love you.' Anybody to whom this happens should count themselves just so lucky.

Of our wedding day itself I will only say that it was wonderful. We had a church service followed by communion in Ursula's local church (St Mary Magdalene, Rodborough, near Stroud). My Dad took the service beautifully. We invited about 100 friends and family. Our ushers were Chris Vaughan (best man), John Pocock, Johnny Gill and Mike Todd, all looking very smart and military but in morning dress, not uniform. Celia, Ursie's sister, a professional oboist, played her oboe as only she can (pieces by Bach and Telemann) and 'Daddy' Sumption, (who was the organist, and music teacher at Cheltenham Ladies' College when Ursie was there), played the organ. It was a warm, sunny day so afterwards at the reception at Moor Court Hotel, guests were able to spill out into the garden.

So on a beautiful autumn day in an English parish church set in the heart of rural Gloucestershire, I married the love of my life and the dearest woman in the world. None of us when we decide to marry, or live with someone, can be sure how things will turn out, and Ursie and I are much blessed in the way our relationship has developed. She remains my best friend to this day, and I hers.

CHAPTER TEN

Making It Happen

'Take your work seriously but not yourself'

– Dame Margot Fonteyn

'One recipe for happiness is to have no sense of entitlement'

– *The Uncommon Reader* by Alan Bennett

My five years at General Foods (GF) in Banbury (now called General Foods International and part of Kraft Foods) was essentially an apprenticeship in the art of business and management. This very well run American company was a good place to observe, and be part of, modern commercial practice at its best.

GF's UK offices and factory complex were (and still are) located just off the Southam Road in Banbury, and since this was the company's sole UK site, everybody from the directors to the forklift truck drivers worked in one place. Everything was on view, and an additional plus point was the fact that the complex was pretty new. It had been built only five years previously as part of GF's take-over of Birds (makers of custard and other foods), whose old factory had been at Digbeth, in Birmingham.

It was a pleasant place to work and learn and my commute, such as it was, took all of 20 minutes by car down winding Northamptonshire country lanes. I can remember the sense of adventure and freedom I had on the first day of work. It was a typical autumn day with quite a wind, but bright and with a freshness in the air. I left 'Roseneath' with Ursula busy getting our new home in order and drove off not really knowing what lay ahead. I was aware that this was the start of a new chapter in my life.

This period brought some wonderful news domestically as while we were living at 'Roseneath' we learnt that Ursie was pregnant with James. She remained well and kept working until the final month of her pregnancy. Naturally, I was excited by the prospect of becoming a Father. I had the same feelings of delight (tempered with a sense of responsibility) when Ellie and then Hattie came along and overall I remember a sense of contentment whenever Ursie was pregnant.

At the time I joined GF, the company was essentially making and marketing two types of product. Instant coffee had been introduced to Britain in the 1940s, and remained popular. GF advertised Maxwell House coffee intensely on TV, so this was a national, well-known brand as well as a big seller. GF also sold a wide range of powdered desserts, including the famous Birds Custard, as well as Instant Whip, Angel Delight and Instant Trifle. The demand for Angel Delight was enormous and the fact that we were constantly out of stock of two or three of the eight flavours at any given moment was the backdrop to my period of tutelage.

As a Production Planner I worked alongside three other men, updating the plans for some eighty or so products in order to ensure a balance between having too much stock or not enough. Our task was to schedule production to maintain this balance and to meet all the sales forecasts, which were supplied weekly by the marketing division. The problem for us was that these forecasts were prone to error and could often be out by 20 to 30%, even sometimes as much as 100%. So to help us with this problem we also received weekly data on actual sales which enabled us to draw four lines on the graphs we had for every product. Two of the lines were 'actuals' (actual sales against actual production) and along with these we also plotted two dotted lines to indicate forecast sales against forecast production. So each graph showed the current situation as well as projections covering the next two or three months. When things went off course we had to produce new plans (new dotted lines) and ask for extra production so as to get products back in stock, and also advise more senior managers what was needed. No wonder all our work was done in pencil!

Although it may not sound very sophisticated, the GF system of production control worked well because it was practical and visual. However, as a new boy, it didn't help me that we had both insufficient production capacity and a departmental manager who was not really up to the job. The working situation was ideal and the hours fairly undemanding (9am until 5pm would sum it up), but this was an age when the culture in UK manufacturing lacked dynamism and the UK work ethic was nothing like it is now.

In fact, during this period I was glad to have the time and space to adapt both to married life and, indeed, to living once more in England. After all, Ursie and I had, in just a few months, undergone three of the most demanding life changes you can make. At one and the same time both of us had changed from being single to being married, moved homes and changed jobs. So in retrospect I can see it was helpful that GF was quite a benign place; that Culworth School was undemanding, and at this stage married life only required us to maintain a small cottage in an inexpensive part of the country.

During the five years I was at GF (1969–74) I had three jobs which, given that I needed experience, was ideal. From Production Planner I was promoted after a couple of years to being a raw materials buyer, with my own office and the use of a team in the typing pool. This is what I wanted and needed, and my learning curve was further augmented during my final year in Banbury by a sideways move into buying packaging. However, I guess the thing which I most remember and value from those years was not to do with GF; it was the link Ursie and I formed with the local amateur theatre group, the Banbury Cross Players (BCP).

We joined the BCP one dark winter evening when rehearsals for the forthcoming pantomime were underway in the upstairs part of an old barn. The show had been written by one of the cast, Nick Baldwin, and was called *The Fairy Queen Who Lost Her Crown.* I was eventually cast as an attendant (male) fairy! From this enjoyable and appropriately humble start we got involved in many productions and events, some of which I've listed below.* I mainly acted and produced, which I loved, while Ursie, who cordially disliked being in front of the public, got involved behind the scenes in such things as the music, front-of-house and wardrobe. Since these were all things she was happy to do, it meant our main social activity was something we could do jointly, a bonus in any relationship.

The main drivers behind the BCP were Sonia and Martin Blinkhorn. Sonia was quite tall and slim with black hair and the most lovely speaking voice. She laughed easily and a lot but in repose her face could convey some hint of sadness. Martin however was short and wiry with a quick easy manner and enough charm to move anybody. He always had rather large, creative projects on the go, either in terms of his business or the BCP. He was the force behind a number of wonderful Old Time Music Halls, a *Son et lumière* and no end of pantos, which he both wrote and produced.

---

* In rough chronological order these were some of the productions Ursie and I worked on: -

The Fairy Queen Who Lost Her Crown, The Cherry Orchard, Ride a Cock Horse, Old Time Music Hall, Son et lumière at Broughton Castle, The Taming of the Shrew, A Shakespeare 24-hour Marathon Reading in the Corn Market, The Anniversary, The Owl and the Pussycat went to Sea, Fallen Angels, Cinderella, Forty Years On and The Lion in Winter.

Martin's family had lived in Banbury for generations. His grandfather had owned the town's first photographic agency while his Father had opened the town's first cinema. Martin took things further by running a family owned audio-visual business. Rather wonderfully his son Tom (the fourth generation) still continues this family tradition from the same premises, which now houses Blinkhorn's Corporate Sound and Lighting Services.

Martin's skills as a photographer were much in demand and one day he found himself taking pictures of a wedding out at the poet John Dryden's family house in Canons Ashby, a village not far from where we had set up home. Peering through the lens he had a strong sense of *déjà vu* and later realised that the position of his camera, the angle and the setting were exactly those his grandfather had used to shoot the same scene over a hundred years before. Martin was a wonderful, kind and talented man, and we were deeply sad when he died too young after we had left Banbury.

The Cherry Orchard was perhaps the BCP's most prestigious production. It commemorated the group's 25th anniversary and you can tell the seriousness of the project by the fact we hired a professional producer called Nova Beer (!) to help put it on. It was a good production. Nova was competent, if a little vague, and more an intellectual than a budding impresario. Certainly the play was a success and I enjoyed acting the role of Trofimov, 'the eternal student'. There's a nice photo of the whole cast including Ursie and myself, with Ursie looking fabulous in the Empire-line cream and brown dress she'd worn as a bridesmaid at the wedding of Inky (her best friend from school).

Our next two productions were pantos and then Martin put on a magical *Son et Lumière* in the grounds of Broughton Castle, as well as writing much of the script. Sonia's production of *The Taming of the Shrew* gave me an easy ride in that, having delivered a few lines in the prologue as the pedlar Christopher Sly, all I then had to do was to stay on stage and watch the action until the end.

At this time BCP felt it needed a better venue than Banbury Technical College, which we had to share with various other groups and which had no space for a workshop. So moves were put in hand to raise funds for Banbury to have its own small theatre and an empty building in the nearby Cornmarket was earmarked. The concept was almost made reality by a local millionaire called Jimmy Black who committed to doubling any money we raised. So if £100,000 was needed in total all we had to do was to find £50,000, which was very helpful of him. Unfortunately, some years later we heard from Sonia that the project had failed through lack of matched funds.

While we were still trying to raise the money, I decided to run and organise a marathon 24-hour Shakespeare 'read-in'. This had its challenges but, since the great man had written over forty plays, a shortage of script material wasn't one of them. To this end I borrowed a flatbed hay-wagon which we parked in the Cornmarket in the middle of the town, and then kitted out with straw bales, some lighting and a couple of paraffin stoves. Over forty BCP members had each offered to do a minimum of one three-hour shift and so, once we'd started reading, we then went on throughout the day and into the night, with people picking up parts as they came and went.

As you might expect, the nocturnal sessions were both slightly surreal and quite memorable. There we were, sitting in the half light on straw bales, reading the parts of characters unknown to us from rarely performed plays, only to find ourselves an hour or so later declaiming some of the most famous and beautiful lines in the English language as we took on *Hamlet* or *King Lear*. Eerie and wonderful. As it got dark, the twilight denizens of Banbury would appear, ranging from bored policemen about to go off duty to local drunks slurringly complimenting our efforts, to young mothers with fretful, sleepless babies, insomniacs seeking diversion or people setting off for the night shift at work. Our audience were a motley but appreciative collection of individuals who, although slightly bemused, also knew they were watching something quite eccentric and very English.

For our next production we changed venue completely moving to the small Oxfordshire village of Duns Tew and a tiny theatre, seating about fifty, in an old house called The Grange, where we put on Noel Coward's *Fallen Angels*, which was good fun. Next, Ursie had a big hand in the music for David Wood's *The Owl and the Pussycat Went to Sea*. We still have a copy of the score, which was excellent. Ursie played the flute and I played the mad and (hopefully) comic Professor Bosch, dressed almost entirely in the uniform I wore when patrolling the jungle in Borneo!

About this time a six-week-old James Wood went for his first public outing which, appropriately enough, was to the College Theatre, where he slept through a rehearsal of the latest BCP offering. He must have inhaled the vibes – many years later James made his mark as a scriptwriter of the successful BBC Television comedy Rev. which won a BAFTA in 2011. This sounds all pretty matter of fact but his arrival in the world was nearly a disaster. He was born on 12 November 1972 at Brackley Cottage Hospital (which contained four beds and not much else). I became aware that, even in these modern times, birth is a messy, primitive and fraught business. Ursie's labour lasted well over forty-eight hours and she went in and out of the hospital twice. Finally, in a period spanning over thirty hours, she went through great pain and trauma due to James's being a breech baby. He arrived safely, but the doctor had to use forceps and if Ursie had not been so strong, both physically and mentally, she might not have survived. I was sent home early in this saga but woke very early on the morning of Sunday 12 November not at all sure what news I was going to hear. Fortunately, in the end all was well, though my own view is that it was at least a year before Ursie was fully recovered.

My only attempt at producing while in the BCP was Alan Bennett's *Forty Years On*, which had been a big success in London a few years earlier, and as I noted in Chapter Nine, has featured significantly in our family life. It portrayed a failing boys' prep school rehearsing its end of term play, and the decline of the school was an allegory for the decline of Britain. Sadly, my efforts received only a mixed reception. To be honest, I wasn't experienced enough to do such a complicated and subtle work and although bits of it were OK I really needed somebody more experienced alongside me.

Our involvement with Banbury Cross Players ended on a high. In March 1975, around the time Ellie was born and we were getting ready to move to Windsor, I played the evil Dauphin Philip II in an excellent production of *The Lion in Winter*, which is all about the power struggle between Eleanor of Aquitaine (played by Sonia) and the domineering Henry II. The play was well produced with a strong cast using costumes borrowed from the Royal Shakespeare Company's wardrobe store in Dorchester-on-Thames, and we had some good photos taken of us wearing these in Warwick Castle. This production certainly brought the name Eleanor to the front of our minds as a possible name for our new daughter. It was good to end our wonderful time at the BCP with such a success, added to which was the joy of having a lovely new baby, whose birth took only a couple of hours.

At this time we began to notice the start of the explosion in house prices that was such a feature of the 1970s. A four-room cottage is hardly big enough for a family, so in 1973 we started to look for a bigger home. Eventually we moved from 'Roseneath' to 'Plumstones', which was in Little Bourton, only a mile from Banbury and close to work. It was an extended Northamptonshire stone cottage, with three bedrooms, a huge inglenook fireplace and a garage. In our new home James kindly learnt after two years to sleep through the night, and how to peddle his green police car down the hill.

We actually moved in 1974, which was a bit of a financial gamble, not only because of the increased mortgage involved but because Ursie was pregnant with Ellie. This, although wonderful in itself, meant we would only have one income for the next couple of years. In fact, during the time between James's birth in 1972 and Ursie starting work again in Windsor in 1978 we made two house moves funded by a single junior manager's salary. Because each move meant more cost and a higher mortgage I'm not sure you would be able to do that nowadays.

The incalculable benefit of Ursie not going back to work immediately was that for six years James and Ellie had their Mum at home to nurture them, until they were ready to go to nursery school. This important precedent was to be maintained even when, some years later, Harriet was born in December 1981. Although Ursie went back to teaching part-time quite soon after Hats's arrival, Upton School was so close to our house that Ursie could nip home and give baby Hattie her lunch. Nowadays I guess many young couples with small children at nursery school would envy the fact we able to look after all three children in this way.

However, this juggling act was not without cost. We were forced to have quite a restricted lifestyle – forget foreign holidays, new clothes, meals out and plenty of socialising or a decent car. Cash was always short and we were constantly looking to economise on an already quite simple life-style. Once I put the phone on incoming calls only, and we decided to save money by not buying orange squash! That's quite laughable now, but in retrospect our financial carefulness was well worth it. Our kids were being properly brought up and, had we known it, we were investing long-term in the increasingly valuable homes we bought and sold near Banbury and, later on, in Windsor. Again it's possible to see a very stable pattern here, since in our married life we have only lived in two locations and four homes. In a period spanning over forty years we have moved house three times and James and Ellie can only remember two homes, while for Hats 'home' has always been Windsor.

During our time living at 'Plumstones' we did have one rather terrifying incident. It was a Sunday afternoon not long after we had moved in, and the Northamptonshire countryside was looking lovely with the sun high in the sky, and a light breeze ruffling the trees down by the river, so we set off for a walk. All went well until with a fierce and angry buzzing noise a large hornet landed on Ursie's neck and stung her very hard. The effect was immediate and alarming. Ursie's neck started to look livid and, worryingly, she said her throat was swelling up and she was finding it harder to breathe. So we staggered back to the car which, fortunately, started first time and I began to think about how to get to A & E, some miles away. Then we had some good fortune. Ursie remembered that a doctor lived not far from our house and, even though it was Sunday, he might be in. By this time, only about ten minutes after the bite, Ursie was already experiencing dangerous symptoms, so we were mightily relieved to find the good doctor at home, with his bag of tricks close to hand. A swift injection of adrenalin saved the day. I do not like to contemplate the outcome had we not found skilled help so soon, and ever since that time Ursie has always carried an EpiPen with her, especially on holiday.

In sharp contrast to this alarming incident and James's protracted and tortuous arrival, I'm glad to say Ellie's birth was without alarms. During the morning of Tuesday 25 March 1975 Ursie said to me she felt a bit unwell and might have flu. This was a mis-diagnosis of epic proportions and, to say the least, eccentric, given that she was eight months and three weeks pregnant! Four hours later, after a fast drive to Horton Hospital in Banbury, Ursie's flu symptoms had gone but a baby girl called Eleanor Lucy Wood had arrived, after less than an hour of labour. This little girl put in a 'quick' arrival and has been quick ever since.

Over these years, I found that settling into civilian life took some time. Quite apart from the emotional upheaval, I missed the sport, which was hardly surprising since in the Army I was virtually a professional athlete. Anything I was going to do in civilian life could hardly hope to replace this level of sport, though as a civilian I did walk the 17 peaks over 1,000 feet in Wales in 24 hours in the company of my friends Mike Falcon and Richard Hughes. However, although that was an achievement it was also just a one-off. While in Banbury I managed to play hockey most Saturdays on a rather rough field (nothing like today's smooth astro-turf) and went for plenty of runs down the country lanes, but it didn't amount to much really.

As a member of the RAC Pool of Officers (Territorial Army) I went back annually to the Regiment (wherever it was stationed) for two weeks. This was part of my TA training, and I did this for about nine or ten years. After 12 years in the TA I got promotion to Major; thus in total I did 22 years for Her Majesty. At some point during my time with the TA I was attached to the Queen's Royal Irish Hussars and won their inter-squadron Cross Country competition, an event I remember well.

'Captain Wood's the winner', said their Sergeant Instructor as I crossed the line ahead of everyone else.

'Doesn't count; doesn't count', snapped Colonel Roderick Jones, determined that one of his own soldiers should be logged in as first. I still won!

In contrast to my work in the TA, daily life in Weston by Weedon was essentially rural and rather feudal. Ursie saw more of it firsthand than I did, as her daily task was to drum knowledge into those local sons and daughters attending Culworth Primary school. In addition she could observe village life as she 'Tiggywinkled' away in our small cottage, strolled to the village shop or cycled back home along the country lanes from school.

During our four years at 'Roseneath' we lived two miles off the B4525, the back road between Banbury and Northampton. In this very rural setting we saw many instances of the unconventional English at work and play in the fields and villages. One memorable eccentric was Stan Ruddlesden, Head of Ursie's school, who had interviewed her for the post while he leant on his garden wall during a break from digging his veg patch. Stan had been in the Navy during World War II and was round and cheerful with a strong Northamptonshire accent. His approach to running a small country school was benign, almost avuncular in manner, but he had bags of common sense and the children did what he said. He loved Ursie's good-humoured, quirky style, and he and she seemed to spend most of their time either laughing or saying, 'Go on then' as the next daft idea was suggested. His aristocratic neighbour was the Lady of the Manor, so to speak, who was called Lady Mildmay. She would summon Stan from her garden to do her bidding, regardless of what he was doing. 'Ruddlesden', she would call in her aristocratic voice, distinctive of that type and that time. Then Stan would sigh and have leave his dahlias and nasturtiums to go and receive his instructions.

The best-known feature of Weston by Weedon was its pub, The Crown. At weekends lots of visitors would fill the car park, leaving the pub free on weekdays for the long established village families the Sekingtons and the Elkingtons to continue their centuries-old feud. We never found out the cause of the row and the families had probably forgotten it too but it kept them occupied and the rest of the village entertained. Nor do I know which side Doug Hatton, our neighbour opposite, took in the quarrel. There was, I'm sure, a Mrs Hatton but we hardly ever saw her, presumably because she had her work cut out tending and feeding several children under the age of six, who permanently had jam on their faces and mud on their knees – as every small child should.

Doug had constructed a series of untidy fences running down from his rather jerry-built bungalow on the other side of the lane from us. True, they all connected, but as this boundary consisted of sample elements of all the fencing materials known to man, the outlook for us was not a pretty sight. The line was formed by rusty corrugated panels linked to old barbed wire which in turn joined broken fence panels, followed by string attached to bamboo canes, not to mention sheep hurdles, concrete posts and even an old fridge. At the time we sensed that this protective line was really intended to fence off land which didn't belong to Doug's house and that he hoped, by dint of occupation and stealth, to secure squatters' rights after several years. He need not have worried, for it would probably have taken quite a while to clear the patch of the mass of junk he had heaved onto it. Imagine an old corporation tip, add a few tired Brussel sprout stalks, some withered potato plants and the odd flower in a pot, and you will have a good picture of Doug Hatton's garden. Fortunately we rarely looked out of our front windows. Nor did we confront Doug about his fence – this was, after all, a man who, having been roused in the night by some noisy youths, took out his shotgun and blasted away with both barrels over the apple tree.

Near Lady Mildmay lived the Rural Dean – the Reverend Sam Brown (I kid you not) and we remember him now mostly for a sermon he preached at Matins. Extolling the virtues of village life and community, he reminded his flock that Mitzi Rogers, an actress who lived in the village, would that night be appearing on BBC TV and that everyone ought to support her by tuning in. His good intentions were not in doubt but, to the delight of most people (certainly the men) Mitzi was performing in a rather lewd 1960s romp in which, for part of the time at any rate, she appeared to be topless. So much for an uplifting sermon.

At some point in the four years we lived in Weston by Weedon there was a general election. When Ursie went along to vote she found Lady Sitwell from the 'big house' in the village encamped in a tent outside the polling station, doing her job as Conservative Party teller. Lady S and her friend had clearly set up camp for the day, with food being brought out at regular intervals from the house and an almost constant supply of wine to offer to those willing to stop by and chat – either before or after voting. Lady Sitwell had a booming voice, an accusatory eye and no doubt the local farmers and villagers who stayed to accept her hospitality were made quite clear about which way they were expected to vote. It was a day of blue favours, red faces and pork pie hats.

My primary reason for deciding to leave Banbury and work in London was the pressure to move jobs. Having started on a pretty low salary and with little experience of the corporate world, I needed to make a quantum leap, above and beyond what any internal promotion might provide. I can't remember the exact figures, but if after five years at GF I was on £3,500 per year I needed to roughly double this if mortgage payments were to be met, children educated and bills paid. Fortunately my efforts to make this happen more or less worked out, and after a protracted period of interviews and delays I eventually got a job as a buyer at Beecham Foods, Brentford.

The national economic background to my move to Beecham Foods was not promising, and we'd had some domestic challenges as well. A year before I got the offer of a job from Beecham, James contracted severe pneumonia. We rushed him to the Horton Hospital and he stayed in an oxygen tent for two days. Then lo and behold only three weeks before we were due to up sticks and move to Windsor Ellie got similarly ill and once again our car doubled as an ambulance for the journey to hospital. Her attack proved less severe but the whole process was pretty distressing.

I mentioned that the economic background at this time was not good. Since it is almost impossible to understand what Ursie and I have achieved (and why we did what we did) without taking this into account, I feel I should try to summarise what things were like in the UK from the mid 1970s until the early 1990s.

My childhood and teenage years largely took place in a period of post-war austerity. In the late 1950s and the 1960s (when I was mostly abroad) there was a period of economic rejuvenation, social change and sexual revolution. All of which was summed up at the time by Prime Minister Harold Macmillan and his famous dictum 'Most of our people have never had it so good.' But a small country at the corner of Europe does not fight two World Wars and lose an Empire without seriously damaging its health and feeling the pain for many a decade. As the legions started to come home so, in relative terms, the economy continued to decline.

At that time many British people assumed that trade and jobs and wealth virtually came along with being British and I was part of that naive and foolish coterie, as were all my family and many others. Thus our financial fortunes as a nation ebbed and flowed but mostly (until the early 1990s) were on a downward path. Other than brief patches in the 1960s, 'Our people have never had it so bad', might have been a more apt catchphrase in terms of the national economy. This depressing cycle was aptly captured by a remark of Sarah Hogg (member of the Cabinet Office, journalist and economist): 'No one should be surprised by the remarkable capacity of the British economy to disappoint'. Quite.

Britain came out of World War II virtually bankrupt. Apart from America, most Western nations were in fact in a bad way at the end of the War. Later, when the free nations of Europe had largely recovered, in relative terms the UK still continued to decline. And to compound things we also awarded ourselves what had long been overdue, namely a Welfare State. This set out to provide everybody, regardless of income, with good schools, free health care, proper housing, decent retirement pensions and social benefits for those out of work, disabled or seriously disadvantaged. The problem was that however deserved the Welfare State added up to an expensive package that could only be afforded by a prosperous nation. Ultimately the Prime Minister, Harold Wilson, had to devalue sterling. This was followed by the IMF giving us a loan and telling us how to run our finances.

Since the Victorian era, manufacturing had been at the heart of our economy. We thought we were good at it but the awful truth was that, measured internationally, we were falling behind and our performance was bad. Thus our payments never 'balanced' and year after year we recorded a deficit of imports over exports, which put us permanently in the red. Part of our problem as a country was that we had no real understanding of the underlying causes of our woeful economic performance. On top of this we had poor skills training; were often badly educated (except for the small percentage who went to university), lacked new investment and suffered from weak management. This last meant that over-mighty unions in obsolescent factories were able to hold managers to ransom in order to obtain unearned wage increases for their members.

On a daily basis in the 1960s, 70s and 80s, TV, radio and the papers were full of news of strikes or threats of strikes; indeed it seemed that there was always someone either on strike or on a 'go slow'. Hundreds of millions of days of work were lost every year, so, not surprisingly, product quality deteriorated and broken contracts meant that the UK's potential clients went shopping elsewhere. Matters came to a head with the Winter of Discontent of 1978–9, when rubbish piled in the streets and the dead went unburied. The state of the nation was even worse than it had been a few years earlier during Ted Heath's three-day week, when all factories closed for two days each week. (As it happened, during the three-day week Ursie and I survived quite well in our little cottage and were fairly snug with oil lamps, an open coal fire and gas cylinders!)

The Winter of Discontent proved to be the low point; almost in desperation, the country voted in Mrs Thatcher and her right-wing agenda who, in time, took on the Unions. 'Never upset the coal miners or the bench of Bishops' used to be an old political maxim. However, successive Tory Governments of the 1980s and 90s took them both on, and the defeat of Arthur Scargill and the coal miners, with its terrible social consequences and still lingering bitterness (especially in the North and in Wales), is now seen as a turning point. Because the Unions were defeated, the UK economy managed to break out of a vicious circle of decline and slowly build towards a position of strength, so much so that in the eight year period from 1999 to 2007 we had sustained growth without high inflation, an unprecedented combination and something my generation never expected to see. Even now in the days of recession, the UK still has the world's seventh largest economy and we are enjoying a manufacturing renaissance.

I have gone to some length to explain these things because they are the background to these memoirs. In the course of the country being economically and socially transformed through the realisation of commercial realities I too was transformed. The establishment child brought up to play his part in large, institutional organisations such as Public School, the Church, the Services, international corporations (General Foods, Beecham Foods, Metal Box) had to grow up. Like the nation, I had to learn to be a more entrepreneurial, more self-sufficient person and one who was able to sell and do the financial sums. I have to say, despite the scars, the worries and the redundancies it has ultimately been liberating. Instead of my identity being an expression of who I worked for, or who my parents were, I have developed my true identity by being…. myself. This journey, socially, spiritually and in terms of marriage and work, has resulted in what psychologists might call 'self-actualisation.' By freeing myself from somebody else's system I have created my own, which works for me.

What was the effect of the changes in Britain's economy and in my career on Ursie and our young family? Well, it meant a lot of uncertainty but that is normal in any business career, particularly any involving start-ups or self-employment. It also meant that, at a time when we were trying to afford housing for a family with three children, the economic situation required us to pay higher and higher interest rates on the mortgage. For example, following the 1974 price hike, when oil went up threefold in a matter of months, mortgage rates followed and continued to go on up until they peaked around 16% in the early Thatcher years. During my business career I was made redundant twice and had to do a fair amount of moving, both from job to job and sector to sector. However, this relatively high level of job market activity may have also been because in the Army I missed ten years of business life and needed to catch up.

We left Banbury and moved to 78 Alexander Road, Windsor, early in March 1976. My work was an unknown quantity; Ursie had no job and no friends nearby; Ellie was still convalescing; it rained incessantly and, worst of all, the aeroplanes that we hadn't noticed on our initial visit roared in just over our roof. So Ellie's first birthday had a background of some tears and a sense of 'what have we done?'

There was, however, one strange bit of good fortune. On the cold, rainy day we actually moved to Windsor, we turned the corner to approach our new home and saw a sign that read 'Upton House School'. 'Oh, look', Ursie said, 'maybe I can get a job there.' In the event Ursie was to work both full and part-time at this happy school, only two hundred yards up the road from our home, for nearly ten years. In addition, all three children had good times there and the headteacher, Miss Wallace, became a close family friend, so much so that she appointed herself Hattie's 'fairy godmother'. Many years later, when she was deeply troubled and terminally ill in the Windsor Hospice, I was able to help her and was very glad to do so.

Number 78 Alexandra Road was one of those typical Victorian family houses built in quite a pleasant red brick. It was on a corner formed by a row of terraced dwellings and Beaumont Road. It had four bedrooms, a fairly skanky bathroom and only a small paved garden. However, it was big enough for our purposes and like most Victorian homes was warm enough in the winter (albeit with storage heaters) and cool in the summer, having been solidly built with a nice front door, cornicing in the sitting room and two bay windows – one up and one down.

I think James and Ellie quite liked living there. James no doubt was influenced by some very colourful (some would say lurid) wallpaper in his bedroom, while Ellie really enjoyed having her own room with a brass bed at the back. Number 78 was just a short walk from Windsor town centre and faced All Saints Church, reputedly designed by the novelist Thomas Hardy when he was a young architect. In later life Hardy became an atheist (though always with religious tendencies), and had an unerringly bleak view of the human condition. The rather unlovely building he managed to create opposite our house perfectly reflected both these traits.

Soon after we arrived in Windsor the Rev John Kerr became curate at 'Hardy's church' and we got to know him really well. John now lives in the States but we are still close friends after nearly forty years and I wish he wasn't so far away. John is tall with glasses, always well dressed and has a scholarly air, which is not surprising since he is the nearest thing to Renaissance man I have ever met, as well as being a leading light in the Society of Ordained Scientists. John has done lots of things supremely well, from flying jets to lecturing in engineering and has a wonderful library of books, including a fine section devoted to the First World War poets.

When I began my new job, I found that Beecham Foods, despite being a major British food company with a string of household brands, was pretty antiquated compared with GF and their American way of doing things. To be fair it was very marketing orientated (quite American and the right emphasis) and I suspect the investment in modern production equipment was also good. But the buying department, which I joined that spring on £4,500 a year, was in the dark ages.

Beecham had a wonderful range of brands, including Lucozade, Coca-Cola (as a franchise), Aqua Fresh toothpaste, Britvic, Ribena, Horlicks and some advanced pharmaceutical products (these had launched the Beecham empire in the 20th century). My job as a buyer was to sit laboriously making out cards each week from which orders would be placed. The ridiculous thing was that every week the orders were almost identical. So I introduced the GF system of placing a bulk order, with a set price for the year, which also had a reference number against which we could phone up and call off whatever weekly amount was needed. I also extended the practice of making supplier visits, so that those who were placing our (often quite large) orders could go and meet the people who made the ingredients and see the sites, the systems and the machinery at first hand. By now I had grasped that business is essentially about relationships, and you don't make good relationships sitting in a Nissen hut (which was 'home' for the buying department) filling out cards or stuck behind your desk. Hardly revolutionary thinking.

These Nissen huts where we worked were situated behind the famous Beecham tower on the A4 flyover. (This building is fondly remembered by many for a line of a dozen or so brilliantly lit Christmas trees, placed on the roof every December, which were the same height as the flyover.) The way we operated was almost as antiquated as the huts we worked in. I remember particularly one occasion which summed up for me how out of date our practices were. I suggested to the Head Buyer that we ought to have some training to develop us as managers, but he resisted the suggestion. Although personal development did have some merit, the day might come when he was asked a difficult question by Senior Management and the person who could answer it might be away on a training course! Similarly, I recall it took Ted Sherlock (my boss) over nine months to sort out my appointment from first advert to arrival – nine months, when my notice period at GF was only four weeks. Ted regularly kept Sales Reps waiting an hour for a scheduled appointment and I never knew if this was just bad time management or some curious way of retaining control.

My journey to work was OK (I used to car share), the pay was better and I had made a move up the ladder but, apart from these factors, the rest was only just bearable. Probably my fondest recollection of my few months at Beecham was arranging a visit to Coleford in Gloucestershire, where they kept row upon row of huge ice cold vats in which the blackcurrants for making a year's supply of Ribena were stored.

Then, at this point I had a piece of good fortune. Johnny Gill, (James's godfather) and I had been at the Junior Leaders together and were good friends. While we were serving, Johnny was kind enough to regularly lend me his morning dress coat for a succession of weddings. This was quite a smart move on my part because if you were going to borrow clothes from someone you could not find a more immaculately turned-out officer than Johnny. Sparkling toe-caps wasn't in it, and everything he wore looked as though it had just been unwrapped. He and I got on really well, for he had a gentle sense of humour and was very kind. There is a picture of him at our wedding holding my sister Nickie's hand and they look rather happy together – but nothing came of it.

Johnny left the army a little time after me, having had a pretty unhappy time in Northern Ireland (where the IRA were on the rampage) and joined Metal Box (MB). In 1976 he was looking for a move within the company, and discussed the new post of Head of Schools Liaison with his colleague Peter Wheeler. Johnny decided not to take the discussion any further but, knowing both my personality and my dissatisfaction with Beecham Foods, suggested to Peter that I might be interested. In consequence I got a call at home one evening from Peter, at the end of which we agreed to meet within a couple of days at Metal Box's splendid new headquarters, next to Reading station. Peter and I got on really well from the start and, having met after work, we went off for supper together.

Shortly after this meeting I came in to see a couple of senior people in Human Resources, and the deal was done. What a contrast to the procrastination and ineffectiveness of my move to Beecham Foods earlier in the year – indeed, because Peter was in a hurry I don't believe my new job was even advertised, but I was thrilled to be appointed.

Despite the brief acquaintance I had with the company before joining, I knew that the first day I first worked there, 7 December 1976, was a seminal moment. My colleagues in the HR department were educated and professional, the company had a high reputation worldwide and the offices were superb. At the time Metal Box was one of the world's largest packaging companies, manufacturing food and drink cans and other related products. It had over sixty factories worldwide and dominated the UK and European market, as well as having a strong presence in the old Commonwealth countries. The company's head office, Queen's House, had two squash courts and a swimming pool, plus an excellent subsidised restaurant; and, as a bonus, my train journey only took about forty minutes. So as I grew into the job I really felt I had made the breakthrough I needed following my Army days.

Working with Peter began to transform my performance. I learnt so many good things from him. Of course, as is so often the case with new jobs, the reality of what I actually did was some miles away from what I thought I was being hired to do. For a start, actual liaison with schools was limited to just the summer months. This was because the bulk of the job was to help Peter and two other colleagues with a demanding and extensive task known as the 'milk round': the recruitment of graduates for the company.

At that time nearly all major British companies took part in this exhausting and very competitive winter sport. This involved visiting universities and polytechnics in order to interview final year undergraduates, in the hope of attracting the best talent to your company. Traditionally, and for reasons that were never clear to me, the accountancy firms were let loose first and were able to roam the corridors of Higher Education freely and unmolested during the Michelmas (autumn) term. Thereafter the universities were invaded by some two hundred companies, often with teams made up of three or four interviewers, all hunting for the best engineers, the best scientists or the pick of the talented all-rounders. MB had recently decided to start taking the 'milk round' seriously, hence Peter's appointment as Head of Graduate Recruitment. Instead of the search for good graduates being just another job for the HR to pick up as an extra, Metal Box had gone for a dedicated team of two (Peter and me) in an effort to improve the calibre of graduate entrants to the company.

Peter was a big, tall man, good-looking and with a ready smile and engaging manner. He was unconventional, and the sort of person who would be equally comfortable in high society or eating cross-legged on the floor with simple food. One evening he came to our house for supper, after which Ursie did her usual kind thing of saying, 'You go and talk and I'll just clear up.' However, Peter wasn't having any of that, and the more Mrs Wood clung to the sink the more determined he got. In the end he just picked her up under the shoulders, with her feet right off the ground, and carried her out of the kitchen. You've never seen anything like it!

Despite being pretty well off (his family owned three or four cottages near Fordingbridge), Peter also had an active social conscience and both he and his wife Margaret did lots of charity work in the area around their Hampshire home. Peter was often on his own there, as Margaret was a great traveller and used to go off on long buying trips to Indonesia to obtain batik fabrics, which she then re-sold in the UK. Peter also had travel in his background. Having gained a Blue captaining the Cambridge Rugby team, he had spent some time travelling the world earning his living as part of the Colonial Service, in the days when we had colonies which needed servicing. In particular he became well known in the 1950s when a volcano on the island of Tristan da Cunha erupted, threatening the lives of everyone. As Governor of the island, Peter sent for urgent help from the Royal Navy, and thousands of people were evacuated by ship. There are famous pictures and newsreels of the event, and I believe Peter and Margaret were the last people off the island, with the Governor resplendent in his cocked hat and uniform.

After leaving this position, Peter joined MB's international side, working particularly in India. Things Asiatic suited his background and his strong desire to be outdoors. It was in India that Peter met and worked with Dennis Allport, who became MB's Managing Director in the late1970s. At the time there was a long running debate about the reasons for Britain's industrial decline. Dennis became pre-occupied with the country's apparent lack of well-qualified engineers, since a good supply of competent engineers was crucial to success for a company like MB. This shortage of supply was put down to a national culture which, it was claimed, valued professions such as the law, medicine and the military ahead of business, and the apparently more prosaic virtues of business acumen, commercial skills and entrepreneurship.

During this period, the UK's educational system was criticised for being out of touch with reality and for putting too much emphasis on the acquisition of what was termed as 'useless' knowledge. The system was also attacked for ignoring the importance of adding value, the need for a vibrant economy and the financial imperative for individuals and nations to earn their keep. Over the next fifteen years I was to become an integral part of this debate and, with many others, an agent for change. Had I but known it I was also about to become a campaigner, a role I have had on and off ever since. Maybe the nervy, dyslexic boy was beginning to find his way.

Peter believed in hard work. Having lived and worked for many years in the tropics, he liked starting early and, as an expression of his personality, also liked finishing late, very much not the culture in Britain's offices and factories at the time. The norm for most people, including myself, was 9am to 5pm with the occasional extra hour thrown in, if really necessary. The concept of 24/7 was unheard of, though it was known that the Germans and the Americans kept long hours, as did some senior managers and employees in City firms. Under Peter's guidance I began to get used to the concept of long hours, which in a way was not so very different from being in the military where, in a sense, you are always on duty.

One of Peter's priorities was to raise the bar in terms of the quality and number of graduates we would recruit by summer 1977. This of course would require new systems, new interviewers, new interview procedures, new universities to visit and, of course, lots more applications to be processed. I think in that first year we went up from an intake of about thirty or forty trainees to something nearer sixty and, in later years, we were recruiting about a hundred a year. The extra effort required for all this was taken as a given and largely not discussed. Peter was really good fun to work with as he was fair, cheerful and warm-hearted, but he didn't understand why everyone didn't work longer hours. For example, under his rule holidays (or 'furlough' in his terminology) were to be earned and not necessarily seen as just part of the employment package. This said, he was never difficult about my taking leave and, indeed, was actually helpful in terms of freeing me up for two weeks TA (Territorial Army) training each year.

I was involved for four years in the long annual process of finding MB its quota of good graduates. I didn't mind the relatively long days, all the hours travelling or the sessions staying behind after work to make presentations. During our first winter together (1976–7) Peter and I developed a system for handling the milk round. The process would start with the five main divisions of MB putting in bids for the number and type of new graduates they needed. These would be turned into raw statistics and then adverts, together with a glossy recruitment brochure, would be sent off to over seventy universities and polytechnics. Despite us being only a small team, Peter insisted we went to as many centres of Higher Education (HE) as possible. He took scant interest in how far away they were, or the general calibre of undergraduate talent we would find there. He felt MB somehow had a mission to 'see and be seen'. Unfortunately in this, I think, he was almost certainly wrong. Though MB gained good reputation in the HE sector through this approach, as a team we spread ourselves far too thin.

From about October onwards, application forms would begin to flood in – sometimes as many as a hundred from one uuniversity. I would spread these over the living room floor at weekends or in the evening in order to do a first sift. I guess most years we had over 15,000 applications in just two months, and of these we actually interviewed some 3,000 people, so roughly eight out of ten were rejected at this paper stage. Everyone who had applied was then written to by a team of five girls working flat out (in those days secretarial teams were the norm and many managers had their own secretary). The lucky shortlisted candidates were told we would see them at their university in the New Year.

Come January we were off on our travels, mainly by train, visiting the various centres by region. Typically we would interview ten or twelve undergraduates a day, which was very exhausting given we then had to catch an evening train to get to the next port of call. On arrival we would grab some supper, re-read the application forms for the next day's interviewees and collapse into bed. Occasionally there were interesting stories to be told, like the one, told me by my predecessor Steve Riley. After a hard week's interviewing in the North, Steve arrived late in the evening at Liverpool University and being in need of food tried the Student's Union Bar. There he asked for something to eat and a drink, whereupon the young guy behind the bar refused to serve him, saying he was closing (it was then just before 10pm), and pulled the grille down in Steve's face. Guess who the first student was who came into Steve's interview room at 9.00am the next day? Quite rightly Steve told him to get out!

Our university visits continued three days a week every week until the middle of March, at which point we went into the next stage whereby some three or four hundred successful candidates were invited to Reading for a two-day second interview. This second interview process was new and largely of Peter's devising. We duly conducted about ten second-interview programmes – each of which lasted two days and involved about twenty students. The process started with candidates making their way to the Great Western Hotel at Paddington Station, where I would meet them and take them to Reading on the train. Over the next 24 hours the students jumped through a series of hoops, including interviews, psychometric tests and an evening presentation about Metal Box, given by me. I used to really enjoy this session in which I outlined the company's structure and values, supported by an excellent set of photographs and slides. A sort of commercial version of the Banbury Cross Players with just me in the cast and a script largely composed of slides about different kinds of packaging!

As part of our second interview process we used a firm in London run by Dr John Howard (not his real name) to run a battery of psychometric tests. John would send various members of his staff to join in the decision-making meeting and to explain the results. One day, the chair of a decision group came to Peter and said, 'That psychiatrist from London, Helen Smith, is a complete moron and worse than useless. Please ring John Howard and tell him exactly what I think and to never send her again.' This Peter duly did, without pulling any punches. A couple of months later we learnt that Helen Smith was actually John Howard's wife.

At the time of my arrival at MB, people were still settling in to the new Head Office. Peter had been given a space between two partition walls, which he hated, so he refused to use this area. He told me that if he did use the space he'd been officially allocated, no one would seriously attempt to find him a proper office. So, arriving very early each working day (often at 6.00am), he would roam the completely empty building like some lost soul, searching for a desk to use. On arrival at work during this period my first job was therefore to play 'hunt the boss – a fun office party game for two people'. He would ring me up, describe roughly where he was and I would go off and try to find him. One day it would be, 'I'm up on the Director's Floor, one of the PAs is on holiday', or another day 'I'm in the Post Room using a table Jack has lent me.'

Peter was a determined guy and this bizarre ritual, caused entirely by an eccentric refusal to fall in line, went on quite a while. Eventually I got Ursie's Mum, Mary, to draw a cartoon showing Peter sitting on the loo, with his coat and briefcase nearby. 'This is fine', read the caption, 'all they need to do now is run in the telephone!' Peter once explained to me that he could sleep anywhere and, pointing to the top of a wooden cupboard, said, 'Up there would be fine!' There is no reason to doubt him, for some time after I had left MB, I learnt that he had sold his flat in Reading and asked him where he was living. He looked a bit sheepish when I questioned him about his arrangements and answered, 'Listen, don't tell anyone, but I stay late in the office and then kip in the car in the car park till it's morning.' Among his other endearing traits was a capacity to know where the sun was at any time of the day even if there was heavy cloud. Consequently he always knew in which direction to head.

Returning to my job, the other part of it was linking with schools and the world of education. This took me all over the country, attending conferences, sometimes speaking at seminars and visiting various colleges and schools. Gradually I became quite knowledgeable about these matters and formed close links with some very good secondary schools – both private and state. For a while I was a member of the Independent Schools Careers Organisation and on the back of that had a week at Aiglon College in Switzerland, doing careers work together with some skiing.

Although I travelled a lot and regularly worked quite late, I was rarely away from home for more than one night and my impression is that I was generally around to read bedtime stories and hear what the family had been up to at school. Certainly Ursula never minded, and if you ask her now I think she will say that my hours were quite tolerable from a family point of view.

In the 1970s and 80s, just as the UK's commercial sector had too many poor manufacturing companies, so too our school system was wanting. In far too many schools, teachers went home at 4pm, homework was not marked for days while discipline was often poor and many buildings dilapidated. This was reflected in low attainment levels at every stage and a general sense of muddle. A survey of the Physics curriculum in the early 1980s found there were 40 different syllabuses, not one of which dealt with scientific discoveries since 1925! Thus I found myself part of a declining manufacturing sector, charged with liaising with a pretty defunct educational system. Looking back, it is nothing short of a miracle that both the country and these two areas of national life have rejuvenated themselves so successfully. Our industrial base is now relatively small but, as the seventh-largest manufacturer in the world, we still very much compete globally, while a great number of our schools (together with the teaching profession itself) have been transformed.

In the late 1970s I got to know Kenneth Adams, also based in Windsor. He was running a campaign backed by the Royal Society of Arts (RSA), which he ran from St George's House in Windsor Castle with the aim of trying to improve the links between UK industry and our educational sector. Kenneth was a bulky Yorkshireman with a thoughtful manner and a good sense of fun. He'd had, as they say, 'a good war', finishing as a Major in the regular Army. Although he could be quite direct and was not one to suffer unthinking opposition he was a very good guy to work with and we got on well. He did wonderful work to raise the image of industry and with his extensive network became a great supporter of what I was doing.

Given the RSA's full remit – 'the encouragement of Arts, Manufactures and Commerce' – it's not surprising that Kenneth's work was devoted to studying the reasons behind Britain's poor manufacturing performance and what could be done to turn it round. Over the next ten years or so Kenneth ran a series of weekend consultations at Windsor Castle and, because of my work at MB and later with 3i, he kindly invited me to several of these. His conferences were convened in the Vicars' Hall at Windsor Castle, which is a beautiful, timbered 16th-century building, set next to the chapel, and is reputedly where the first performance of *The Merry Wives of Windsor* was held in front of Queen Elizabeth I. In these rather Oxford-college type surroundings we would debate and discuss the social, political, scientific, and economic reasons for our inability to compete with the rest of the developed world (especially Japan) in terms of making things. Industry was something Britain believed it had always been good at and which had underpinned Victorian prosperity and the building of Empire. Lots of 'the good and the great' attended these seminars including people like the Chair of the CBI, MPs, directors of major companies, journalists and prominent academies. I learnt a huge amount about the subject from being with such people, and in a way these conventions were a sort of mini-university, where I sat and listened and took notes.

Increasingly, by virtue of my job I was also able to contribute and even lead on these issues. In fact I became something of an expert on the subject of theories attempting to explain Britain's industrial decline and possible solutions. My contribution to solving the problem was dwarfed by the massive changes brought in by Mrs Thatcher, whose reforms of the mid-eighties swept up this issue as part of her revolution. In general terms Mrs Thatcher's view was that manufacturing, like the railways, was passé and defunct, so if it didn't function it could go to the wall, while we built up clean, new shiny service industries. And to some extent this happened. Certainly during the 1980s and 90s the country's service sector grew fast and began to dominate the economy, while sub-standard industrial concerns were allowed to die.

The arguments that were developed at these conferences and in the press helped me later when I eventually led a campaign on precisely this issue. Over time I became a long term member of a quite successful movement which achieved two things. First, we made links between the business world and schools not only respectable but necessary. What's nowadays seen as part of a 'company's license to operate' often includes links with education. Secondly, we got much of the educational system to accept that students needed other things as well as academic qualifications, including the life skills to help them get jobs. Of course, the real answer is that we need to keep a proper balance between these two conflicting ideals.

Alongside these messages our campaigns also helped to offset the idea that 'profit' per se was a dirty word. At the time many people believed it was better to work in the public sector, in social services for example, than to do the capitalists' work for them. Along with many others, I promulgated concepts such as 'added value' and the idea that people needed to earn, and companies needed to make a profit. Without this income we would be unable to pay for education, the NHS, social services, the Army and many other things. This seems blindingly obvious now but at the time we were pushing the proverbial stone uphill, and not helped at all by the ineptness of many managers or the generally insalubrious nature of manufacturing.

The thinking behind this movement is best summed up by a rightwing journalist, Paul Johnson, with whom I would normally disagree. In a quote, which I have carried with me for over thirty years, he said, 'For we are an island people and our future is necessarily commercial. It will be a poor one unless we can make a better job of bringing our educational system more in line with the needs of a trading nation.' This malaise, which was very deep and went back much further than anyone imagined, was well analysed in two seminal books published about this time. One was *The Audit of War* by the historian Correlli Barnett, and the other, by Mark Werner, an American academic, was (I think) called *The British Disease and the Decline of the Manufacturing Sector.*

The point both books made was that the downward spiral in manufacturing actually began in the latter part of Victoria's reign. It could be that complacency and arrogance played their parts. As industrialists and traders made their money, they became preoccupied with using their new wealth to try and imitate the landed gentry, who historically had used their influence and wealth to run the country. With their new-made money, Britain's entrepreneurs and industrialists bought themselves large houses and estates, took up country sports and during World War I helped Lloyd George by buying titles. In other words, too many successful people turned their backs on the very occupation which had made them rich in order to try and move up the social order. Britain's industrial decline was at heart an issue of class.

We can see an example of this snobbery at work in India, a key part of the British Empire. The British in India were serviced by a network of people providing everything from the supplies needed by the Army to the furniture, pens, and paper required by the British (Indian) Civil Service, as well as the whisky drunk by them all. The providers of these vital items were derisively known as 'box wallahs' and for many years they were not allowed to use the clubs and facilities frequented by the officers and their equivalents. They were socially ostracised for being traders.

Things got worse. By the start of the 20th century we were short of engineers; technology training was limited and, compared with the rest of Europe, the mass of our people were badly educated. At the start of World War I we had virtually no aniline (chemical) dye industry and, tellingly, in 1916, at the battle of Jutland, Admiral Beatty declared, 'There's something wrong with our bloody ships.' This was at a time when the Royal Navy was the pride of the nation, and this critical comment about the fleet casts further doubt on British industrial supremacy. People often say that such criticism of our manufacturing base can't be true, citing as an example the quality and performance of the Spitfire. However, in his analysis Correlli Barnett argues that though the Spitfire was designed in the UK it was built in large numbers on machine tools brought in from America and, while its aerial performance was slightly better than the Messerschmitt 109, it actually cost over twice as much to build and took longer to service. Thus, in a peacetime market, it is likely that the Spitfire would not have outsold the competition.

* * *

As the country's economic condition declined further, so did that of Metal Box. The odd factory was closed (MB had 60 worldwide); posts were cut; graduate recruitment curtailed and profitability fell. Finally, in 1981 the Board called in McKinsey Consultants to review all our activities. Every department was asked to fill in forms justifying their existence, and a feeling of great insecurity spread through Queen's House. It was like being in an Army unit on stand-by and not knowing where you might be sent – except in this case the worst place to be sent was back home.

Peter seemed quite sanguine and saw the process largely as another aspect of the business cycle but I felt it was more serious. I didn't see how we would be allowed to spend time and money on a large-scale graduate recruitment programme when contraction was all around. So, with Peter's blessing, I applied for a sales job with Metal Box Portsmouth, which sold plastic bottles to all the major food, automotive and pharmaceutical companies. I felt I wanted to get into selling because sales and accounts are the bedrock of most businesses, and I needed to move more to the centre of things.

Before I actually joined MB Portsmouth an incident occurred which rather clouded my relationship with Peter. During my interview at Portsmouth I was asked when I would be free to take up the new post. 'Well', I said, 'We are not in the recruiting season and my personal diary is pretty free but you'll have to speak to Peter.' MB Portsmouth interpreted this to suit their needs and made me a job offer starting in only two weeks. Peter, who, I think, had never really believed I would leave, reacted furiously and accused me of being disloyal to him. Obviously this stung, as I felt I owed him a lot but that he was overreacting. It is true that my sudden departure did leave him in the lurch and diminished his operation. On the other hand, he wasn't prepared to accept that I had told them to speak to him about dates. I'm glad to say we made up over this misunderstanding later, as he was a great man and a good friend.

I took my new sales job for three reasons. First, it offered a salary increase and a car during a period when mortgage interest rates were very high. Secondly, you can only do so much intensive interviewing, and I needed a change. Finally, I had become aware that in business you need some kind of qualification or basic training, preferably in either accounts or sales.

Along with my job change, some cheerful incidents occurred during this period. During my time at Metal Box I became a fellow of the Royal Society of Arts (FRSA) at the second attempt. Up until then the RSA had only awarded fellowships to graduates, but Kenneth Adams challenged the fact that my application was rejected for my not having gone to university. As a result the RSA changed its mind, for which I am indebted to Kenneth. This kind of recognition mattered, and I used to go to for lots of evening meeting at the RSA in the Strand and to other seminars round the country.

In particular I wrote the Metal Box submission for an RSA project called The Campaign for Capability, and we became one of its lead companies, as well as strong supporters of Industry Year 1986, which was the follow-up. In my time as Head of Schools Liaison, we commissioned a former advertising executive called Jo Graffy to produce some MB-sponsored promotional literature on behalf of manufacturing. Together we worked on a series of posters and booklets called *Industry in Perspective* and *Industry in Close-up*, which were very well received and launched by a junior minister in London. My favourite part of the campaign was a fine poster that Jo produced showing the amazing technical feats required to produce the humble two-piece drinks can.

As you will have gathered, graduate recruitment Peter Wheeler style was a hard grind. Inevitably, getting overtired played to my weaknesses in health terms and during my time at MB I had a series of bouts of tonsillitis. The worst of these occurred about a year after we'd moved to 53 Clarence Road and laid me out for a week. The pain was so intense that I couldn't swallow or sleep, so, although our doctor, Dr Thomas, had given me some extra-strong medicine and unhelpfully advised me *not* to have an operation I ignored him and had my tonsils out. It was one of the best decisions I've made, and after a couple of days in an NHS hospital in Queen's Square, Soho, I came home able to eat raw cornflakes and all things 'spiky', and I'm sure that thereafter my energy levels and general well-being improved. This was despite the efforts of an endless succession of people who advised against having my tonsils out saying how dangerous it was and how it wouldn't really work.

* * *

Generally, I have been blessed with remarkably good health and have managed to keep away from the medics. Obviously there is a degree of good fortune in all of this, but I think there have been other contributing factors. For a start, I was born skinny and throughout my boyhood and teens I was very thin. Put me in the sea or a swimming pool and before long I would emerge shivering and blue with my ribs showing. But in certain ways my slim build has been a help. Being a non-smoker and moderate drinker, together with my light frame, has helped to keep me fairly slim and able to run and ski.

So far I've only discussed the physical side of things. Given both my Mum and my brother Michael's susceptibility to depression and obsessive behaviour it would be wrong and foolish to ignore this aspect of well-being. But depression has never hit me seriously. At heart I have the capacity both to give and receive affection and the probability surely is that both my parents gave me plenty of love. From about the age of seven onwards, because of Mum's illness, this would have mostly come from Dad. They say the first two or three years are key in this respect, so my Mum too must have been the gentle and caring person everyone said she was. I guess also that the experiences of soldiering and adventure have contributed to strengthening me mentally. The equation looks to be that competitive sport, strange places, active service and being away from family and familiar places all put more into me than they took out. Feeling angry and being down are normal emotions and though I now try hard to stay in control I guess there is still a 'Splinter' side to my personality which will always be there. But I have become better balanced with age.

Finally on this subject of maintaining mental equilibrium I do seem to have a useful degree of self-knowledge. I instinctively know, on the whole, what is good for me and, as I get older, I am more inclined than ever to follow this instinct, – indeed maybe that's one of the plus points of getting older. These days I feel beholden to no peer group and my values are, I believe, a healthy combination of some of those I grew up with and others I have acquired for myself. I have learnt to be reasonably comfortable with the person I've become.

* * *

During my time at Metal Box we decided to take a bit of a risk and have the third child we had always wished for. In the spring of 1981 we went to Crete, and it's nice to think that lovely Hattie was conceived on that beautiful and civilised island. Ursie and I were thrilled at the prospect of another baby, albeit after a gap of six years and Ursie's pregnancy was, as I recall, pretty uneventful. (However this is a man's point of view and the good Mrs Wood may have a different memory). Despite Ursie being medically classified at the relatively young age of 35 as an 'elderly primate' Hattie arrived with no complications at ten minutes to midnight on 22 December 1981. This was a joyful event which has continued to give joy ever since.

On Christmas Eve I collected our new babe plus her Mum from the Heatherwood Hospital and we drove home over Windsor Great

Park from Ascot. Halfway across the park Carols from King's came on the radio. As a boy treble's voice rang out with the first lines of 'Once in Royal David's City' it started to snow, and we all shared a very special and magical moment.

CHAPTER ELEVEN

A Different Kind of Campaigning

'Far and away the best prize that life has to offer is the chance to work hard at work worth doing'

- Theodore Roosevelt

In 1981 I left the comfortable confines of Queen's House, Reading, for the rather more uncertain delights of what was called Portsmouth Bottles. This, as the name suggests was a factory making plastic bottles, located quite close to Portsmouth harbour. My new base was still part of MB and was a fairly large, modern factory, about two hours by car from Windsor.

Metal Box gave me a car and a pay increase but my remit was, to say the least, pretty daft. From a factory right on the south coast I was expected to service a key client on the outskirts of Manchester – while living in Windsor. Not many people know that it is exactly 203 miles from 53 Clarence Road to the Cussons factory in the heart of Bolton. However I do, as I did the journey remorselessly every ten days for about two years while I was part of the Metal Box sales force.

The idiotic geographical aspect of this arrangement was compounded by the fact that Metal Box also had a very large plastic bottle making factory in Wexham, North Wales, about an hour from Cussons HQ. My outward journey was normally about three hours, but the return home could take longer if the evening traffic was bad, so the logic of the arrangement was difficult to work out. The reason this strange situation was allowed to continue was because of inter-factory rivalry between Portsmouth and Wexham, exacerbated by competing egos on the Board of Directors. In his autobiography (called *Iacocca*) Lee Iacocca tells of his many years in the US car industry, where he became President of Ford and then CEO of Chrysler. In the book he remarks how useful his early training in psychology had been during his business career. 'It helped me understand and deal with the many paranoid individuals who frequent the boardroom', he observed. Quite.

I started to learn how to sell packaging and about the intricacies of blow moulding, which is the process used to make millions of plastic bottles daily, to very high tolerances. This included going on an expensive but very professional sales training course held in an old country house in Kent. This sales training has stood me in very good stead ever since, in terms of fundraising and campaigning. At the heart of the course was a simple message. If you want someone to buy from you don't 'sell to them' or 'talk at them' but try to ask questions about their needs and really listen to the answers. Once you know what people actually want, you are then able to offer the benefits of your product in a way which resonates with your client. We were taught that the key word here is 'benefits', because customers buy benefits, not product specifications. Thus, if you're selling mowing machines you don't say the blades go round at a certain number of revolutions a minute, but that your machine will enable people to cut the grass when it's wet. Simple stuff really, but often ignored. I enjoyed the learning process but never really had the technical grounding or the temperament to become expert in my new field.

Apart from looking after Cussons, I had to try to find the company new clients. So I would research the market and arrange to visit potential new customers, all of whom used plastic bottles. Then, having listened (as instructed) to my putative client I would say, 'Very good. MB can supply you with the best quality bottles in Europe, at the cheapest price, to your unique design and with full service backup'. 'Wonderful', my new friend would say. 'I'd like to order 10,000 for delivery asap.' At which point I would have to explain that he didn't really want 10,000 but one million, which was our smallest delivery quantity. 'But currently I don't sell one million bottles in five years', would be the answer and, frankly, the end of the conversation. Thus, the chance to acquire a new and, possibly, expanding customer was gone. Some other company which was more nimble and with more flexible production facilities would pick up the business and the growth. Sadly, this example was not untypical.

The unhealthy situation I now found myself in was the result of an over-emphasis on engineering quality and the technical integrity of the product. Quite wrongly, these concerns were allowed to override the market place and the needs of the client. Instead of a factory completely geared to high-volume, beautifully engineered products, Metal Box Portsmouth should have had an area given over to machines capable of small but worthwhile production runs. Fast turn-around from initial client interest to prototype to small batch production should have been the order of the day, which would have met the needs of the SME (Small to Medium Enterprise) market.

As it was, there were probably only 15 to 20 companies in the whole of the UK who required minimum deliveries of one million bottles and these were already being looked after by the respective factory managers at Wrexham and Portsmouth. What was the point therefore of my job and sending me off round the country to tell would-be-clients, in effect, that what they thought they needed was wrong? In the end, my year and a bit at Portsmouth taught me the invaluable lesson that it is the client who determines the service you should provide – not you. As the Duke of Wellington remarked of his first major campaign, 'At least I learnt what not to do, and that is always a valuable lesson.'

While I was absorbing this lesson the hard way, other things were going on in my life. For twelve years after leaving the regular Army I had a happy time serving in the Territorial Army (TA). However after several years in the Pool of Officers, the rules said I had to leave so I took a TA Staff job at the Headquarters of South East Command, in Aldershot. The role itself was pretty undemanding but I did manage to work it in with being at MB Portsmouth and I and a group of about six other TA Staff Officers used to meet once a month for a dinner in the Officers' Mess in Aldershot for lively and happy meetings. The late Richard Holmes, the military historian (not to be confused with the literary biographer) was part of this group, and it was good fun discussing battles and books and the strange ways of the military with him and the others.

During this period I took myself off for a fortnight to the Staff College at Sandhurst to attend the TA Staff course. This was not a good experience, and looking back I can see that most, though not all, of the fault lay with me. I didn't get on with the officer in charge of my 'set' and was not good at the details required in quite low level staff exercises. Our Instructor (a Major in the Signals) wrote a fairly damning report on my abilities and suitability for promotion. This may, at the time, have been fair, but it shook me and I appealed against his finding – not so much because I wanted a promotion but because I thought he was making a point at my expense. Little came of my efforts to alter his comments, just the predictable 'nothing can be done' response. So once again I had some evidence that staying longer in the Army could have been not entirely pleasant, and also that I still had some maturing to do.

I did enjoy the lectures at Sandhurst given by visiting high level speakers, both civilian and Army, and one was particularly memorable, albeit for the wrong reasons. A senior officer from the RAF was giving a long and essentially technical lecture about a piece of equipment. During his talk, he paced about the stage and, at one point, lost his footing and nearly fell. The convention is that at the end of these lectures officers are expected to ask intelligent questions. In this case, sensing the audience's ennui, the officer in charge pretty well demanded a question. When none came he repeated his demand even more forcibly, not once, but twice. Finally, somewhat hesitantly, a hand went up.

'Ah, good, a question. Ask away.'

'Did you hurt yourself when you fell of the stage?'

As part of our TA staff duties several of us found ourselves on a panel to select TA Warrant Officers as potential officers. These panels were run over the weekend, and we used to conduct five or six a year. On Friday evenings we would meet up and go through the volumes of paperwork detailing the background of the candidates. They would then take written tests; make a presentation; take part in a discussion; attend one-to-one interviews and carry out practical leadership tasks in groups of eight. Assessing each performance and trying to make a fair and balanced judgement was very interesting in itself and also laid down the basis for the task-orientated courses on teamwork and leadership which I later ran in the 1990s.

Meanwhile, things continued to go badly for the economy, including Metal Box. My job at Portsmouth was increasingly untenable and things got worse after Mrs Thatcher arrived in 1979. Amongst other things her monetarist economic policies were designed to reduce inflation while allowing unemployment to rise, which happened for most of the decade. Many factories and offices closed or were forced to work below capacity, which had the effect for me of reducing the chance of a new customer to virtually nil. I was left with hardly any stock to sell and just one solitary client 200 miles north of where I lived.

At this point an opportunity came along, which I heard of by chance from a friend. Ursie was still teaching at Upton School and one of the small girls in her class was the daughter of a couple named Hannafi and Hannifa. (Although British by birth they had recently become Muslims, hence their Eastern first names.) It turned out that Hannafi, a very pleasant, well-educated man, was something of an entrepreneur. Quite how much of an entrepreneur we weren't sure but were shortly to find out, because he invited me to join his team, based in offices formed from a converted chapel in Egham – about five miles from home.

So sometime in 1982 I left MB (again!) and joined the small but energetic firm of SED Holdings. Meantime at MB, although Peter Wheeler and the others soldiered on at Queen's House, MB's once great commercial empire never recovered. Its patents and factories worldwide were sold off, many people were made redundant and, in the words of the poet, 'nothing besides remains'. Sadly, the main reason for the company's collapse was pride. The Metal Box Board thought they could do without US technological know-how, as provided by the vast Continental Can Company, and went ahead on their own, severing its links with the USA. All that now survives of this major UK company is a residual offshoot, called Stelrad, which makes central heating boilers and radiators.

Fortunately I was now out of this painful process of decline and fall, and about to embark on the strangest 15 months of my life in business. Hannafi and Hannifa, plus about fifty other people, were members of a spiritual movement called Subud. Subud had been founded in the 1970s by Muhammed Subuh, an Indonesian guru, and it had various branches around the world, all small. It was one of those organisations that had no problem in making a strong connection between the commercial side of life and spiritual values, a bit like parts of the Evangelical Church in America. I never went to a Subud meeting, as I was just a hired company hand, not a member of the group. The meetings seemed to be held rather privately in an upstairs room, some time on Sunday afternoons, and only full members of Subud could attend.

What I now gather is that the guru or leader would go off every so often into the jungles of Indonesia to meditate and seek guidance on what the next commercial venture should be. After a time he would come back and send a message to the elders of the group, telling them what to get involved in next. They would be expected to borrow the money from the City or the banks (even in a recession), hire the people, find some premises and set to work.

When I joined SED it had been going about three years and had about sixty employees. They were engaged in as disparate a set of commercial activities as you could imagine. SED included a division making hearing loops to help deaf people in conference halls, an offshoot dealing with the import of bananas (which Sachlan, Hannafi's brother headed, and which got into difficulties), and another team working with lasers. There was also a subsidiary working to create a conference centre from a former merchant banker's mansion, and a franchised restaurant in Windsor, belonging to the Country Kitchen chain. The conference centre was called Anugraha and there was also a hotel called The Aurora Garden, so you get the picture. To describe SED as mini-conglomerate hardly does it justice. Finally (though there could well have been other enterprises) there was a 'world beating' moisture computer.

Initially, I was hired to help run the Country Kitchen restaurant, which was on the first floor in the newly built King Edward VII shopping precinct in the middle of Windsor. And therein lies the first problem. Talk to anyone in the catering world, and they will say you should never take space on the first floor. Customers can't see in to suss out the ambiance, passing trade passes on and your most powerful client incentive which is the delicious smell of coffee and cooking, goes unnoticed. Also, as our Country Kitchen was located in a shopping centre rather than being on the High Street, we closed at 3pm and thus missed out on the evening trade. So we were something of a lame (or uncooked) duck before we'd even opened.

Of course I knew nothing about the restaurant business nor, to be honest, was I very interested in the whole eating out thing, for eating out was at this time very much the preserve of those with disposable income. Nonetheless, there were bills to pay, so I set to and enjoyed the task of trying to fill a 120-seat restaurant at lunchtime. The essence of the franchise was 'wholesome' food, so the interior design was light and airy with heavy country-style wooden tables and benches and pine chairs. The food was good and we gradually built up a reasonable supply of customers. I liked the team too, although I felt that the two women in charge of the cooking and service side were quite resistant if any of my marketing and sales ideas impacted on their side of the house. In particular I had a number of run-ins with Anne of the auburn hair and green eyes.

I suppose to begin with the operation more or less broke even, which wasn't bad, but after a few months I was asked to do a different job so never really saw if our plans and strategies bore fruit.

My new job with SED Holdings was with an organisation called Microfin. Our main product was a new high-tech invention to help farmers, sold under the brand name 'Sinar Agritech'. And so, during my first few weeks there, I started to learn about the farming industry. I discovered that cereal farmers lead a precarious financial existence due to the fact that all their efforts during the agricultural year hinge on the success of the harvest. Effectively the outcome of 12 months of work depends entirely on a few weeks in summer, and until then farmers are short of cash. Consequently during most of the year they are dependent on bank loans or savings made from the previous July/August and the end of summer is a very tense time for them. Understandably, if things go wrong, they become pretty irate. How irate I was about to find out!

A crucial element at harvest is not just the weather (though that of course is important) but also how much moisture has been retained in the grain. After the huge combines have transferred their newly harvested crop into large mobile carriers, it goes off to the grain merchants to be weighed and dried. Dried is the key word here because the amount of moisture the grain merchants claim is in a farmer's consignment will determine the price paid. Speak to any cereal farmer and they will tell of unscrupulous grain merchants who provide false moisture readings in order to pay the lowest price.

It was this imbalance in the commercial relationship between the farmers and the merchants that Sinar Agritech's high tech gizmo was intended to address. Sinar Agritech had hired a very clever newly-graduated Oxford physicist called Howard, who had invented a small hand-held moisture computer that could calculate in seconds the moisture content of a sample of grain, via a digital readout. With our hand-held moisture computer the farmer could stand next to the grain transporters and take a dozen or so readings to determine for himself what the average moisture level was across the crop. He was now armed with information that could be used to challenge figures from the merchant. At a stroke the balance between the two parties became more even – a level cornfield as you might say.

The moisture computer itself was about the size of a thermos flask and at one end there was an open cup, into which a sample of grain was poured. Below this was a small screen showing the read-out, and the rest of the machine was taken up by five or six push button keys, which were simple to use. It was portable and the only requirement before dispatch was for it to be calibrated, which we did in our small laboratory at Egham, using samples of grain with known moisture content. Sir Keith Joseph and his officials at the Department of Trade and Industry liked it enough to award it a prize for innovation.

The machine was clever, met the needs of the market and was well priced. (It cost around £600 – about £3,000 in today's money). All we had to do was sell lots of them and then expand production into Europe and the rest of the world. This optimistic assessment of the way things could go was correct – up to a point. We went to agricultural shows as well as doing all the usual advertising and, as a result, we sold lots, probably 600 that first summer, in a very conservative market place.

But there was one snag and it was a big, even insurmountable one. Once out in the field doing its job the damn thing broke, constantly, regularly, repeatedly, and even after it was repaired the same unit would come back to us, sometimes three or four times in one year, which must be some kind of record if you reckon it was only being used during an eight to ten-week period! The problem lay not with the basic concept or the production or the electronics, nor really in the design, pricing, service back-up or marketing. The fault which lay at the heart of Sinar Agritec's failed moisture computer ironically mirrored that which bedevilled much of the UK's manufacturing sector and which lay at the heart of the campaign I had led while at Metal Box and was later to take up again. Within the moisture computer's body lay a spring balance whose job was to weigh the sample of grain. Howard, because he was clever, decided to design and make his own spring balance, and part of the device he developed included two fragile wires soldered onto a plate. Once in the back of the farmer's car or on his tractor in a bumpy field these connections generally broke and the machine failed.

During that summer of 1982 I sat doggedly (and I hope patiently) taking calls from furious and very worried farmers demanding instant action. We would call their machine back in, mend the fault, re-calibrate it and pack it up for return to the rural depths the next day. Some machines received this treatment two or three times in as many months, and tempers did not improve with repetition. Vexed, incensed, fuming, livid – take your pick because all these epithets and more would apply. I must have received hundreds of calls during this period, and each working day I had to deal with mini-crisis after mini-crisis. I'm not sure what I learnt from all this but, looking back, I seem to remember dealing with these justifiably angry customers with a degree of professionalism and some skill.

What this saga did re-enforce was how amateur we Brits could be in manufacturing terms in those days, and all because we had a system (and it goes wider than just education), which was bad at providing, encouraging and 'forming' a sufficient number of good young engineers. You do not achieve commercial success by putting nice, able young physicists like Howard, in charge of engineering new products. If the engineering is faulty, the machine is faulty and it doesn't matter how clever or academically gifted the inventor is.

The weeks passed and gradually our defective moisture computers returned to doing what they did best, sitting on the shelf in the barn looking impressive and measuring nothing. There was one more twist to come. As autumn turned to winter it became clear the whole Group, not just Sinar Agritech, was ailing and for me it was time once again to either leave or be pushed. At this moment, when

I was pondering what to do, I learnt that spring balances had in fact been around for ages and there were several robust models made by major companies out on the market, any one of which could have worked for us! The fault that killed Sinar Agritec and its potentially world beating product was totally unnecessary.

I'm not surprised Sinar Agritec failed since it had deep-rooted problems. As the moisture computer fiasco developed it became clear that the endless new start-ups, poor credit arrangements and weak cash flow were threatening our survival. As a result some of the secretaries came to me and said they had not been paid for two weeks and could I speak to someone. Now a sensible person would have ducked this invitation, which had 'poisoned chalice' stamped on it. But I thought there was an injustice, and given my known preoccupation with the idea that wrongs were there to be righted, you will not be surprised that I agreed to speak to the MD. I'm not sure how pleased he was to see me, nor did my message – 'why haven't the girls been paid?' – necessarily endear me to him, though, not long after our meeting, the money for the wages was found. Soon after this incident I was told Sinar Agritec was going to be wound up and if I knew of another job I should take it. Are you surprised given that this is a wicked world and behaving properly can carry its own dangers? Incidentally, despite the risks I like to think I would behave the same today, for if a company can't pay its staff it is technically bankrupt and should stop trading.

What was the effect of all this on Ursula and the children? Since leaving the Army and getting married in 1969 I had had a fairly settled five years with General Foods, followed by this period of hiatus with four jobs in eight years. These job moves were carried out against a background of financial uncertainty, a failing economy and Union militancy. So, my life at this time was altogether a bit of a rollercoaster and one which could have adversely affected our young family. Funnily enough, our children don't recall any great drama and, if it wasn't for this memoir and the occasional chat about the past, they would not know how tight things were and that on a number of occasions we were reliant on Ursie's pay.

By the time I left Sinar Agritec and my connections with Subud in 1983, James was eleven, Ellie nine and Hats just two. One of my principal reasons for leaving the Army was to give our children a proper home and the best chance in life, and I ought to now take stock of that intention.

In his early days James was a sensitive boy with bitten fingernails, and fairly unsure of things. At one point, we needed to take him away from school, which points to a guy finding his way. From an early age he was obsessed with film and he and I both remember our first outing to the cinema in Slough, where we saw a movie about snow tigers called *When the North Wind Blows*. We also enjoyed games of Hide and Seek, in which we would crawl around in the sand dunes or creep about in a wood trying to find each other's camp. (Shades of the Rectory garden crossed with my military training). James's passion for film continued, and, when he was still quite small, we used to see him talking to himself and waggling his hands in front of his eyes in order to simulate the effect of a projector. I remember once trying to divert a small squabble with Ellie in the back seat of the car by asking him about the new James Bond film. He started to describe the first scene. Twenty minutes later, unbelievably, he was still on the same scene and I was wishing I'd never asked.

Despite the fact that James found his métier early in life, the pattern of uncertainty that had characterized his behaviour at primary school continued until his early teens, when he was boarding at St Edward's School, Oxford. During one tricky period when the other boys rounded on him I offered to take him away, but he eventually settled down to make friends and began to get seriously interested in drama, producing and acting in a number of school productions. From this point on he rarely looked back. He began to enjoy the school's sporting and social scene, and did increasingly well academically, eventually going to UCL to read English. Once there he decided quite early on that most of the lectures could be missed (those given by Dr David Daniels were an important exception) and spent much of his degree course sitting in the dark in the Odeon Leicester Square!

In comparison, the girls had an easier time growing up and were less anxious – they simply did their thing. At the age of four or five, Hattie had a dressing up/shoe fetish and spent her time wobbling around the house dressed in shawls and various adult-sized high heeled shoes. At one point she set up a library in the hall, and you couldn't get from the front door to the kitchen without agreeing to take out several library books, with the attendant form-filling and rubber-stamping. For her part, Ellie early on became as taken with dancing as James was with film. We spent many a Wednesday evening and Saturday morning ferrying her to classes in Stoke Poges or Uxbridge and eventually, when she got a County Scholarship to the Royal Academy of Dance (RAD), all the way into Chelsea. In her teens, Ellie became wonderfully eccentric. She developed a passion for leg-warmers and brightly coloured headbands, which she wore all the time, and she would constantly do headstands and cartwheels in front of the TV. Every so often when we were trying watch the screen, a pair of legs would somersault across it. From an early age both Hattie and Ellie were very much their own women. Hattie's motto was 'I can do it' while Ellie was famous at school for talking through every lesson, not in a rude way but just because her chat with her friend Kate was clearly so much more valuable to her at that point than the efforts of some poor teacher to get her through History GCSE.

I went once to Lady Eleanor Hollis School (LEH), which they both attended, and spent an hour with Ellie and her friends in the Lower Sixth, talking about careers in industry. The girls were very polite, but all the time I was in the room there was a happy buzz of conversation, with my daughter, in particular, pretty oblivious to her Dad droning on! This independence of mind and force of character has in the end done her nothing but good, and the same is true of her sister. They gained good grades in pretty well all their exams, with Hattie, perhaps the most academic of the three, showing a useful scientific bent. Ellie worked hard, got her A Levels, a degree from Durham University, a top qualification in dance and a teaching certificate from RAD. The equally hardworking Hattie went to Leeds to read Psychology (getting a 2.1) and is now a producer of television documentaries. Ellie also makes TV programmes, which means, curiously, that all three of our children now work in the same world, though fulfilling very different roles. James's expertise is in ideas, words and comedy; Ellie is a storyteller with a passion for characters and plots; while Hattie is a fixer with a special ability to solve problems, handle people and make programmes.

Returning to the end of my career at SED – I was beginning to wonder what my next move should be when I bumped into 'Tolly' Taylor during a parents' evening at Upton School, where Ursie was teaching his daughter. Tolly was a tall, relaxed ex-Gunner officer with a good sense of humour and a passion for rally driving. He was easy to talk to and was sympathetic when I told him how dodgy things were at SED Holdings. He knew about the work I had done in schools with Metal Box, as I had been on the Steering Committee of a project he was running called Understanding Industry (UI).

This conversation led to me meeting Tolly's boss, Gerry Richardson, and I joined UI quite soon after. Eventually, UI became the Understanding Industry Trust (UIT) and, after my time, transmogrified itself into Business Dynamics. It is still running and on its website claims that since it started in 1977 more than half a million young people have benefitted from its work. I was there for over ten years (1983–94) and became its first Director. Working for UI got me into calmer waters with regard to earning my living, since I was doing something I believed in, and the job was a stable one for which I had some of the necessary skills.

To start with my job at UI was based in an office in Victoria Street in Windsor, five minutes walk from home, which was ideal. Apart from Tolly and myself there were two part-time UI employees in the office which otherwise was staffed by business consultants and their support team. This was because the premises were really the home of 3i Consultants, a subsidiary of 3i (Investors in Industry), a venture capital company whose headquarters was near Waterloo Station. Both the part-time workers made an impression on me. Marise was a statuesque lady in her forties. Although she was beautifully turned out with a pleasant manner, you could never really get to know her and she had an aura of mystery. Jenny Wiggington was somewhat different, a very down-to-earth character who had a healthy suspicion of all organisations, including consultancy! Jenny now runs her own catering business.

3i itself was a fascinating entity. It had been created by an entrepreneur called John Kinross who had been thrust into a business career when, as a teenager, he had to find the money to pay the family's debts after his Father's early death. Soon after the end of World War II the government acknowledged that there was a problem with the opportunities available for small (mainly manufacturing) businesses to borrow money. This was called the Macmillan gap, after a famous economist, and it was noted that there was a gap in the lending market between merchant banks and the high street lenders.

So 'Investors in Industry' was born during the austerity years following the War to plug this gap and to lend long term. Since then it has never seriously looked back and in my time it was UK-wide, well known, profitable and highly regarded. In the 1990s it became more of an international company dealing in billions of pounds; was part of the FTSE 100 and re-branded as 3i. Eventually the over-ambitious Sir John Cuckney turned it into an investment bank, in which guise it suffered badly in the financial crisis of 2008 and, as I write, is still languishing. Even though UI was actually just the not-for-profit offshoot of 3i Consultants, I still went on the payroll of a major player. Good fortune indeed at a time when unemployment was to reach nearly three million. If I could make a go of UI I would be in a safe place.

From 1976, when I joined MB, until 1992, my work was to immerse me in building closer links between industry and education, a national issue of the time. However, UI was not concerned so much with analysing the problem, but with tackling it. The method UI/3i Consultants, led by Gerry Richardson, proposed to adopt was novel. The idea was that we would organise volunteer managers to spend an hour or two in schools, talking with students about what they did and how the various elements of business fitted together. The UI course, when fully developed, consisted of seven modules covering an introduction, marketing and sales, finance, design, production, HR (known then as Personnel) and management, with a summary session to pull the whole course together. UI's job was to find schools and companies who wanted to participate, train the volunteer managers and provide outline material for them to use. Given my experiences with Metal Box and SED Holdings and the generally dire state of manufacturing in the UK you can imagine that I threw myself willingly into UI's work. It also helped that 3i's pay package was always likely to be ahead of the market.

I assumed on joining that everyone involved in the project was coming from the same direction and had the same motives. Mostly this was true, but looking back, I'm not so sure that changing the attitude to manufacturing of the nation's students was the only reason that Gerry Richardson originally dreamed up the scheme. Gerry was Tolly's boss, based in Windsor and the Managing Director of 3i Consultants. He had been an accountant out in the West Indies and when I knew him was very much the dominant figure at 3i Consultants. He was bald with a florid complexion, and used to sit at his desk in his braces with a pencil, which he twirled as he talked, held horizontally in both hands. His style was to summon you and, in a fairly genial way, tell you what he had decided. Although I got on OK with him I could see his methods were a bit dated. Nonetheless, along with Peter Wheeler he gave me my best break since leaving the Army, so I don't want to knock him too much.

Gerry had picked up on the case that was being made almost daily in the media, that a major cause for the decline in our economy was the failure of many schools and universities to take seriously the need to prepare students for working life. He wasn't alone and it's significant that a number of organisations were started at this time all seeking to take action about a complex and deep seated problem. Young Enterprise, the Schools Careers Industry Partnership (SCIP), Understanding British Industry (UBI – fostered by the CBI) and the Trident Trust, were just a few of the early players, and all competed with UI for funding and access to schools. In 1978 the movement was given an added boost by the then Prime Minister, Jim Callaghan, who gave a speech on the topic at Ruskin College, Oxford. This was the first time in living memory a British Prime Minister had taken education as his theme, and it generated considerable coverage. In essence his message was that there must be something wrong with the UK's educational system if so many of our citizens were not ready for work when they left school or university.

At the time schools were very much the preserve of Local Authorities and therefore the syllabus for each school and how it was taught varied depending on the Local Education Authority (LEA). As a result education was primarily in the hands of teachers and academics, who often had little experience of management; tended to dislike outside interference or attempts to measure their performance and whose preoccupation was often knowledge for its own sake. While there is a strong case for academic study being used purely to develop people's minds, a country cannot survive economically unless this is balanced by sufficient education in those subjects which can be applied to actual careers. Also, not everybody is academically clever. As it was, by the late 1970s, Britain had proportionally a higher number of children leaving school at 16 with no qualifications than most other developed countries. There was a chronic shortage of good engineers and a strong case could be made for saying, as indeed the Prime Minister did, that the whole system was under-achieving.

I believe Gerry Richardson probably had mixed motives for wanting to be involved in this issue. Certainly he knew about the shortcomings of our schools and colleges, since quite a few of his consultants were earning their money trying to put right defects caused by poor management. Indeed 3i itself could be said to have had a stake in the issue. But I think what Gerry also surreptitiously wanted to do was to train some of 3i's consultants to deliver the UI course and for them to be paid by UI (a charity) for doing so. Other companies could put in additional (unpaid) volunteers if they wanted. This manoeuvre, if agreed, would help Gerry to achieve his budget, which was under pressure at this time. It was only much later that Gerry's rather dubious intentions came to light. Of course, he had kept these ideas pretty much to himself and when, eventually, 3i and the Chairman, Lord Caldecote, did discover what had been in his mind they swiftly acted to disassociate 3i from this kind of behaviour by changing both the Trustees and the name of the Trust. I'm pretty sure I was the whistle-blower in this case and would happily argue that this was the right thing to do.

However, this all came later. In the early days I had no reason to be suspicious of anything or anyone and I got stuck in enthusiastically, though there were one or two warning signs. For a start my pay package was lower than had been indicated – it turned out to be £13,200 instead of over £14,000 – and the promised car, when it eventually came, was second-hand. I remember this all caused some grief to Ursula, but there was no accommodation by Gerry when I rang to discuss the problem with him. The other warning sign was when I went to ask the Finance Director Ted Barker for £300 to buy an over-head projector, so UI could make professional presentations. He refused my request, saying that Understanding Industry had no money at all, which was rather a salutary piece of information, given that I had just joined.

Despite these worrying incidents the basic 3i deal was very good, as it included a non-contributory pension and a company mortgage fixed at 3%, when mortgages were generally in double figures. Like the car these 'goodies' mostly kicked in after 12 months, but nonetheless it was a generous deal, and over the years 3i got Ursie and me out of quite a mess. Certainly it enabled us to hang on to Number 53 Clarence Road and I felt really comfortable with my actual job of going round schools and commercial organisations to drum up support.

However, about eight months after I'd arrived, UI entered something of a crisis. It was caused, if I remember rightly, by 3i Consultants hitting hard times and Gerry deciding he had to reduce staff. The upshot was that Marise and Jenny Wiggington left. Tolly took umbrage at the decimation of his team and went off to look for something else to do that might get him closer to his real love of rally driving. Suddenly everything was changed. From being part of a team of four and part of a national organisation I was a team of one and very much an 'add on' stuck in a back office. It looked and felt like trouble.

I survived, and was probably lucky to do so as my rather direct approach to things had caused a small stir. Sometime in the first year when we were still a team of four the whole of 3i Consultants flew via Caledonian Airways (which 3i partially owned) to Ibiza for a three-day conference. The UI team was invited to the opening session and then told to go off and do other things. This was probably sensible as we were not actually consultants, but it was also was symbolic of a general consensus that UI was not mainstream and should be kept at a distance. At a question and answer session I raised this point in some guise or other and it was batted away. On our return Gerry got me in his office and pointed out my remarks were inappropriate. This rather stung and surprised me. However, I had the good sense to reply that if some fences needed mending then I would happily apologise. Thus this dangerous, but fairly trivial, moment passed.

I remember this reprimand from Gerry with particular vividness as Wavell, our first dog (named after Lord Wavell, Viceroy of India, and editor of a fine poetry anthology called *Other Men's Flowers*), had been run over the day before. Wavell was a handsome brown Labrador with unfortunate roving tendencies. Given the slightest chance, either in Banbury or Windsor, he would nip out to see if he could find a girlfriend. He was brought back to us on numerous occasions, sometimes within a few minutes, sometimes the next day. He once came back in a taxi, another time; in the cab of a coal lorry and uniquely, his greatest triumph, in the back of a Rolls Royce! Shortly before his death he had discovered two friendly bitches living on the edge of the Great Park at the home of Kate and David Beresford. He was on his way there when he was knocked down by a speeding car halfway down Bolton Avenue. The passing of an animal in any family is always upsetting and as Gerry attacked me, I'm afraid a few tears came into my eyes. He must have been surprised and possibly a bit discomforted by his fairly mild criticism producing such a result.

Fortunately the family's grief at Wavell's death was tempered with excitement when a new canine friend arrived in our household. We were determined to get another dog, and Ursie started to ask round and look in the papers. After about a month, she saw an entry in one of the national papers advertising Springer Spaniel pups for sale at an address in Guildford. Given Wavell's propensity to roam, we decided to buy a bitch rather than a dog. Unfortunately, on calling the owner, we learnt that all the bitches from the Guildford litter had been sold. So, a little disappointed, we renewed our search. About three days later we got a call to say that one of the puppies had been returned as the buyer had developed severe eczema, and consequently the pup was back with the litter and up for sale at a reduced price. This seemed providential so we decided to go and see said small animal. We were keen to involve the children, but kept the details of what we were planning a secret from them.

The following Sunday afternoon we all piled into the car on the pretext of 'going for a walk in the Surrey woods.' The kids must have been surprised when we eventually pulled up at a small house in the suburbs and I suggested we all call in. Once inside, we were shown the area where the pups were kept, and as we approached we saw the sweetest, rather anxious little brown and white face peering cautiously round the door. What we thought might be a tricky and difficult decision proved to be no decision at all. There was unanimous agreement that this was our pet and about ten minutes later our little Spaniel was cradled in Ursie's arms in a red blanket, ready for the journey back to Windsor. Finding the right name for our new arrival took a day or two but we soon settled on Beth — what clinched it was the rather Elizabethan ruff round the top of her neck.[*]

Returning to my job, the abrupt departure of the whole UI team in 1984 left me on my own only a few months after I'd arrived. UI still had no money but the scheme had potential and I felt I could make it work, particularly as it resonated with the times. I knew that I had to make the crucial decision whether to stay with this vulnerable campaign or to seek another post. Fortunately I decided to stay and this proved to be the start of a very happy and pretty successful 11 years.

In part I decided to stay because I was damned if I was going to put myself back onto a pretty unfriendly job market yet again. Also, I knew Gerry was leaving, and saw this as an opportunity. Once I had made my decision, the main uncertainty was whether I could find my own salary, for Gerry had made it fairly clear that unless I could start fundraising the company would have to take a tough line and might close UI. I had never done any fundraising before, so this felt like a difficult call but I really had no option. At least my Metal Box sales course was going to prove useful.

---

[*] Beth proved to be the best of dogs, with all the special Springer Spaniel qualities of loyalty, playfulness, good nature, being wonderful with children and lovely to look at. She lasted with us well over twelve years, but in the last two years of her life she got quite ill and had to have an operation. This meant that she had to go round with one of those white plastic funnel shaped hoods round her neck, making her look like an inverted HMV dog wearing the gramophone horn instead of looking down it. Poorly dogs can often look deeply mournful and none more so than a spaniel under treatment. I sometimes worry that we may have contributed to Beth's decline as Spaniels want to always be with their owners, and with Ursie out teaching in the day and me up in London she had perforce to be left on her own for quite long periods. By 1996 the vet confirmed that her quality of life was going to be poor from then on, and we made the heartbreaking decision to have her put down. Her ashes are buried in the garden, next to a plaque saying 'Beth, our beautiful dog, 1984–1996', with a special rose bush for her planted alongside.

At this point Gerry had a good idea with regard to our course literature. Historically, this had taken the form of some rather drab looking pamphlets with ugly line drawings on the front and some fairly boring prose on the inside. It was suggested that we edited and changed these pamphlets and adapted them into a course handbook. So I settled into the task of converting eight pamphlets into a book, which suited some of my skills. At the time 3i Consultants had invested heavily in IT in the form of Wang personal computers, which was one of the earliest personal computer systems. There were plenty of terminals in the office, and every afternoon for about three months I sat myself down at one of them and started to amend the rather anodyne prose of the original pamphlets. The opening words of the introductory chapter set the scene with a majestic first line: 'Industry is about people and their work.'

Meanwhile, with Gerry's retirement looming, he began to search around for things to do, with special interest reserved for those that might be fee earning. He wanted to keep his hand in with UI, particularly, I thought, with a view to becoming Chairman of the Trust. I didn't fancy this idea at all, because having a retiree in charge would weaken our crucial link with 3i. Also I didn't like Gerry's general view that UI (a charity) should somehow keep him in pocket nor, to be honest, did he and I get on that well.

Very boldly for a new employee, I told my then boss that I didn't want him to become Chair of UI. Although this was nerve-wracking at the time, it turned out to have been absolutely the right thing to do, as events over the next ten years were to prove. Although Gerry was predictably underwhelmed by my response, the outcome for me was wholly beneficial. Somehow Lord Caldecote, then Chair of 3i, heard about Gerry's manoeuvrings and decided to take on the role of Chair of UI himself.

Robin Caldecote was a tall, incisive man in his early sixties. He came from the famous Inskip family so his manner could be a little patrician at times, but I never minded that. Originally, he had been an academic and then moved on to run various engineering firms, including Hawker Siddeley. He was an engineer by training and was committed to doing something to stop the decline in British manufacturing, which he thought unnecessary. He told me he caught the engineering bug when he was young from the family gardener, who taught him how to make things in the potting shed during the school holidays. In his role as Chair of a House of Lords' Committee on Industrial Performance he bravely took on Mrs Thatcher, but sadly got nowhere.*

I flourished with Robin Caldecote's support. He used his contacts to give UI access to all sorts of people and about two years into his time as Chair he encouraged 3i to commit £50,000 a year to us for five years. At the time I guess we were turning over about £200,000 a year, so this was a hefty and immediate increase, which helped us to grow quite fast. Later, I went to him saying that personally I was struggling financially, and he immediately upped my salary by 25%. Robin Caldecote and Peter Wheeler were the two people who really believed in me during the important years after I left the Army, and I am deeply grateful to them both.

I spent my first 18 months at UI purely in survival mode, both for myself and the project. However the production of the new

---

* Incidentally, the other direct dealing he had with Mrs T was over the appointment of George Carey as Archbishop of Canterbury. Robin was a devout Christian with an evangelical slant which, unusually for someone of that ilk, he kept quiet about. My only inkling of how he felt about Christianity was gained from my attendance at some of his lunchtime meetings at the Charing Cross Hotel. These were avowedly religious, and involved high level speakers such as Virginia Bottomley and John Selwyn Gummer (both then in the Cabinet), William Rees-Mogg (editor of *The Times*) and the US Ambassador. Lord C and his committee thought the then Archbishop, Lord Runcie, was too liberal. When Robert Runcie retired, they sought someone of a different cast and came up with George Carey.

handbook and one or two good slugs of sponsorship helped us turn the corner, roughly at the same time as the national economy began to improve a little. With the book safely edited I had another small run-in with Gerry over whose name should be on the cover. He wanted just his, but I insisted that my work as the actual editor should be recognised. Just in time we compromised (British and liberal to the last!) and *Understanding Industry Today* finished up as being edited by Gerry Richardson and Antony Wood.

We needed somewhere to launch our new book and, ideally, someone well known to be involved. I knew that 3i, despite being a private company, had quasi-official status and strong links to government. The Governor of the Bank of England, Robin Leigh-Pemberton, was often in the news, and his brother Jeremy was one of our Trustees. I won a lot of brownie points not only for inviting the Governor to launch UI's new handbook but for actually persuading him to come. We did the launch in 3i's smart tower block office opposite Waterloo Station, and the company kindly paid for lunch. Not bad for an organisation that only a few months before couldn't afford an overhead projector!

While on the subject of *Understanding Industry Today*, I ought to mention that during my time as Director of UI we changed both our publisher and the format twice. Over the years the original text began to look dated, and in its hardback form the book was too expensive for use by students. So about five years into my tenure we dropped our original printers and publishers David and Charles and moved to Heinemann, who were then the largest school textbook publisher in the UK.

Initially, I had thought that our small annual usage of about 7,000 a year wouldn't interest a big company. Then I realised that, as our pupils moved on every year, we would of course need a new print run annually. Assuming even modest growth in annual pupil numbers over a five-year period we would issue well over 40,000 copies. This was serious business even for Heinemann, and I wouldn't have minded a quid for each copy myself! The books cost us about £4 each and we sold them to pupils (via schools) for around £6 which gave a considerable boost to our finances.

Later, the book underwent further changes. Elspeth Howe, who became famous as one of Mrs Thatcher's most serious critics, was a Trustee and also Chair of the Equal Opportunities Board. She felt the text talked about 'he' too much, and wanted something done to improve the gender balance. The alterations needed to fix this late in the day could have meant a lot of extra work and consequent delays. However, I got over the problem by the cunning wheeze of making all the male pronouns plural, so that 'he' and 'him' became 'they' and 'them', which was relatively easy to sort. Alongside a new publisher we also got in a new author called Rosemary Stefanou, who was an ex-teacher. Rosemary worked really hard, putting in long hours, and produced a modern, lively book with lots of pictures which made it eminently readable. We got on really well for a couple of years – until she decided her contract wasn't fair. Despite the terms being pretty standard and similar to nearly all Heinemann's educational writers, almost without warning, she took serious umbrage and the ensuing row went on for well over a year.

In the meantime, we continued to improve the accessibility of the book. We sent a draft of our new version to a couple of schools for their Lower Sixth pupils to read and comment on. We then invited them to London and spent a day with about a dozen of them discussing the text, and many of their comments were ultimately included. This may be standard practice nowadays but at the time it was quite forward thinking, especially with a textbook of this kind. Finally, just before I left UI, we commissioned another author to do a new edition of the book, rewriting Rosemary's text, and also explored changing publisher. One way and another, editing the book and dealing with publishers was good fun and the book benefited UI a great deal.

Although my job at UI had many advantages, I found fairly soon that I was having to get used to the life of a commuter. In the early stages of my time at UI I was fortunate enough to be able to walk to work. For a couple of years I enjoyed an easy and simple walk from Clarence Road to my office at the back of Victoria House: a five-minute journey. However change was beckoning – again! Gerry's replacement as Managing Director was Rodney Drew, who had an entirely different view of UI – he didn't want it! He didn't want it near him; he didn't want it in the building and he didn't want the Director of UI reporting to him. So on his second day he told me that I needed to find a new boss and a new home. In the event, the solution to one of these imperatives also led to the solution of the other. Lord Caldecote was the obvious person to head up the Trust since *de facto* this had been his role and by staying on he would ensure continuity. So from quite early on I reported to him and he in turn undertook to find us new offices, which he managed to do in a couple of weeks. Gerry, notwithstanding his ambition to run UI, remained just as a Trustee, but got his own back eventually.

Just down from 3i's tower block in Waterloo Road was an empty office called Mercury House, which 3i was holding, pending a possible need for more office space. In fact they never did use the building, and we were able to move into a large empty room at the back of the first floor for some years. It meant that I had to commute to London but fortunately Windsor Riverside Station was only about ten minutes walk from Clarence Road, while Mercury House, our new home, had a front entrance which faced Waterloo

Station. The drawback was that the train was slow and took about an hour to reach London, but I always worked on the journey and if I was on top of things could read a book.

This routine became my life for about the next seven years and I rather enjoyed it. One of the things I looked forward to on the journey up to town was to sit opposite and chat to our neighbour Peter Hywel.* Peter regularly caught the same train in the morning and sat in the same seat in the same carriage, which was about halfway along, always with his back to the direction of travel, reading *The Times*, while I studied my papers. We always found time for a chat, and I learnt a lot about his working life and current pre-occupation, which was industrial fishing. Peter was editor of *Fishing International*, and if he wasn't on the train I knew he was at some large fishing conference in a distant port. I remember him telling me how much he loved New Orleans for its atmosphere, constant street music and friendliness.

Various unusual incidents happened on my journey from Windsor to Waterloo. In the mid-1980s there was a period of several years when the word 'incident' was likely to refer to an IRA bomb threat or an actual attack. During one 'alarm' Waterloo Station was closed and I had to schlep over to Paddington and join a very crowded train. A rather anxious American visitor had a long conversation next to me with her friend about how the change of destination to Slough would affect those waiting for them in Windsor. I gallantly intervened to say that we could share a taxi from Slough to Windsor,

* Peter had a very interesting background. A South African, he got married and had a family when Apartheid was dominant. Very much a liberal politically and socially, he took a public stand in opposing this evil. Once in an outlying township he gave a long speech which was received with only a scattering of applause. Slightly dismayed, he sat down to hear the next speaker receive a rapturous reception when he had finished. 'How come the crowd liked that speaker so much?' he asked the man next to him. 'Because', came the reply, 'He's just given your speech – only in Swahili!' When Peter realised that his family was being threatened by the police, he decided that they had to leave South Africa, and they relocated to the UK.

which they thought would be great. Less gallantly, indeed rather acidly, I added an unnecessary afterthought. 'And if I had one of those new, expensive mobile phones, we could ring your friends' hotel and tell them the situation.' At which point the guy next to me said, 'Well, I have one, do please use it.'

My other memorable train gaffe shows that even trying to be helpful can sometimes get you into trouble. On a particularly dark and rather unpleasant winter's night I was travelling in the rear part of the train, and as we neared Windsor the carriage gradually emptied. During the journey a young girl with a huge rucksack kept getting up to look at the route map on the carriage wall. Eventually I asked her if I could help and she explained she didn't want to miss getting out at Windsor. 'Ah', I said, 'There's no danger of that. I'm getting out at Windsor and I've done this journey hundreds of times.' Trusting my reassuring words she settled back and we continued the journey until, almost without warning, the train came to a halt. Looking out, you could see nothing but 'the black bat, night', and there was complete silence. There we sat, with nothing happening until suddenly there was a sound of running footsteps, the push button doors crashed open and an out-of-breath figure jumped on board. Almost at the same moment the train started off back up the line from where we'd come. Completely unnerved, I sought an explanation. 'This is disgraceful. They've stopped the train short of Windsor because it's running late and we're going back to London.' This explanation could not have been more wrong or my outrage more unfounded, as a few minutes later we pulled into Datchet Station. In fact we had been in the station at Windsor all the time but in the dark I 'who had done the journey hundreds of times' hadn't realised. All the time we were stationary we had been at our destination. My discomfiture was complete when we had to get out at Datchet, cross over to the other platform and spend 30 minutes together waiting to go back to where we'd just been. I don't think we spoke much!

Up at the UI office in Mercury House, we initially rather rattled around, but gradually as UI grew our two desks became eight and the room filled up. John Warner joined us on secondment from Berkshire County Council Education Department, and after a while decided to stop being a teacher and become a fulltime employee of UI. He and I were very different people – while I found him occasionally prickly, I'm sure he found me too bouncy and unworldly. However, John made an important contribution to our work, including the development of an excellent programme of teacher training courses, which enhanced our reputation and very much helped our finances. His partner Dorothy joined us as a fundraiser but after some success she moved on to raise money for Malvern Theatres. When Dorothy and John got married they kindly invited us to the excellent post wedding reception and also the ceremony itself, held in Luton Registry office. This part of the day was, I thought, somewhat marred by the spectre of the local traffic wardens marching up and down outside the Town Hall putting parking tickets on the bridal party cars.

The star during our early days in Mercury House was undoubtedly our secretary Rosanna. In those days most managers had secretaries, and indeed my desk generated a sufficient volume of letters to warrant such help. Rosanna could type faster than the speed of light and often our Wang computer system literally couldn't keep up with her flying fingers. She had the endearing habit of regularly kicking off her shoes and wandering round the office barefoot. After a while, Rosanna decided to move up North and was replaced by a very different person. Diana Clarke had worked for various senior figures in the finance world, and brought a fairly sophisticated approach to the role of PA. She was always well turned out and could sometimes have a slightly severe manner. For many years she kept everything running smoothly and I came to rely on her a great deal. Unfortunately she started to want to run the show and her style began to be resented by our team. Increasingly Diana began to be seen as a professional gate-keeper (which neither I nor the team wanted) and I sensed I was being 'controlled'.

By the time I finished in 1994, UI had grown in eleven years from a small team of three or four key players, plus ten or so part-timers in the regions, to a Head Office team of eight or nine, with nearly sixty part-timers in the field. Initially the bulk of the money to fund this expansion was found by me though, in the last two or three years, I was increasingly helped by a dedicated fundraiser.

About four years into my time in London I had my one and only run-in with Lord Caldecote. This, as is so often the case, was to do with money. It was my job to prepare the draft budget for the Trustees to approve, and in the early days one of the biggest entries on this was my salary. Unsure of what figure to put in, I took my current figure and added a percentage based on the RPI as a forecast for the next year. This went down badly, and Lord C wrote me quite a stroppy letter criticising me for trying to bounce him into a salary increase. This wasn't the intention, so I wrote to him apologising and saying I had handled the matter badly. He immediately accepted my explanation, and I realise now how lucky I was to have a boss who was so supportive and yet who didn't interfere.

Shortly before Lord Caldecote left 3i and UI, an incident occurred which underlines the importance of taking care what we scribble on internal memos, or in more modern terms, taking care to check the distribution list of any emails we send. One of Lord Caldecote's many roles included fundraising on behalf of one of the royal charities to which 3i had made a large donation. Some time after 3i had made this gift, I wrote independently asking for help of any kind, including money. In time I got a reply back from one of the trustees which referred to my letter, enclosed a copy of it, and told me they couldn't help. On my original letter the Chief Executive had written a comment, faithfully reproduced on the photocopy I had in my hand. 'Alex', it said, 'Be careful how you handle this request for help from Antony Wood at UI, bearing in mind the large amounts of 3i money still sloshing around in our coffers!' Ever since then I have been extra careful about what I write on the bottom of letters, or latterly, what I put in e-mails. I guess it's sensible to ask ourselves the simple question: 'If this email/letter got into the wrong hands would it cause a problem?', and if it might then bin it.

Eventually Robin Caldecote's time as Chairman of 3i came to an end and with it his role as Chair of the Trustees of the Industrial Training Foundation (ITF, as UI's parent body was now called). He was succeeded by the late Sir John Cuckney of whom more later.

The thing I enjoyed about being Director of UI was that I felt I was always learning. For example, the Trust paid for a trip to the USA in 1987 where I attended a week long convention in Washington on 'Education/Business Partnerships' and about this time I also became a Fellow of the RSA. This last mattered more to me for the value of being connected to this famous, old organisation than for the award per se. In fact, the only way of viewing such things is not to take them too seriously, which was the view Ursula took with an estate agent who rang up one day. Being conscientious, he wanted to check my title so that any further correspondence would be correct.

'Is it Dr or Professor or Mr?' he enquired.

Ursula replied ironically '*Sir* Antony, if you don't mind.'

So for several months after this conversation we continued to receive letters incorrectly addressed to 'Sir Antony and Mrs Wood.'

At the very least they might have made Ursula a 'Lady' as would normally be the case.

Trains continued to feature in a number of odd incidents during the UI years. I remember an occasion in 1987 when James was due to go to America as an intern to see the film industry first hand, courtesy of the parents of a friend of Ellie's. His flight went from Gatwick so he needed to catch a train from Slough to Paddington and from there make his journey across London and on to the airport. I drove him to the station in good time and as we waited for the train we checked that he had all he needed: his tickets, money, phone numbers, passport... passport!

'My passport's at home.'

'Where?' I asked anxiously.

'In the pocket of my black winter coat, hanging in the hall', was the surreal reply.

Our only option was for me to rush back to Windsor to get it, so I ran across the footbridge, raced home – crossing red lights – and retrieved the vital document from what was apparently its permanent home, in the pocket of a coat. I now know that the fastest return journey you can make between the centre of Windsor and Slough Station is seven minutes and twenty seconds, because that's how long it took me that day. Hurtling over the footbridge on my return, I arrived in time to see the train pulling out of the station with James on board, his face white and his hand outstretched. Remembering my early athletics training, I ran alongside his carriage as it gathered speed and passed his passport in through the window, rather like handing over the baton in a relay race

During my years at 3i/UI I got to know some interesting people. These included my contemporary Bob Finch, Head of Academic Affairs at ICI. In those days ICI was a real power in the land, a key part of the UK economy and British industry. It was also seen as a rather conservative organisation and somewhat as a creature of the establishment. Notwithstanding this the Board took the decision to appoint the ebullient, witty and definitely unconventional John Harvey-Jones as Chair. Sir John wore his hair long, smoked a pipe and sported loud, kipper ties. Along with his flamboyant appearance he had a very clever business brain and was a man of fierce integrity. Bob Finch (who referred to him as 'Sir John Hardly-Phones') kindly arranged for him to speak at UI's dinner at the Institute of Directors in 1990, and we got to know each other a bit.

That Sir John took on the role of After Dinner Speaker for UI shows his good nature, for a couple of years earlier I had rather messed him around. In 1987 we had needed someone prestigious in the business world to write a foreword for the new edition of the UI book. Sir John readily agreed and quickly wrote an entirely appropriate piece. Some two months later, with the book about to go to print, British Rail quite separately replied to my request for sponsorship, saying they would donate £10,00 (a very large sum for us) and that their chairman, Sir Bob Reid, would like to write the Foreword. I therefore had to bite the bullet and ask Britain's best known and probably most influential businessman if it would be OK for us to drop the piece he had written specially for us. Sir John thought this was very funny and, appreciating our need, pulled out most graciously. I think I did have the nous to soften it a bit by saying we would use what he had written another time.

The Bob Finch connection continued with his and my involvement with Radley College. If you combine my time at UI with the five years I had in schools/university liaison at MB I spent over fifteen years working alongside the UK's educational system, so during that time I was able to build up quite a network of contacts across the UK, with state schools featuring large in my activities. I also worked with ISCO (The Independent Schools Careers Organisation) and the Year in Industry Project and Radley College by helping to set up and run the 'Radley in Industry Group', which met quarterly. One of the ideas we put forward to promote careers in business/manufacturing was to have a debate on the subject, 'This House believes that British Manufacturing should be allowed to die.' This idea took off, so we got Cecil Parkinson (a local MP and Cabinet Minister) to propose the motion and Bob Finch agreed to take the stand on behalf of industry.

On the night of the debate I found myself chatting to Mrs Parkinson and after a couple of pieces of small talk she cut to the chase. Looking across the room at her husband, she said: 'Ah, there's Cecil. You know I made up my mind to marry him as soon as I saw him!' This flummoxed me completely, as I had no idea what to say in reply. During the debate itself I thought Lord Parkinson (as he later became) spoke rather poorly, while Bob Finch was lucid and witty. However, rather predictably for the time, the Radley boys thought the City and the professions were right for them and consequently kicked industry into touch. However, it was an enjoyable, imaginative event and worth doing.

My connection with Radley continued and at one point Dennis Silk, the Warden (Headmaster) of Radley suggested I might join the staff there. Dennis was an amateur cricketer of note and eventually became President of the MCC. He was charming and effective, but I'm afraid I didn't really take to him. I suspect he was a high Tory of the old school, for he ran a very traditional establishment. Joining Radley to help run the Cadet Corps (CCF), teach English and Scripture to the lower forms and help with the sport would have been a big mistake. I suspect that as I grew more liberal the rather establishment culture in the Staff Room at the College would have grated, leading to an inevitable clash.

I knew Radley College was not right for me, and we assumed this would also be the case with our son. Instead, we put James down for Radley's great rival St Edward's School, Oxford, as a boarder, which nearly back-fired on us, as he was bullied and quite unhappy in his first years there. However I don't know if Radley would have been any better, and I'm glad to say that in his later years at St Edward's James flourished, largely due to the brilliant teaching and care of the witty John Trotman, as well as the opportunity to do endless drama. He directed a great deal, including a shortened *Macbeth* (with Duncan being drowned in a water tank), a very funny *Seasons Greetings* and – shades of my first outing with Ursie – *Forty Years On*.

The story I like best from James's years at St Edward's comes from his time in the Sixth Form. By this time he had developed his night-owl habit and used to work very late in the library, sometimes till 1.00 or 2.00am. On one occasion he overslept and was missing for the first lesson. Although the other boys tried to cover for him, this didn't fool his geography master Kris Spencer. 'I think I know where we might find James, so pick up your books and come with me', said the rather clever Mr Spencer. So the class dutifully collected their things and trooped across the quad to Segars House, where they found James fast asleep in his room. They roused him from his illicit slumber by jumping on him and sitting on his bed while Mr S gave an A Level Geography lesson in the dormitory, with a very surprised and tousled James still in his pyjamas.

As I mentioned earlier in the chapter, Ellie attended LEH (Lady Eleanor Holles School) in Hampton, where she was very happy. By the time James was doing his A Levels, Ellie had been joined at LEH by Hattie, who entered via the Junior Department. All three of our children have had largely happy and educationally excellent schooling, which has provided a base for their adult life. In an unguarded moment I could admit to some pride in this, mixed with considerable surprise that we actually achieved it. One of the ways I augmented the fees at LEH was to offer my help via the Headmistress, Miss Candy, to Jenny Barnes who ran the Careers Department. I chaired three meetings a year and helped to set up the termly careers fair, and in return got a 50% reduction in my daughters' fees. For about two hours each term I was effectively getting the sort of hourly rate normally reserved for QCs and directors of merchant banks!

Despite periodic financial worries we still managed to create interesting family holidays, at what the travel firms might call 'budget' prices, and were fortunate enough to go twice to Glyndebourne, once with Teresa and Ian Cadell to a Benjamin Britten opera and once as guests of Hugh and Catherine Stevenson, (parents of pupils of Ursie), to Verdi's *Falstaff*. We managed to get abroad a fair number of times, and, wherever we were, the main memories are of funny incidents and of laughter. When Hattie was three, we got in the car on a whim and drove all the way to the Loire Valley. The only problem was that we hadn't booked anywhere, and on Day One we ended up sitting 'homeless' on a pavement in Blois, before we finally found a place nearby, courtesy of a friendly local. On one holiday we had a wonderful time in the French Alps; while on other occasions we whizzed around Paxos on scooters or had good times exploring Crete and Sicily. Best of all our children remember the holidays we took on the beautiful North Devon coast, near Woolacombe, when Mike Falcon generously lent us his home.

I spent eleven years working for UI, and in career terms it was the making of me. I had my own show in a cause I believed in, which used my abilities as a speaker, front man and campaigner. I managed in the early days to raise funds to keep the Trust alive and as UI grew, with the support of 3i and the benevolent Lord Caldecote, I got the chance to grow with it. I didn't mind the daily commute to London or the long hours, as I realised that mine was a largely enviable situation and that I could cope with the demands on stamina this schedule required. As my confidence developed I began to shake off the more controlling and hidebound attributes of my personality, which the Army might have encouraged, and to manage people better.

One of the key things in life is to have work which allows you to learn and therefore to develop. This I have had in abundance. By the time I left UI at the age of 53, not only was it time to go, but I was increasingly starting to show the independent and entrepreneurial tendencies that I have mentioned before. This was fortunate, because during my final months at UI I would have to dig deep into my reserves of strength and resourcefulness. For in my departure from the Trust there lies an unpleasant tale of disloyalty and foolishness.

CHAPTER TWELVE

The Best of Times and the Worst of Times

'Of old, unhappy far-off things and battles long ago'

- William Wordsworth, 'The Solitary Reaper'

When Sir John Cuckney took over from Robin Caldecote, the atmosphere at UI changed. I found myself working for someone who was not outgoing or really interested in being involved in 'good causes'. At heart Sir John was a City man, set on making 3i an investment bank rather than a supplier of funds for small and medium-sized manufacturing operations.

Sometimes when you first meet people you can scent trouble, and so it was with Sir John. One day I had to go into the 3i building and caught the lift going up to the top floor. As the doors opened I was faced by a broadly-built, very well turned out man in a classic grey and chalk pin-striped City suit. Sir John was at this stage in his early sixties. He had a square face with bushy eyebrows and positively oozed gravitas. This was the man who had recently dealt with Margaret Thatcher over the Westland Helicopters affair, done well in the City via merchant banking and had also, as I learnt from his obituary in 2008, been recruited by MI5 in the 1950s. He and I were likely to be on different planets and indeed we were, so I guess it was not surprising that I may have had an inkling of trouble to come as we ascended in the lift.

The fact is that Sir John found UI a rather homespun operation, and his heart was never really in it. Our slightly 'seat of the pants' approach clashed with his armoured personality, and he was concerned that he might be too closely involved with a not-for-profit organisation that might someday lose money and become an 'actually-for-loss' operation. Some months before he finally gave up as Chair of UI he prepared the ground by bringing in some of 3i's internal auditors to check how we handled our finances. Of course they found lots of things to complain about (most of them quite small) and this confirmed Cuckney's view that we were better held at arm's length. In fact nearly everything the auditors complained about was quite easily put right (and we set about doing so) but not in time to stop our lovely Treasurer, Bill Siddle putting in his resignation. Bill felt he had no option but to resign. He was an old 3i hand, having been Company Secretary, and was a good friend to both me and the Trust. He did sterling work for no payment and did not deserve to go – certainly not with his tail between his legs.

After this, the next step was plain to see. Unfortunately, when Cuckney announced his intention to resign as UI's Chair I made some mistakes. In my usual bouncy 'can do' way I took it upon myself to find another Chair. I guess I thought that if I knew who was being recommended then I would feel more comfortable and have a degree of control. But in truth this view was flawed since my job was to run the Trust, not mill around with the good and the great trying to find someone who would echo Mr Humphries in *Are You being Served* by saying 'I'm free.' This was not my world, and it was deluded to even contemplate the hunt on my own. What I should have done was turn the problem back to those who owned it and whose responsibility it was to find the solution, namely the Trustees and Sir John himself.

My second mistake lay in the person I sought as Sir John's successor. I forgot the old adage that 'servants should choose their masters with care' and what I did was to grab onto the coat-tails of virtually the first genuine contender to pass by. No search, no soundings, no compiling of a shortlist, no involvement of wiser heads and wider experience, just me being dazzled by a CEO who had the ear of the Prime Minister and good connections through his PR business and his MP brother. At my suggestion, Peter Gummer, then the owner of Shandwick Public Relations, came to see Sir John to talk through what being Chair of the Understanding Industry Trust involved.

* * *

We sat in the Chairman's office in 3i in the tower block opposite Waterloo Station. As we were on the highest floor of the building, this office had fabulous views over London, including the Thames, the House of Commons and the many rail tracks curving outwards from Waterloo towards the South and the West. It was all very pleasant and, what with PAs bringing coffee and important phone calls being put on hold, there was an atmosphere of power and importance which, in my case at least, was entirely unjustified.

Peter Gummer was tall and well turned out, with greying hair and a long face. When Ursula first saw him at our third UI book launch she said she had her doubts about inviting him to chair UI, as she felt his smile was too appraising. What good intuition. But Peter also had considerable charm and some style. My second meeting with him was at the Shandwick Head Office in the West End. It had snowed, and he came in at the front door wearing blue wool-lined ski boots with a long black overcoat and singing hymns. The latter was not all that surprising since Gummer Senior was one Canon Selwyn Gummer, who used to sell his sermons to less fluent members of the cloth.

Peter's brother John Selwyn Gummer was a Cabinet Minister (and a friend of Lord Caldecote) so at this time both the Gummer boys were making names for themselves. It was John Selwyn Gummer who encouraged Margaret Thatcher and then John Major to link the Conservative party with Shandwick for PR purposes, and of course Peter's company benefited from having the Tory Party as one of their high profile clients.

This then was the background to Peter's arrival on the UI scene towards the end of 1991. For over a year things went pretty well. In his capacity as Chair of UI I saw Peter quite regularly at his office and he helped me with one or two stubborn problems. Once he signed over 400 fundraising letters, topping and tailing them all personally by hand and he also hosted two dinners at the Institute of Directors. At the first of these the guest of honour was the MD of a new mobile phone company called 1-2-1 (now T-Mobile) and Peter helped to get him to come and speak. At the second dinner the main guest was Sir John Harvey-Jones, who did us proud, as I mentioned earlier. I noticed Peter included being Chair of UI in his entry in *Who's Who*, which implied that he valued his connection with us. Indeed, before things got difficult he also initiated a six-month strategy review to help UI redefine where it was going. We were now much better known, operating UK wide (apart from N Ireland), with a staff of eight full-timers and over fifty part-time people and although our finances were stretched we were OK.

In addition Peter had a deft hand when dealing with the Trustees, who, though less weighty than when the link with 3i was clear, were still members of the good and great. I recall that at the end of one rather long meeting Peter played an excellent practical joke on some rather startled Trustees. He said UI had a long tradition that when meetings finished Trustees would be asked to hand in those pieces of paper with their 'doodles' on them. Sir Christopher Ball (ex-Warden of Keble College) was up for the joke, however, and smilingly replied, 'That will be fine, Chair. I've just been doing the prime numbers up to 7,043 – you might like to take them further?'

In 1992 I had taken on two operations called Pegasus and Index and these gave us extra reach in terms of the education market. Pegasus was an attempt to move into the HE sector as the scheme focused on the development of inter-personal skills for undergraduates. As more and more people went straight to university from school, it became clear that a virtually undiluted diet of academic work was producing a generation of students many of whom had missed out on a whole range of skills and training. Attributes such as time-management, presentation skills, assertiveness, working in a team and leadership were not given enough attention during pupils' time at school or university. Such skills can be transferred across any aspect of our lives be it family, work, artistic, personal, sport or other interests, as I know from my own experiences. They are of huge value to business but also matter a great deal in terms of each of us living a full life.

Pegasus set out to redress what was seen as an imbalance in the formation of young people, but sadly it never quite took off. Even now, when this approach has had a considerable boost from Howard Gardner's work on the 'eight intelligences' and the consequent realisation of the importance of, for example, emotional intelligence there is still a gap to be filled. Employers still complain about graduates coming to them with a reasonable degree but without decent transferable skills.

Index, which was backed by Sir Anthony Burney, then Chair of Debenhams, aimed to tackle the same problem, albeit in a different way. I first met Sir Anthony in his luxurious office in the West End when he was looking for a home for Index. He was probably in his seventies by then, but still influential as he had a marvellous network from his days as a senior partner at one of the 'big five' accountancy firms. He was a cultivated person and his office was unusual for a business premise in containing as it did a number of figurines, statuettes, and some fine paintings.

Sir Anthony was passionate about industry needing to be more professional and, in particular, about the way it failed, in his view, to invest in the next generation and develop young people of ability. He saw talented young graduates as a precious resource that neither the country nor business was investing in properly. We got on well and he ceded Index to UI on the basis that we would find places in major manufacturing companies for undergraduates of special promise. This was an approach that sometimes attracted criticism from those on the left of politics as they perceived it as elitist. I'm glad to say, that, belatedly, society has recognised the 'special needs' of particularly able people and many schools now have policies for talented and gifted pupils.

Unfortunately, Sir Anthony then became rather ill and I visited him in the King Edward VII Hospital for Officers. That same week *Time* Magazine did an article on the revival of the UK as a business force, as opposed to being the 'sick man of Europe'. The article was full of good news, and it pleases me to think that my last conversation with this cultivated man was positive and that we shared together a feeling that somehow our small efforts were making a contribution. It would still take many years before British manufacturing as an entity became truly professional and only now, in the early years of the twenty-first century, is it seen as a global player, with many excellent small and large firms. As I write (2012) manufacturing is growing faster than it has done for many a decade and the UK is the world's sixth largest producer of manufactured goods; albeit one which, because of increased productivity, now employs far fewer people than it once did.

But back to the Peter Gummer saga. It is the autumn of 1993 and for the last ten years I have happily been building up UI and enjoying the role of Director. Despite a predictable number of ups and downs the Trust has generally prospered and, unlike many people, I am happy in my work. However I am also aware that funding continues to present a serious problem both in the short and the long term. As the winter approaches Dave Cox and myself are working to produce a five-year strategy, which keeps bringing us back to the fundamental problem of funding. Dave had joined us after an entrepreneurial stint with Quasar. He came to UI having built and successfully sold this modern business and his input was invaluable since he had a younger perspective, a good strategic grasp and was well up on the importance of IT.

* * *

By 1993 we have one or two possible big donations in the offing and on this day in October I am about to go and see a potential donor. John Willett is a very successful entrepreneur who owns a company making date-stamping machinery for the providers of food products, both in Europe and the USA. His machinery is a market leader and he is very enthusiastic about what UI is trying to do. John is a stocky, dark-haired man with lots of energy and a decisive, pleasant, manner. After coffee at his house he turns to me and asks me what I want.

'What UI needs', I reply, 'is a serious donation to pump prime a properly run and professional fund-raising campaign.'

'That sounds sensible', says our man. 'I'm prepared for my company to donate £50,000, provided it is matched pound for pound by others.'

This is wonderful news and something we have been trying to achieve for years, so as I leave John Willett's office my head is full of ideas as to the best way to use this money in order to raise even more. I am in effect a farmer whose barns have suddenly become full of seed corn.

By pure good fortune, or so I thought, the same day I have a morning meeting scheduled with the Chairman, so I can go straight to his office and tell him the good news. To celebrate I use a taxi to save time and as we are driving round Trafalgar Square I determine to remember this day, 15 October 1993, as something special. Special indeed.

'Good morning, Peter', is my cheery greeting as I arrive at the offices of Shandwick Ltd. 'I have very good news for you.'

His response however is not the one I was expecting. 'Sit down', he says, 'I have something to tell you.'

Alarm bells start to sound, though the level of clanging in my head is not as loud as it should be. After a few preliminaries Peter explains that he is sending me a letter and that this letter will set out that it is the duty of the Trustees to ensure that they have the best person as Director of UI. Although I do my job very well, the Trustees feel it is necessary to check who else is out there. Consequently, the job of Director of UI will be advertised in the Sunday papers at the weekend and I can, of course, apply for it. Alternatively, I could choose not to apply and instead help to choose my successor. If the latter (though he didn't say this) I would be out of work, seemingly of my own volition, and would need to start a job search. But he would like an answer from me right now as to whether I would be applying for the post of Director of UI. In blunt terms the question is: 'Are you willing to apply for your own job?'

I feel various emotions when I receive this deeply unattractive proposal, none conducive to making a clear, sensible and (needlessly) instant decision. However despite my total surprise at his behaviour, my anger at being so poorly treated, my fear for the future and my justifiable feeling of hurt, I answer his question. 'This is my job, Chairman, and I intend to keep it.'

'Good', he replied, 'I thought you would say that.' And our meeting is over.

In retrospect I realise that Peter's evident pleasure at my agreeing to fight on was because his plan required me to do just that. Had I said I needed time to think and to wait for his proposal to be put in writing, I could have started immediate proceedings for constructive dismissal. The likely outcome of that would have been an industrial tribunal, significant compensation for me, and I would also have kept my job. But Peter gambled on my willingness to fight for my rights and the probability that I had never heard of constructive dismissal. He was right on both counts, but totally wrong in what he was setting out to do. This was to remove someone from their post without any kind of written or verbal warning while all the evidence was that they were being successful. The £50,000 I had raised that very morning being a good example.

So we set out on a pretty ghastly six months. I continue to enthuse about my job despite everything and carry on opening the innings even, though, to use Sir Geoffrey Howe's cricketing metaphor, re his treatment by Mrs Thatcher, 'the captain has drilled holes in your bat'. I regularly visit expensive lawyers who tell me I have a real case and from time to time I am summoned to see even more expensive head-hunters (based behind Harrods – yes, that expensive) who ask me to give reasons as to why I might make a good Director of UI.

(Like having done it well for the last ten years?). Meantime Dave and I battle away on the five-year plan and three people move into the office to start a six-month fundraising campaign. It is a frantic, surreal and tense time during which I continue to carry out my role as Director and at the same time fight for my job.

Everything is clouded in uncertainty, but what is most unsettling for Ursie and me is the sense that something else is going on which we don't know about. In particular we aren't able work out what the Trustees are up to. Having previously been pretty supportive of me, they become distant and refuse to help. To a man and a woman they appear to back the Chair's line. So what is Peter up to? Why is he spending the Trust's hard-earned funds on very expensive head-hunters searching to replace a perfectly good Director? There is something mysterious about all this and we can't work out what it is.

About three months later, this air of mystery deepens when my London lawyers (one of the 'big five') ring to say they want to drop my case, ostensibly on the grounds that as we get nearer to any tribunal then my costs will rise disproportionately and they are worried about whether I can afford them. Unwittingly, I decide to go along with this and transfer, not to a solicitor of my own choosing, but to a small, rural firm they recommend, based in Swindon. I find the advice of my new solicitor, 'You have a good case for compensation but we advise you not to fight it', pretty unhelpful. This bizarre turn of events forces me into conjecture about what is going on but without any sense of what the answer might be. So, while the UI team and the education/business links world continue to support me, events move to a climax with a splendidly surreal meeting.

Eventually I find myself sitting in Gummer's office with a new Trustee. Shaun Woodward had married into the Sainsbury dynasty and I know him to be both wealthy and a politically well-connected member of the Tory party. He is pleasant enough, but I get the impression that he is there largely to lend respectability to whatever decision is made. I know also that Peter Gummer has links to the Prime Minister and so, I thought, had Shaun (though in the event these links were to prove quite tenuous).*

So there we were in the Shandwick Office, in March 1994, six months after Peter had started the tortuous process of getting me to apply for my own job, with me again being asked to explain what I brought to the position of Director of UI. At this point it will occur to you (as it did to me) that my position was pretty hopeless. Clearly the trust was not going through the charade of sizing me up against other candidates in order to keep me in post.

Whatever strange games they were playing, I still felt at this point that I couldn't walk away from UI, for more reasons than one. I had been told that if I lost my job and went to an Employment Tribunal, conducting my own case would go down well (quite apart from being much cheaper) and I'd got it into my head that in order to be sure of my case I needed to get a letter from Gummer confirming his decision. With hindsight I'm not sure about this as what they had already tried to do almost certainly infringed employment law. So I stuck with the whole process until I got the result of the interview, which, surprise, surprise, confirmed that I had lost my job and am being replaced by someone called Stuart Bishell. Once again a surreal element crept in as the letter from Gummer confirming that someone else had been appointed Director of UI took three weeks to arrive, with him protesting all the while that it was 'in the post'. What on earth was going on?

---

* At one point Shaun Woodward was the director of communications for the Tory party (1991–2) but several years after my meeting with him he changed parties and stood successfully for Labour. This change of heart was, I'm sure, genuine as he was strongly opposed to the homophobic nature of some of the then Tory party and their stance on legislation concerning gay teachers. In 2007 he became Secretary of State for Northern Ireland and as part of the Labour Cabinet was reputed to be close to both Blair and Brown.

The full answer didn't materialise for two or three years, but when it did the machinations surrounding my sacking were as unpleasant as we suspected. Eventually I went up to see my erstwhile colleagues at UI and they told me they thought I had been manoeuvred out of my job in order to create a vacancy for Stuart Bishell. I have no way of knowing if this was indeed true, but the whole thing was very odd. Such tales of the darker side of business and government abound and I believe that in the years to come people will look at elements of our much vaunted capitalist system and wonder how various powerful individuals could treat quite so many people so badly for so long.

Since that time Ellie has married George, whose father is the eminent QC Ron Thwaites. With Ron's skill as a lawyer and George's journalistic abilities I might have been able to handle the whole thing better. Certainly had we but known the Thwaites family at the time I would have felt less alone.

Once I was officially 'sacked', I served notice on UI that I was taking the Trust (or rather the Chairman) to court for unfair dismissal. After I was made redundant a long delay ensued, during which James, (who was now trying to build up his film business from our home) and I used to travel in together every Thursday to the Employment Exchange in Maidenhead, where we would collect our weekly unemployment pay. Sounds like the basis for a rather dubious TV sitcom called something like *Generations on the Dole*.

This slightly bizarre ritual went on for a few months until we both found work. At home we shared the same computer, the same room, the same desk and even the same chair, but our working methods were somewhat different. James was in his 'messy' phase (like Picasso, he had 'periods', but his were not quite as lucrative) and so papers, books and scripts were scattered everywhere. As far as he was concerned the floor made an ideal filing cabinet and everything lay where it was last put. In those days when writing he needed complete silence with no interruptions and if he was on the phone, no one could use the Hoover or ring the doorbell lest his contact suspected he was not in a 'proper' office. (Incidentally this scenario appeared again 15 years later in James's successful script for the TV comedy *Freezing!*). I on the other hand, both through my Army training and by temperament, am pretty tidy. I like to clear up at the end of the day; to be able to find papers and generally to have a place for everything. Fortunately there was one important and 'saving' difference between us. Whereas I was happy to work normal daytime hours James was still a nocturnal animal. Like some literary bat he functioned only after dark, and so between us we invented a domestic form of hot-desking, to the point that if I met James in the kitchen in the morning it was because he was on his way to bed, not about to have breakfast!

It was a hard time for all of us, but ameliorated by two or three pieces of good fortune. Firstly, we were all basically kind and considerate to each other and despite flashes of temper and occasional arguments didn't let the stress of events divide us. In these situations you just put your head down and believe things will get better: 'Keep buggering on (KBO)', as Winston Churchill so admirably put it. Secondly, Ursie's love and strength supported us all and her income teaching at Davenies School kept us afloat financially. Thirdly, I managed to ensure we kept our home. Two years before I left UI, I had taken out a mortgage insurance policy with the Halifax which meant that, for a moderate monthly charge, they guaranteed to pay the mortgage if you were out of work. This scheme actually worked, and for some months they paid the interest on our (then) huge mortgage of over £150,000, so that at no time did I or the family feel that our home would have to go. This sense that our physical and emotional base was actually safe was a vital ingredient in keeping us from going under. Ever since those days I have believed that no one should be allowed to buy a home without first having to take out insurance to protect their monthly payments – just like car insurance.

Of course, the stress got to us in different ways. I remember once just breaking down at home when I got another job rejection. 'Oh God. What do I have to do? I have tried so hard for everyone.' My distress was no more than that endured by millions of my fellow citizens and, after all, my pain was just about the loss of a job and a sense of failure. Many suffer greater pain and have bigger problems with no solution in sight. But being jobless is still a terrible situation to be in, even if you are lucky in other ways. Also tension can lead one to make mistakes, and I remember going to a CBI dinner to hear Michael Heseltine speak and, having failed to read the invitation properly, finding that I was the only person wearing a suit, with everyone else in dinner jackets! That evening I also failed to follow-up an offer of help from a Trade Union legal specialist. How stupid that was. Also I waited too long to go to court.... and so on.

My final evening as Director of UI was an odd affair. As chance would have it UI had booked the Whateley Hall Hotel, Banbury, for its spring conference. So the town where we had had many happy Banbury Cross Players meetings and performed Dickens at Christmas became, in a rather surreal way, the venue for my disgraceful exit from UI. About sixty people from the Trust came, and they were universally kind to me and Ursula. We sat on the 'top' table with Gummer and his wife which was all pretty tense. Stuart Bishell, my replacement, was there too, wearing by strange coincidence the same tie as myself.

The evening at the Whateley Hall Hotel passed and I moved into the twilight, difficult world of redundancy. My understanding is that Bishell didn't really fit in at UI and after a couple of years he left. During his period with UI it was rumoured that he worked a four-day week and the Trust often paid for him to fly back to his home in Sheffield at weekends. Bishell's replacement turned out to be a guy I'd asked to take charge of UI Scotland, whose name, I think, was David Miller.

During the time I was redundant I did take the issue of my dismissal to court and was prepared to conduct my own case. In the event the solicitors acting for the Trust phoned me up the day before the tribunal and we reached an out-of-court settlement. I emerged from this saga with some scars, but in reality I was just one of many to suffer in this way, and, in the event, came away not too badly damaged. The challenge implicit in the whole saga lay in whether I could cope with such an experience and that is the next bit of the story.

CHAPTER THIRTEEN

Leadership Challenge

'A man's true delight consists in doing the things he was made for.'

- Marcus Aurelius

In the middle of 1994 I was out of work in an economy which was dormant, if not actually in recession. This was the second time round on the carousel of unemployment, but I was determined not just to lie down and accept my lot. I took the advice of Marcus Aurelius: 'Cease to fume at destiny by ever grumbling at today or lamenting over tomorrow.'

The depressing thing about being out of work is that you can't quite envisage the scenario that will get you back into the workplace. It's easy to think your bad situation will go on forever, and you feel this at double strength as you get older. Also things feel worse if, like me, you haven't trained in anything particularly specific (law, medicine or accountancy, for example) or truly found your métier. But, had I known it, help was at hand, albeit not immediately and in the next year I was to find my vocation.

In the meantime I kept in touch with my friends at UI and refreshed my network, as is the approved course. Not much happened for a few months, then Helen Holmes (UI's fundraiser) rang me to say she'd made contact with a fairly senior Labour MP who was looking for someone to drive a campaign. So I went up to the House of Commons to meet Barry Sheerman MP.

Barry was Labour MP for Huddersfield, with its attendant large majority, and had all sorts of schemes on the go, one of which was called 'Made in The UK'. The purpose behind Made in The UK was to help and support British manufacturing by encouraging companies and consumers to choose products produced in Britain. So here was another national campaign, but this time one aimed at a national audience rather than UI's limited remit of those in education.

In those days (as now) MPs were routinely disparaged, but what I learnt from my few months on the periphery of the Houses of Parliament was how influential MPs actually were. Journalists hung on their words and the magic letters 'MP' seemed to summon powerful people and even the most critical individuals. On behalf of Made in The UK, I sent out many invitations to receptions in Parliament and put through calls to top business people. All I had to do was mention Barry Sheerman MP and the job was done.

Despite not having a particularly strong hand to play, I managed to get the job and an excellent salary of £40,000 per annum. Easily the best deal on pay I ever did. I have often felt that when seeking a job we shouldn't have to discuss our salary and terms with putative bosses. It might be useful (despite the fact that they would take a cut of the eventual salary) to have an agent, as actors or musicians do, to haggle for us before the terms are agreed. Footballers lead the way on this, and employees whose rates are agreed via negotiation with the Trade Unions are following the same principal. The average man or woman, though, has to manage for themselves, and often ends up having to bargain with their potential employer.

Barry found me an office courtesy of BP, which was going through a torrid time. Virtually all of Britannic House (BP's erstwhile Head

Office) was empty, so there were times when I felt like I was the only person at work in a 20-storey tower block in the heart of the City. Britannic House is now no more as, after it was sold, it was knocked down to help BP's cash flow. Curiously at almost the same time as its 20th floor was biting the dust, developers were creating Portcullis House as plush accommodation for MPs. Having spent some time in Barry Sheerman's tiny cubbyhole in the back corridors of the House that Pugin built, I can see why MPs needed a new study block across the road.

I had some administrative assistance, a computer and access to Barry in his office in Parliament. And I battled away at restoring the battered image and dubious credentials of manufacturing industry. I remember speaking at a conference up in Huyton in Lancashire, writing articles for the press and attending functions at the House of Commons. We also put on one or two events ourselves and the good John Pitt, whom we had known for years kindly came. He donated £5,000 that night and on the strength of it took Ursie off to dinner at Wilton's Restaurant, probably spending almost as much on dinner for two as he gave to the campaign!

It was becoming clear that Tony Blair's New Labour Team was likely to win the next election and I had hopes of our project getting closer to Government. Then a *Sunday Times* attack on Barry Sheerman used an unwise quote by Peter Breen (Barry's political assistant) as the basis for an article full of innuendo about his activities. Barry was furious, as he had his eyes on a Cabinet post. I unwisely said that perhaps Peter had been misquoted. In his fury Mr Sheerman took my 'middle line' as tacit support for the article and after that I was on a slippery slope. About a month later Barry introduced me to a young woman who had recently worked in Hong Kong selling wickerwork furniture to the Russians. Not hugely related to the UK's industrial scene, perhaps, but Barry announced he was bringing her in 'to help me'. Well, that was enough. For once I got really angry and it showed. Calling in at his office I found two members, of his team and told them it was lucky their MP was out as otherwise 'I'd punch him on the nose'. Excellent salary or not, I was glad to leave. Barry Sheerman never did make Junior Minister or the Cabinet, though he did eventually become chair of the influential Education Steering Committee, and is still MP for Huddersfield.

The upshot was that two years after leaving UI I once again found myself both needing a job and wondering what I wanted to do. This in turn begged the question of who I really was. You could say that by the not-so-tender age of 54 (retirement age for some!) I should have known the answer to that particular challenge, to which I would reply that if you do, then you're lucky.

I would argue that ten years in the same regiment and eleven years with UI were fairly strong evidence that I am neither disloyal nor difficult to work with nor am I by temperament permanently in transit. My occasional work crises were, I think, partly due to the fact that I didn't train for one of the professions, and in part a reflection of the poor economic conditions which dominated events from the 1960s through to the 1990s.

Fortunately that summer two things happened. As part of my job search I logged in with the Officers' Association, run by the British Legion from their office in Pall Mall. Having done the usual thing of providing my CV, sending a small fee and attending an interview, I got sent a weekly and extensive digest of available jobs. Admittedly many were repeats from the week before, and a lot were for weapons specialists. Nonetheless it was a good service and I was grateful for it, not only as it led me to my next job but also because it helped me to find my métier.

At the same time as I was joining the Officers' Association Ursie's sister Celia and her husband Howard offered us the use of their beautiful penthouse flat down in the ancient seaside town of Lyme Regis in July, so our summer holiday question for that year was easily and inexpensively solved. This flat, their second home, was in the eaves of Farnham House. It slept six comfortably, even eight at a push, and was so lovely that Ellie apparently willed herself back there when giving birth. It was ideal for us, and one of my favourite memories is of being in the sitting room, with the dormer window open on a hot summer's evening, looking over Lyme Bay with Golden Cap in the background, and the music of Fairground Attraction filling the room.

Generally the weather seemed good when we were there. The fudge shop was always worth a visit and the putting green overlooking the bay in the Ornamental Gardens was both a must and the scene of fierce competitions. One holiday I took along our old boat, a converted Enterprise called the *Comfy Pew*, which didn't have a mast but did have an outboard motor. It had been given us by Mary, Ursie's Mum, who, in her slightly eccentric way, thought it would be something the family could do together, 'to stop the children taking up drugs!' Alas, the family will tell you that it plus Dad as captain were a nightmare. I was permanently tense and they were either slightly seasick or overcome by the smell of diesel from a less than efficient second-hand motor. The only drugs they were likely to take up were tranquillisers as a result of sailing with me.

We already knew Lyme Regis well, for in our early married days we had had many Christmases at Lyme. These involved the whole family including Mary and Reg and at these happy gatherings we would often number a dozen, with ages, ranging from those in their eighties to a new born babe. Such simple, indeed obvious delights, should never be taken for granted and, Celia and Howard were always generous with their hospitality, so much so that holidays in Lyme remain a happy memory for all our family.

The summer of 1995 was sunny and hot, so I took just a few casual clothes down to Lyme. I was pursuing a number of leads via the Officers' Association, including one to do with leadership and a franchise calling itself Leadership Challenge. Out of the blue I learnt that the organisers were inviting people with an interest in the project to an open day and since what was on offer was so much 'me' I knew I had to go, holiday or not. I solved the problem of only having T-shirts and shorts by raiding Howard's wardrobe. Howard is much bigger than I, and I finished up wearing a shirt three sizes too large with a tie that didn't match and an enormous jacket that I quickly took off.

The meeting was held at a large hotel in Gloucestershire and as I came down the drive a large banner proclaimed 'Leadership Challenge.' Just as I had when we first arrived in Windsor and we saw a sign saying Upton School I had a feeling that this was going to be an important part of my future.

The event was being run by the 'Board' of Leadership Challenge (more a loose grouping of associates), whose principal protagonists were Jerry Witcher, Julian Tyson-Woodcock, Peter Page and another ex-officer, all of whom had either an RAF or Army background. After a presentation about Leadership Challenge, Jerry then beguiled us with figures explaining how, for a down payment of only £8,000, the franchise would earn us good, or even very good money of up to £40,000 a year. For your £8,000 down payment, operators would purchase a geographic area of the UK, where they would be licensed to run the product. The Challenge programme was targeted at the education system (a market I knew extremely well from my Metal Box and UI days), offering courses in teamwork and leadership to students and teachers. The actual delivery needed more thought but in essence the idea was to take Leadership Challenge to our client schools. The course would involve a whole year group for one day, with residential courses as a possible further option.

Over the next five years many people learnt to be cautious about Jerry's rather over-optimistic view of things. Indeed, of all the people who bought franchises, I think I finished up as the only person able to make the thing work financially. At this first meeting, I said I was happy to consider buying in, but had I been more commercially adroit I would have suggested a lower franchise fee. At the start, Jerry also proposed that we contributed 25% to the centre for every course we ran but this proved to be way too high and eventually it was decided that 12 -15% was a more realistic figure. What we didn't factor in sufficiently was that Leadership Challenge was a start-up operation with an unproven market and an untried product.

Jerry's set-up in Shropshire proved to be costly. He had rent to pay on buildings, a large photocopier, plus a Land Rover and people hired to do the administration of the project. You could tell that he was an Army man, because generally military people do not have to find the money for overheads and they tend to like plenty of admin back-up; historically, it used to take about eight people behind the scenes to put one man in the field with a rifle or a gun. In contrast, well run, lean businesses keep their overheads as low as possible. For example in the 1980s a large corporate called BTR was able to run its global manufacturing organisation with only 24 people in its London office. Indeed the audit team provided by their accountants Ernst and Young had more staff than the whole of BTR's International Head Office.

In my view Leadership Challenge didn't really need a Head Office and I believe what Jerry should have created was a model with Head Office being just himself. He could have worked a computer and a mobile phone from his front room and spent at least three days a week either selling or running courses, which would have funded the centre plus his own costs and salary in one go. For a start-up operation the initial concept was too expensive, and the idea that we, the franchise holders, would be able to pay for Jerry to career round England in his Land Rover like some Alan Sugar of the training world was unrealistic. Also I don't think we really needed weighty manuals telling us how to operate or an expensive consultancy to provide a classy looking method for conducting a Training Needs Analysis. Because everything was new, such difficulties were to be expected, but it took time to suss out these problems and create realistic ways of delivering consistently good courses. In the end we managed, but over the next five years at least a dozen franchise owners failed to make anything from it and fell by the wayside.

At this first meeting with Jerry, still wearing my oversized clothes, I said I was interested in being involved, and so some three weeks later found myself again meeting the members of the Board. As all had Service backgrounds you can imagine there was many a smart suit worn, and polished shoes were de rigueur. Peter Page was an ex-engineer who I liked a lot, very bright and keen for the project to succeed. He was immensely loyal to Jerry and later got quite angry when I suggested that the mileage rate we were all getting for driving around on Leadership Challenge business was too low. He thought, I suppose, that I was questioning Jerry's judgement. Although I half see his point, I think he may have been carrying the concept of 'obeying instructions' a bit far.

Julian on the other hand was a tall, pretty easy-going ex-Etonian who had been in the RAF and had very much enjoyed his time in uniform. Julian was always pleasant and a good team player who quietly got on with what he was good at. Stuart was another very different character. He came straight out of the Parachute Regiment School of soldiering where he had been an NCO (non-commissioned officer). At the time he was very taken with the poetry of World War I and I remember him reciting the first few lines of Wilfred Owen's *Dulce et Decorum est* at breakfast in some slightly run down B and B.

Following my interview, Leadership Challenge offered me a franchise, so I borrowed the money from the local bank manager, the good and green-fingered Bob Davis. Bob left NatWest a couple of years later to set up his own gardening business as The Jolly Gardener and we now see him regularly since he comes quite often to help us with the garden. (Having left banking Bob is now much slimmer and happier!). With my bank loan, the deal was done and by October 1995 I was the proud owner of a new business, operating as a sole trader but as yet with no office, no staff, no working capital, no income and no clients. No problem!

What a long road I had travelled from the days when, as a 20-year-old, the security of a regular income and the respectability of a profession were the criteria for job selection. Of course this was a journey many of my fellow citizens were taking at the same time and thousands more have done so since. But at the time it felt as though I was on my own. I had become an entrepreneur, with just the suspicion that being a trainer was the job for me and therefore, at the age of 54, I might even have found my vocation!

As the owner of a franchise, I had to get on and get the project off the ground. I converted the study into an office, using a Victorian table which dear Lizzie from next door had inherited from one of her many aged aunts. I think my first computer was an ex-UI Acorn (to call it basic would be an exaggeration) but with the arrival in the same room of Mountain Films (proprietors: James Wood and David Thwaites) we upgraded to something better, courtesy of Ron Thwaites, QC, David's Dad. Letters were sent out both by me and Jerry (sorry, Head Office) and old UI contacts in the education sector were phoned. For some while not much happened, which is a rather English way of saying nothing happened, and we drifted into 1996 with no income and no real prospect of any.

However, early in the New Year I made a presentation at Windsor Girls' School to members of the local Education Business Partnership (EBP). By pure serendipity this particular Partnership was the Windsor manifestation of a national movement, largely started by Julia Cleverdon of Business in the Community (BIC), which I had strongly supported. (I don't mean by this that I had materially contributed to the process, but at a meeting where the concept was outlined I had spoken positively from the floor about the idea.) As is sometimes the way of things my good deed that day in 1993 materially helped Leadership Challenge to get off the ground a couple of years later.

Soon after I had spoken at Windsor Girls' School, Slough EBP phoned to say that they wanted to talk to me. This conversation led to a useful contract with them for the spring and summer, which enabled us both to hone our product and also to demonstrate to other potential customers that we could deliver. The first course we ran for the EBP was at a school for children with quite severe physical and mental problems, which was very rewarding. I also remember getting close to a really useful deal with Portsmouth Grammar School but in the end the vexed question of price defeated us. However, it was a good lesson, because thereafter we adjusted our prices slightly downwards and began to get more schools involved.

I ran Leadership Challenge from our first course in 1996 until I sold the business to Charlie Rigby (of whom more later) in 2001. In about five full years our turnover went up from roughly £17,000 in the first full year to nearly £100,000:

Leadership Challenge (SE) – Annual Turnover

Year 1: 1995-96	£4,000 (part year)
Year 2: 1996-97	£17,000 (during which year Nikki joined)
Year 3: 1997-98	£37,000 (Nikki full-time)
Year 4: 1998-99	£73,000
Year 5: 1999-00	£92,000
Year 6: 2000-01	£99,000 (part year)

This was pretty good growth from a standing start with an unproven product in a market not famous for being awash with money. However by the time we had paid 'Head Office' the franchise fee I never really made any money. Anything left over I treated as salary, and I don't believe I ever took more than £14,000 in pay from Leadership Challenge in any one year. Actual profit therefore was non-existent (which makes the events of 2001, when we come to them, all the more remarkable).

Towards the end of Year Two of Leadership Challenge (1996) I had a stroke of good fortune that in many ways accounts for the leap in sales from £4,000 in Year One to £37,000 by the end of Year Three. It is a good example of serendipity at work and a reminder that chance meetings are not to be scoffed at, especially if the key introductions are effected by a dog! Phoebe was a beautiful brown and white English Springer Spaniel and we got her as a 16-week-old pup from the Gornes, friends of Ursie's who were vets and whose children were in Ursie's class at Davenies School. She arrived in the spring of 1997, rather nervous and quivering after a short car journey from Beaconsfield, and we all fell in love with her because she was so pretty and had so much personality. I remember once sitting sideways at the kitchen table and suddenly Phoebe appeared on my knees with her nose about four inches from mine and an

'Aren't I clever' look on her face. Her favourite game was to chase a bouncy red rubber bone up and down the hall, and she would only give it back when we weren't looking. Also if anyone came to the door she would bring them a present of an old towel or slipper, just to make them feel welcome.

Leadership Challenge was just getting off the ground when Phoebe came to live with us, and because our courses were nearly all run outside I was privileged in being able to take Pheebes with me. If we were working in a wild or open area she would be running around with me all day and of course the pupils loved her. She was a good asset to a team too. If Phoebe had one defining characteristic it was that if we were out walking in a group and someone stopped to get something from the car or tie a shoelace she would hang back and draw everyone's attention to the fact the 'team' was one member short and we shouldn't go on without them. How could you not love an animal such as that, especially when we were teaching teamwork? We did indeed all love her quirky, slightly nervy personality and were devastated when she had to be put down in November 2010. Her loss hit me particularly hard and we all miss her still.

Phoebe's role in Leadership Challenge proved to be far more than just team mascot. One day Ursie and I were out walking with her in Windsor Great Park and while we were wandering up Queen Anne's Ride, Phoebe decided to chase after another dog's ball. The ball was being thrown with some vigour by a tall girl with blonde hair tied back in a pony tail. Such 'doggy' incidents, although common, are always potentially embarrassing so I went across to apologise and as a result got talking to the girl. It turned out that her name was Nikki Chance (now Bartlett) and that she was currently working as a temp for British Gas helping them organise conferences. We chatted about what we were both doing and while I explained about

Leadership Challenge I gathered from Nikki that she wasn't very happy in her part-time job, stuck in an office.

'So, what would you really like to do?' I asked.

'Well', came the surprising answer, 'I really want to be out in the fresh air, preferably working with young people.' I then pointed out that this was exactly what Leadership Challenge did but wondered why she didn't think of becoming a PE teacher or something similar?

'I've thought of that', said Nikki, 'But my problem is that I left school at 16 and haven't got the necessary A Levels.'

Within the next twenty minutes or so we had agreed that Nikki would come and work with me. Initially she would keep her part-time work at British Gas, but, if things went well, we could think of a full-time job at Leadership Challenge.

Well, within a few months Nikki became an integral part of my embryo operation and, in fact, our fortuitous meeting made the business. What I loved about Nikki was her hunger to learn. She gobbled up everything I and the other trainers could tell her, worked tirelessly, was always on time, and her excellent IT skills complemented my sparrow-sized ability. We were a very good team as we each had the strengths the other lacked but also got on so well. There was the odd point of conflict but most of the time we laughed, worked fast and agreed on everything.

So there you have the story of how a middle-aged man with a public school and Army background, who loved theatre and books, built a successful business partnership with a young woman from Croydon who left school at 16. I think the glue which kept us together was personal respect for each other (which we still have) plus Nikki's tenacious determination to learn and my willingness to tell Nikki everything I knew. We were training people in teamwork and I guess it must have been quite impressive for students on our courses to see such starkly contrasting types as Nikki and I working well as a team right in front of them. Nikki now runs her own training organisation called Zest, and has a list of qualifications and clients only slightly shorter than these memoirs.

We provided onsite personal development courses in team building and leadership training, working with whole Year Groups (roughly 100 to 150 students) but always concentrating on individuals. Generally we went to the client's school and used their facilities. This saved money but, of course, also meant that every course was an 'away game' for us. We would agree to provide seven or eight qualified instructors if the school would match this with seven or eight teachers for the day, which gave a ratio of about one adult to ten students. This had two advantages as not only did it save both parties money but it also provided a degree of 'buy-in' from the staff. Teachers working with us on the course were able to advise us about particular children and to see first-hand how we worked and what our outcomes were. For some children the positive effect was quite staggering and easy to see, after only a few hours.

Unfortunately Leadership Challenge had two quite serious flaws in commercial terms. Firstly, it was very cyclical. We were too busy between March and September with hardly anything to do in the winter. This was because those schools who wanted to develop leadership and teamwork didn't like to take on anything which would disrupt classroom studies in the winter term. This is the term when each new Year Group is 'bedded in' and which lays down the groundwork for the next academic year. Added to this was the fact that as our programmes were essentially outdoor it made sense to run them in the spring and summer terms, when the weather was better.

The other commercial flaw took me some time to discover. Over the first two or three years it concerned me that, one by one, my fellow franchise holders came to realise they couldn't make the license work and dropped out – why was this? They were all experienced, capable people and many had a mix of service and business backgrounds. It took me a while to work out that the answer lay in the range of skills required to run this apparently simple business. We were all sole traders and the business required each individual to be capable of three rather contradictory attributes. You had to be able to actually deliver the programmes and to do this you needed to understand the basics of how training works, how young people learn, and precisely what motivates children from very different backgrounds. Fortunately, Ursula had taught brilliantly for over thirty-five years, and during our many conversations together I had learnt a lot about schools, the educational system and the challenges which teachers face every day.

In addition, two other skills were needed. One was that you had to be able to sell. Of course prices have to be affordable; the product needs to be presented in a way that is attractive to clients; the deliverers have to be credible on first meeting; you need persistence and stamina in order to chase every lead and, above all, you have to be happy to talk money with strangers. Despite my rather cloistered and correct upbringing, over the years I had learnt how to do these things and I was helped by the fact that, in general, people in schools are a pleasure to deal with. Their approach was not cut-throat or aggressive and, significantly, once we had earned their trust they were only too glad to invite us back the following year – especially if they felt we had been working with them to develop all the pupils, not just some. I think our repeat sales level was something like 65%, which is high and provided an ideal base from which to grow the business year on year. Just as I had survived in the Army I was now beginning to survive in the commercial world.

Finally, to grow the business we needed to administer it properly which meant, for example, being able to work the computer; control the cash flow; and turn up for every gig on time with the right people and the right kit. Here my reasonably organised approach to things came into play, along with the experience gained in 25 years in business and the training I had picked up in the Army. Over the years I had perhaps become qualified by experience to run a business, albeit a small one.

If one had the right balance of these three attributes – training experience (including dealing with young people), sales ability and basic business skills – one's Leadership Challenge franchise had a reasonable chance of success, but you did need all three and in roughly the same proportions. In general most of my ex-Service colleagues struggled with the sales side, as it was not that easy for them to see things from the customer's point of view or negotiate over price.

So what was it Leadership Challenge (SE) provided for schools in South-East England?

The days for me and my green-shirted team were long and demanding. Often Nikki and I would leave my house at 6.15am and spend an hour or so on the M25 getting to our destination. Arriving at the school, we would split. Nikki would go off with the trailer and other 'green shirts' to set up approximately a dozen team tasks in the school grounds. Meanwhile the caretaker would let me into the school and I would start to set up in the main hall, organising my flip charts, setting out the chairs and tables theatre style and preparing for a teachers' briefing at about 8.15am.

Over the next half an hour I would go quickly through the day with the staff, explaining their role, expanding on our culture and how Leadership Challenge worked. This was crucial to the success of our programmes, as trainers approach the business of learning differently from the teaching profession. Trainers see themselves as facilitators, and this means they are not there primarily to blame, correct or tell.

During the day we would set tasks for the various teams to undertake and observe what happened in order to draw out from the participants what they felt had gone well or what needed improving. This process is known as 'reviewing', and only really works when led by the participants. At the end of each task a review would take place and teams of young people could be seen sitting on the ground in a circle, discussing what had gone well, what not so well and, crucially, how they could improve. These learning points could then immediately be taken forward to the next task and applied as actions. Thus teams went straight from discussion and theory into implementation. Cumulatively these reviews built up during the day so the effect on both the team and the individual was very powerful, with many students feeling empowered and in charge of their own learning for possibly the first time. Even if at first some pupils disliked not having someone older to tell them what to do, most soon adapted to our novel way of doing things. It enabled them to learn a lot about themselves and the gentle art of working together with others. As we ran course after course, we saw the old training mantra proved many times: 'Hear and I forget; See and I remember; Do and I understand.'

As our business grew it became clear that we would need more staff. Because money was short there was no question of taking anyone on full-time, but fortunately the training world is characterised by having a large body of freelancers, many of whom like to work part-time. I therefore advertised for 'associates' to apply to us for occasional work, stipulating that I didn't want any CVs. I don't believe in the value of these potted biographies, as I have had my hopes raised by many glowing one page résumés only to feel let down on actually meeting the person whose name is at the top of the paper. So in the advert, alongside asking candidates to provide just the barest personal details, I also asked for anything – a poem, a drawing, a story from the applicant's work – which would show some personality or creativity.

I had five or six replies but none matched the sangfroid and sheer force of personality of a woman called Sharon who sent me a drawing of a running shoe. Her drawing of a 'trainer' highlighted the shoe's soul (sole!), the tongue, the strong construction, sound base, flexibility and its suitability for a variety of roles. Small, mid-blonde and very pretty, Sharon brought calm, wisdom and huge experience to our little group. I learnt so much from her about the art of listening, of letting the client speak and generally how to help people move forward from where they are and grow. As Leadership Challenge expanded we all benefitted immeasurably from watching Sharon at work and from her delightful company. She is someone I much admire and a dear friend of Ursie and mine.

As a team we soon began to take on quite tough assignments. For example on one occasion we ran a course near Newbury for over 600 pupils. A successful school was being forcibly amalgamated with another that had been deemed to be failing and, despite the offer of a brand new campus and financial incentives, none of the students or the staff of either school wanted the marriage. We used our skills and, notwithstanding the huge logistic task, at the end of three days a helpful spirit of co-operation was beginning to emerge.

I was fortunate in having good people around me at the time to help with such challenges and I learnt much from them about the gentle art of training. The techniques we used on our courses were experiential (based on learning by doing). However, eventually I decided that I also needed (and wanted) some form of academic qualification to underpin what we were providing. I reasoned that a better understanding of training theory would help me personally and make Leadership Challenge more credible.

For some time I had been amazed at the number of semi-literate people who sported degrees, let alone 2.1s. For too long I had been in thrall to the 1950s mantra espoused by schools like Aldenham that 'there are only two universities and you need to be very bright to go to either of them', without acknowledging that the world of academia had changed. I began to hunt for a distance learning course that was relevant to my life as a professional trainer. In this I was very much helped by the excellent Phil Whittaker, whom I got to know on Leadership Challenge's initial training day, who himself gained a PhD after leaving the Army and who taught for a while at Ashridge Management College. I found the course I needed following discussions with Leicester University who, despite my only having two A Levels, still took me on their Education and Training MSc programme, a three-year distance learning course.

Looking back, I realise I was not at all sure of my ability to complete the course, let alone successfully. I am fairly quick-witted but academically untrained and my mind is not that rigorous. For example, in the 70's I had dropped an Institute of Personnel Management degree-level course, while some years later I failed to achieve the Institute of Marketing's postgraduate diploma - albeit by a small margin, after a very short course.

All this is a roundabout way of thanking Leicester University for their faith in me, for being so supportive and understanding of their distance-learning students and for providing course material that I could not only read but (mostly!) understand. The vocational element of the course must have helped, as did the fact that it was all about education and training, two subjects about which I felt passionate. The old enthusiasm, so obvious in that little guy growing up in the 1950s, was rearing its head and once again seeing me through. In July 2000 I went up to Leicester with Ursula and, clad in a hired gown and mortarboard, was photographed clutching my MSc certificate. Hurrah! After three years of study I had a degree and academic success at last, at the age of 59.

Running Leadership Challenge courses gave food for thought and also led to a number of amusing incidents. The most memorable of these occurred after I had run a course for potential prefects at St Paul's School, London, some time during my second or third year of operating the franchise. The course took place on a Saturday, which I sensed the Prefects rather resented, but though I had to leave the boys briefly on their own, we got through the day OK – or so I thought. However just as with the Olympic Games, there was going to be a legacy!

For our next engagement we had to go all the way up to Yorkshire to a rather expensive girls' school, all ponies and tennis. I say we for at the time I was lucky enough to have the help of Giles Smith-Walker, the son of our good friends Jean and Malcolm and a willing and capable helper. Giles was a cheerful, well-built guy, a good sportsman who at one time had seriously thought of the Army as a career. Unfortunately a nasty rugger injury put paid to that. At the time of working with me Giles was in his gap year. Later he went into the wine business, where he has since done very well.

The day's programme at the girls' school started with me facing about seventy or so well brought up, demure 16-year-olds and a lot of the staff, seated firmly in the front row who resembled so many hospital matrons attending a convention. Nothing daunted I launched happily into my spiel on the subtleties of working as a team, writing up my words of wisdom on many a sheet of flipchart paper as we went. There was absolutely no warning for what was about to happen as, with a flourish, I turned to what I thought was the next blank page. Immediately I realised something, was wrong for shame and surprise were writ large on the girls' faces, while most of the staff regarded me with horror.

Turning back to the flipchart I saw that the prefects of St Paul's had indeed left me their legacy in the form of a drawing of a large, anatomically correct penis. As the cold hit my stomach and the shock registered I managed to utter the absolutely correct if banal words, 'that shouldn't be there', and both physically and metaphorically turned over a new leaf. The only person to enjoy the joke was Giles (hugely!) and, of course, we were not invited back for the following year. Ever since then I have treated flipcharts with some caution and each pad gets inspected carefully before a new course.

Despite the odd incident of this kind I'm glad to say lots of schools did in fact invite us back and we went to them regularly, year after year. One of our frequent clients was King's Ely, where Gill Smith, who was in charge of the prefects, thought Leadership Challenge was good news. One year we decided to create a new course at King's Ely by combining our standard outdoor team tasks with some map reading and initiative exercises in Thetford Forest, about ten miles from the school. This large tract of pine forest was owned by the Forestry Commission, who inevitably had any number of rules governing its use and, no doubt, plenty of forms to fill in and send to Head Office for approval. I wasn't going to get involved in any of that, mainly because I didn't agree with the principle that as a tax payer I should have to pay to use a forest. I did make gentle enquiries with Forestry officials about access, but it was all made as difficult as possible. So I decided to drive into the forest and set up our tasks there, ignoring the system and without telling anyone.

It was dusk on a clear, cool summer's evening when I finished putting out the tasks and started to drive to the exit. This kind of English forest, full of pine trees, heather and scrub, is curiously quiet at that time of the day and you sense that a whole world of small creatures is getting ready to chance their arm in the gathering dark to find something for supper. Foxes, rabbits, hares, stoats, weasels, field mice and owls are preparing for another nocturnal adventure which, for the smaller ones at least, might be their last. As I drove out I was enjoying this atmosphere, blithely unaware that an adventure of my own was beckoning, until I drove along the metalled exit road only to be confronted by a large, securely locked gate.

Nearly two hours later I had discovered an interesting albeit disturbing fact. At dusk the entrances to Thetford Forest are closed, bolted and securely fastened against anyone wishing to enter or, more importantly from my point of view, wanting to get out. I was faced with the distinctly uncomfortable prospect of 'overnighting' in the forest. No food, no water, no bedding and, significantly, no communication, as the phone companies hadn't yet seen the commercial worth of putting up masts where nobody lives. Back at King's Ely I would be classed as 'missing, believed gone home'. As I wondered what to do next, I noticed that the thick undergrowth either side of the gate was protected by large wooden blocks designed to keep out deer rustlers. Looking at it another way, they also appeared pretty good at keeping 'unauthorised' visitors in! There was a small ditch protecting these blocks on the forest side while, on the other, tantalisingly close, lay the road to freedom and supper and all sorts of good things not normally found in a forest.

But your hero hadn't spent ten years in an armoured regiment for nothing. I also saw that one or two blocks were only loosely set in the ground. Backing up the car, I fixed the tow rope to the towing bar and wrapped the other end tightly round the first stump. My "cunning plan" worked. Slowly my trusty Rover took the strain and the wooden block was dragged at an angle from the ground. Hurrah – now for two more. They all responded and, filling the shallow ditch with brushwood, I was able to escape from my rural prison. What I now think of as 'the breakout from Thetford Forest' was complete and supper back at the school tasted rather sweet that night.

Leadership Challenge also gave me some interesting insights into how to deal with people. Generally my approach to those around me is to smile and say 'Hi' pretty well everywhere I go. Of course some folk will let you down but I'm sure it's wrong to assume that they will fail you from the outset. My approach has its merits, as became clear one day when Nikki and I were running a course for about a hundred and fifty students in Basildon, Essex. It was one of those rather drizzly autumn days and we needed to make an early start. Essex was looking particularly unlovely as Nikki and I drove east and we had been warned by the link teacher that we were about to work in 'a rough old school'. So what with one thing and another, we set off knowing we would have to be quite determined about things. Later in the day our rather grim view of the task ahead was confirmed when the whole school had to be evacuated while several fire engines dealt with an arson attack on the boys' loos!

Nonetheless, as normal we set up our outdoor tasks on the patch of ground allocated to us and ploughed on through the morning until it was time to do some outdoor work. At this moment Nikki came to me and said, 'We have a real problem. Look out there.' On the area we needed to use there were a large number of young men of varying ages enjoying an extended mid morning-break. We couldn't delay the programme for any serious amount of time so some sort of action was needed.

'Don't worry', I said, 'I'll deal with it.' (though, actually, I had, no idea what 'dealing with it' might involve).

'How?' said Nikki, very reasonably. 'You can't stop their break, and these are potentially pretty stroppy kids.'

After only a slight delay I replied, 'I'm going out there with a smile to ask them if they could please take their break somewhere else.'

And so I did and so they did. As nice as you like, they gave this strange man with his inconvenient request a short stare and with half a nod went to another part of the sports field to talk, play footie or, possibly, to plot more attacks on the school buildings. To this day I'm pretty sure that it was the sheer element of surprise that an adult should smile and ask politely for their co-operation that worked.

If I got it right at that school in Basildon and in Thetford Forest it wasn't always the case and these two tales should be offset by another. One year I decided get a present nice and early for Ursie (either for her birthday or our wedding anniversary, I can't remember which). I purchased a rather lovely looking plant in a pot, but needed to hide it carefully for a few days until the due date. Cunningly, I found a space in the spare room under the bed, and, with the job done, thought no more about it. On the morning of the happy day I went and retrieved said plant from its hidey-hole and gave it to my lovely wife. She was suitably grateful, and it wasn't until a few days later that I found out she had not only discovered her present but, more importantly, had been watering it punctiliously for the last few days. She had kindly became the custodian of the gift intended for her! This incident demonstrates three things: women are aware of everything that goes on in the home, men are sometimes not very bright and the female members of my wife's family have keen noses!

At this point I needed to divert slightly to recount a series of significant family events. They concern Ursie's parents Mary and Reg Nicklin, of blessed memory. We often went to see them in their home in Stroud, especially on family days, anniversaries and the like, particularly after my Father's death in 1977. Mary and Reg lived in Stroud for many years after Ursie and I were married, leading a generally quiet but comfortable life together.

Sadly, Reg died in 1998, aged 91 and we held a lovely memorial service for him in Marling School Hall. James read a Shakespeare sonnet and I contributed with that famous description of a village cricket match from A.G. Macdonell's *England Their England*. The music was stunning, with most of the members of the family contributing, and it included a violin solo from young Ursie Gough (now Le Huray), who played *Méditation* by Massenet most beautifully.

After this Mary was on her own up in Gloucestershire, short of support, quite frail and with her various aches and pains getting worse. The house was quite isolated and we learnt later that she kept a water pistol full of ammonia by the door in case of intruders! Not a good situation for someone in their eighties. Mary adored Gloucestershire and her roots there went back pre-war. There was a strong case for arranging for her to stay in her home, close to what was left of her friends but how to do this always seemed to elude us. In the end the perennial 'what shall we do with Mother?' problem was solved, up to a point, by bringing Mary down to Teddington to live in a well appointed flat, with full-time staff on call day or night. Her apartment there provided a level of sheltered care which was only possible because Reg had put aside enough money to provide for her in old age. I remember some years before his death standing with Reg in the garden at Stroud, when he turned to me and said, 'Make sure she's all right when I'm gone.' I think we did and I hope we did.

However, notwithstanding our efforts, I don't suppose you could say Mary was entirely happy in Teddington. The one saving grace of the move to London was that virtually the whole family was within a 30-minute drive. In her final three years Mary saw someone from the family most days and, in addition, regularly came over to us in Windsor for Sunday lunch. However, she did have diabetes and high blood pressure and in 2001 the inevitable happened. Late one night in July we got a call from the night staff to say Mary had collapsed and been rushed to Isleworth Hospital. We went there straight away, and all the family attended her over the next two days as she lay unconscious and virtually untreatable in her hospital bed. We talked lovingly among ourselves and recalled happy days when she was at home in Stroud with Reg, in the strong belief that unconscious people can hear what you say. Her end was painless and peaceful, and she was surrounded by those she loved and who loved her. Following a funeral service in Teddington's beautiful Georgian church (which she went to often in her last three years) Mary was cremated and her ashes lie next to Reg's in Rodborough churchyard, surrounded by the countryside she adored. God bless.

Back at the office, Nikki and I ploughed on working together as a good team and building up the business. They say that if you can keep a start-up venture going into Year Three then it will probably survive and do OK. Leadership Challenge was a case in point, though I have to say that during the first two years the only thing keeping us going was the residue of my redundancy money from 3i, Ursie's salary as a teacher, unemployment pay and my mortgage insurance policy. During my early years running Leadership Challenge we had people looking round the house as we thought we might have to sell, but fortunately we were able to cling on.

You will have seen in the table on page 274 that after Leadership Challenge the letters SE (standing for 'South East') appear in brackets. These were added deliberately to differentiate my operation from other Leadership Challenge businesses as they bit the dust and even Jerry found he was unable to keep going. To help him (and myself) I extended my franchise by buying the rights to operate in various parts of Kent, Sussex and Surrey, which was potentially lucrative territory. I was encouraged to do this by my friend and colleague from Leadership Challenge Steve Adams and I am eternally in Steve's debt, as his advice proved crucial when the time came to sell.

The thing that's best about running your own business is that you don't have a series of bosses telling you what to do and changing their minds every two minutes. The worst thing (apart from being on your own a lot) is the financial uncertainty. You can't ever be completely sure if enough money is going to come in month by month, but in our case by Year Three I'm glad to say we had the best of both worlds. As our programmes became more sophisticated so we got slicker at delivering them and our turnover began to climb.

Nonetheless, when you start a new business you ought to have some idea what you want to do with it and how you see the business developing. Without claiming to be a leading strategist, I had always sensed that I wanted to grow mine sufficiently to be able to sell it, and this incipient purpose became clearer as I realised I was unlikely to ever earn a proper income from the business. I needed to sell the operation to create a capital sum to pay off a chunk of our mortgage. Once an outline strategy is in place, really good business people then put a plan together to make the agreed strategy happen. I did have a plan but it was not much of one – it consisted of carrying on for as long as I could in the hope something would turn up! The experts call this approach 'trusting to luck', so not only was I fortunate that a buyer arrived on the scene, but I also had another slice of good fortune just before we clinched the deal. Being twice lucky was exactly what the strategic plan required! To be fair I did throw in a little bit of low cunning, and had also, of course, developed the business to the point where it was actually sellable.

Sometime in 2000 Charlie Rigby, who now ran most of Leadership Challenge, surveyed all that he owned and, rather like God, saw that it was good. Good, certainly, but it could be better. He felt there was an opportunity to float the whole of his World Challenge business (which comprised of overseas expeditions for Sixth Formers, and the recently acquired Leadership Challenge) on the stock exchange, which could make him a rich man. The only snag was that he hadn't been able to get the whole of the operation from Jerry, and an important and sizeable chunk called Leadership Challenge South East still belonged to Antony Wood. The upshot was that in order to implement his plans Charlie Rigby needed my business. Fortunately I had got wind of this and therefore decided to bide my time and say nothing until I heard more from him. Eventually Charlie approached me, letting me know in an off-hand way that it would 'tidy things up' if I sold him my bit of Leadership Challenge.

Now, the thing to realise about people like Charlie Rigby, (and there are plenty of them around) is that they like to feel they are in charge. Some might call this paranoia, others bullying, others just strong management. Whatever it is, you don't really want to be near it or to have to work for it, as generally it is a manifestation of the need to control. I realised from the start that if I wanted to negotiate with Charlie I would have to let him think he always had the whip hand. I knew that for his plan to work he needed to buy my franchise, but that it would be fatal if he once guessed I knew he was vulnerable. Since he needed to buy but I didn't need to sell Charlie was not actually in control, and this could be dangerous for me. So I adopted a style that might best be described as 'jokey naivety'. My tone was, 'I haven't sold a business before but I guess you know the form and it'll be OK in the end'. Rather low behaviour, you might think, from the boy brought up in a vicarage?

The whole thing dragged on for over six months as Charlie hesitated and his lawyers faffed round. During this period I remember going to Acton to discuss the selling price with him. I had just bought a book called *Twelve Essential Points When Selling Your Business* and putting this on the table I said: 'There you are, Charlie. I'm doing my best to catch up with you and have just started Chapter Two!' In fact although this was a ruse the book was full of helpful tips, including the idea that, as you prepare for a sale, you should 'invest in taxes'. This means that in the years when you are building up an operation you spend all you can on it, which keeps the profits down but in turn means you pay less tax. On the other hand, in the year you plan to sell you spend very little on the business and work hard to make the profits as high as possible. This may mean a bigger tax bill for one year but it also inflates the value (therefore the price) of the business. This strategy is what we followed, aided by my accountant, the splendid David Watts.

However, in all these things you also need good fortune and I did have two bits of good luck; one small and the other very significant. The first came in the form of an excellent piece of advice from David, who had a good knowledge of the art of selling businesses. He explained that as I was not a Limited Company I was classed as a self-employed owner-operator and therefore did not have to supply accounts as part of the sale. All I was required to give any potential buyer was the turnover (that's the value of sales) for the current year. In fact World Challenge already had the turnover figures for every year I had been operating because they needed to levy their 15% franchise fee. As a result, World Challenge never knew what Leadership Challenge's profitability was or the fact that it was so low I could hardly afford to pay myself.

So the discussions meandered on with me cheerful, apparently naive and without urgency and Charlie seeming cool, but in fact slightly paranoid and forever in touch with the lawyers. After a few months I began to sense things might go wrong and I would miss my chance, for the price offered was excellent, and included a consultancy deal for the next three years. So my second, and important, piece of good fortune was when Steve Adams encouraged me to get on with the sale. Timing is crucial in most things and I am eternally in Steve's debt for his advice.

Charlie and I were very close to finalising the deal at the same time as Mary died. Charlie wanted my business in order to float his company and he also needed to lock me into World Challenge. In outline the deal was that he bought Leadership Challenge South East for a six-figure sum (paid in two instalments) and in addition took me on to his staff as a consultant, working one hundred days a year for the next three years, on a good salary. About a month before Mary died Steve and I had this feeling that I should move the deal to a conclusion and so I gave Charlie a deadline. Later, I heard that not long after signing the contract Charlie discovered that World Challenge's financial position was not nearly as good as he had thought. On this occasion I had moved just in time.

Things moved on speedily once I had set a deadline, and the lawyers quickly agreed the detail so the sale documents could be drawn up. Then an extraordinary piece of serendipity occurred. Mary's funeral in Teddington was scheduled for 11.00am on the very morning Charlie's accountant asked me to come in to sign the contract. So, in the end, this financially life-saving and important event took place the day we said goodbye to dear Mary, and I found myself leaving the World Challenge office in Acton to go to Teddington to attend Mary's funeral.

CHAPTER FOURTEEN

The Greasy Pole

'When you are old and grey and full of sleep,
And nodding by the fire, take down this book,
And slowly read, and dream of the soft look
Your eyes had once and of their shadows deep.'

– W. B. Yeats

'And the end of all our exploring
Will be to arrive where we started
And know the place for the first time.'

- T. S. Eliot

For a year or so after selling Leadership Challenge South East I kept myself occupied by doing various assignments as a consultant for World Challenge. This mainly involved training their staff in such things as making presentations (my favourite), negotiation, networking and time management. During this time I also helped the local Liberal Democrats with leafleting, canvassing and running events and I joined the Executive Committee of the local (Windsor) branch of the Liberal Democrat party.

Like many people at the time, Ursie and I had come to support the Lib Dems via the Social Democratic Party (SDP), which we joined in 1982. We had heard David Owen speak in Slough (most impressive) and felt that he and Roy Jenkins (briefly the SDP leader) represented a set of political and social values that matched ours. Increasingly I became more involved in Party work (known in the trade as being an activist) while Ursie, who viewed politicians and political activity askance, remained on the sidelines, though she was supportive of me and the SDP in general. She intensely disliked the vituperative nature of the political world and the unpleasant element which is always just below the surface – what Douglas Hurd used to call the 'sour' aspect of politics. For my part I took this as a given, and indeed felt that part of my personal remit was to get involved in order to help speed the arrival of a different kind of politics, based on proportional representation and the need for cooperation between parties, as in Europe.

One evening, about three months before the 2003 local elections, I attended a local Lib Dem meeting in the Windsor Liberal Club. We were deciding how to contest the coming local elections and who should stand in which Ward. It rapidly transpired that the Chair, Bryan Hedley, had too few candidates for too many Wards which, as I now realise, is a common problem. Trying to be helpful I volunteered as follows: 'I'm happy', I said, 'to stand as a paper candidate in an unwinnable seat, to be an actual candidate or just not stand at all.'

Bryan had a bluff manner and an ability to upset people from time to time, but he was also someone who for decades had served the local Liberal cause wholeheartedly. He had been a councillor for many years and was Mayor of Windsor and Maidenhead in the 1990s, so his record was impeccable. However, I heard nothing from him; there was no discussion of my proposal nor did he ask my views. Eventually, about a month later, during the next meeting, Bryan confirmed who the candidates were and then added, 'Antony, you'll be standing in Clewer South.' Given that I didn't even know what or where Clewer South was, this decision and the way it was announced could be described as neither Liberal nor Democratic. But there you are. Welcome to local politics and the small groups of slightly mad people of all parties (including myself!) who take part in them.

Undaunted, I got out the map to find where I was supposed to be standing. Clewer South lay about a mile from home, in an area known as Dedworth. It is one of the few Wards in the Royal Borough designated as an area of social deprivation, which nonetheless rather debunks the myth that Windsor is full of rich people living in big houses. In Dedworth, much of the housing was small and poorly built, with many ex-council houses. As I went out knocking on doors and asking people to vote Liberal Democrat I found that the area had more than its share of people in need of help. A good proportion were quite poor or elderly or sick and, in some cases, all three and as I went round I increasingly wanted to help them.

I was therefore delighted when, some six weeks later, in May 2003, the citizens of Clewer South voted myself and my colleague Richard Fagence (who had been my ever-helpful tutor during the campaign) to be their elected representatives on the Royal Borough of Windsor and Maidenhead (RBWM). The voting figures were:

Richard Fagence:	742
Antony Wood:	706
Two Tories:	about 220 each

A majority of around 500 for Richard and myself.

This trend was repeated with other candidates throughout Windsor and Maidenhead, with the result that the Lib Dems found themselves back in power and in charge of the Borough for the next four years. Being appointed as a councillor felt like an achievement and an honour, but of course the learning curve from then on was massive. I owe a debt of gratitude to Richard and other local Lib Dem councillors for their help both in terms of campaigning (which was a quite unknown art to me) and for their good advice during my initiation period.

I soon realised that being a councillor suited my temperament. For example, for the first time in about thirty years I really began to understand the place where I lived. Debating in the Council Chamber allowed me to use my communication skills and held no terrors. Also I enjoyed trying to find the essence of some complicated topic which was made all the more obscure by the myriad papers and reports without which it seemed RBWM could not move. My view was, and is, that much of council life is unnecessarily complicated, and therefore unbundling the dross from the essence is a key role for councillors. This was a challenge I rather relished.

Trying to find ways of helping vulnerable people with mundane but to them serious problems was work I took to. I helped residents get their allowances; fought Thames Water to unblock the local church's drains; visited schools to show support and interest; reported pot-holes; campaigned against aircraft noise; battled to improve provision for young people and, memorably, helped obtain 1,400 signatures on a petition to stop the night-time closure of Windsor's fire station. And lots more besides.

Being a local councillor is a much misunderstood activity, and what I've described is merely the meat and drink of being elected. Regularly one failed to win against an entrenched system, so if a particular piece of casework brought success it was always a special pleasure. I learnt that many issues (be they a matter of long-term policy or routine activity) are not as they might seem initially. I tried to do my best for every resident. Some were confused or had an unreasonable expectation of what was possible. Some were angry, not always justifiably, and a few were simply trying it on, so managing expectations was important.

After a year or so of this kind of work, including lots of evening meetings, I was prompted to think about standing for Parliament. The catalyst was a conversation with an old teaching friend of Ursie's, Lynda Cottrill. Lynda had been one of Windsor's first Lib Dem Councillors and she suggested I should stand as candidate for Windsor at the next general election, which would probably be in 2005. At first I gave her suggestion and the compliment it implied little thought but gradually the idea grew on me. As with any new venture, the fear of failure had to be overcome, but after 50 years I was at last getting over the lingering inheritance that such a step was 'not for the likes of me'. I have always enjoyed politics and my experience as a councillor, plus the many different things I had done during my working life, also gave me more confidence.*

Our political system was seen by most people as producing too many MPs who were 'dodgy' in one way or another, unnecessarily aggressive or just plain mendacious. But the system can only choose those who put their names forward, and if the talent pool is poor it's no use complaining unless you are prepared to enter the ring. I didn't seriously think I would get elected but I thought that if

---

* During my working life, I have worked in virtually all major sectors of the economy:

Public Service –	The Army
Private Sector –	International Companies – General Foods, Beecham Foods and Metal Box
Private Sector –	SME (Small and Medium sized Enterprises) – Anugraha
Not-for-Profit –	Made in the UK and UI
Self-employed / Start Up –	Leadership Challenge
Self-employed –	Consultant to World Challenge/Executive Coach (Praxis)
Local Government –	Royal Borough of Windsor and Maidenhead

I could at least be a decent candidate I would have done my bit by trying to change things. So, at last, the young man who once had been afraid to take the Army's Staff College exam in case he failed, had now grown up sufficiently to risk failure.

Despite having been a councillor for less than two years, I put my name forward in the early part of 2004 to be Windsor's Lib Dem Prospective Parliamentary Candidate (PPC). I filled in various forms and then waited for many months while the Lib Dem Head Office got its act together – or more accurately didn't. Having chased and chased, I found my anger rising over the inability of the Party to match me with a selection panel. Eventually, on a Thursday evening in the autumn of that year I got a call saying could I be in York (over 200 miles away) by 9.30am that Saturday? By this time I was so frustrated by the delays I would have happily flown to New York, so didn't hesitate and two days later I left home at 5.00am to drive to York. Notwithstanding a 45-minute delay on the M1 (on a Saturday morning!), I managed to arrive with five minutes to spare.

The day was taxing, thought-provoking and professional and to my surprise I got clearance to stand as a PPC on the first time of asking, which is not always the case. The next hurdle was the Hustings, which is where local Party members vote to select the candidate they think will best represent them and their party in the General Election. I had prepared myself well and quickly made over two hundred calls to local Lib Dem members to seek their support and their vote. My main opponent, Martin Rimmer, had been 'round the block' as they say, and was well known to older local party members, as well as to various people at Lib Dem Headquarters in London. So I needed to work hard.

But the truth was that during the past few years Martin had been 'coasting' and had not actually done much for the Windsor party. My approach was certainly more passionate and in one rather over-the-top moment I remember clutching the Lib Dem Policy Manifesto and saying to the audience 'and this is my Bible!' In the event I beat Martin pretty comfortably in the vote. I was surprised at his pitch, which seemed very negative. He seemed to be saying that the chief task of whoever was selected as Lib Dem Candidate for Windsor should be to spend their time going off to help someone else in a nearby target seat, which in our case was Maidenhead, just down the road. At the time I was very dismissive of this approach as my view was that we should fight hard for Windsor, get the Tory majority down from about 10,000 to somewhere between 4,000 to 5,000 and turn the constituency from a very safe Tory seat to one that was marginal. If this plan worked we would, in theory, have had every chance of winning next time round.

After my selection as Windsor's Lib Dem PPC we campaigned for over a year and a half and I also worked hard to obtain the help of three mid-course students from Brunel University, who all contributed a lot. Darshna Ladva was the first and she brought an infectious manner and great loyalty to our work for a year. Later, partly as a result of conversations we had together, she became a teacher and a family friend. Darshna, whose family was originally from India, was followed by Omar Hussein and Marlene Nwoye, both of whom helped the cause and made my study look a bit like a mini-United Nations.

With hindsight, I can see that I didn't press hard enough on two issues that would have made a big difference. I should have taken my outline campaign plan (which took nearly six months to prepare) away from Region, who showed no interest in my efforts (refusing even to read the document), and gone straight to ask Chris Rennard (now Lord Rennard), who was in charge of the actual campaign, to back me with some money and some support. I didn't grasp the nettle and go to see him and I can see now that I should have been more ambitious and hungry for success. My other mistake was not to hunt harder for a good agent to help me in the last few months. I thought having a professional, very experienced agent, Simon Werner, down the road in Maidenhead, would be enough but, in the event, Simon understandably got immersed in the Maidenhead campaign.

During the campaign I also learnt something else which surprised me. Apparently the stance that Martin Rimmer had taken up at the hustings would have been seen as correct party policy at the time. For some years the Lib Dems had prospered under the guidance of the aforementioned Chris Rennard, a canny Lib Dem campaigner. His mantra, which was enforced in a fairly peremptory way by his acolytes in the agents' team (who reported directly to him), was 'concentrate resources and throw everything into a relatively small number of target seats', which in 2005 numbered about thirty-five, out of more than six hundred constituencies. Over the previous ten years this policy had proved to be pretty effective, and the number of Lib Dem MP's went up from a handful to about sixty-five. So Martin was right. The official view was indeed that if you weren't likely to win the seat your job as a PPC was to go off and work in another area.

I never agreed with this approach for two reasons. First, it is an 'all eggs in one basket' approach, which is dangerous. Of the 35 seats targeted in the 2005 General Election only ten or eleven produced a Lib Dem MP. During the actual campaign each target seat received about £60,000 of funding from the centre, so the 25 that failed cost about £1.5 million in total, and thus used up much of the very limited Lib Dem general election budget, to marginal effect. Secondly, such an approach is massively demoralising to the six hundred or so prospective candidates who form the shock troops of a party in election year. They work night and day, give their soul to the cause, donate quite serious money and are then left, so to speak, to 'die in the trenches'.

Another way of putting this is to say that the work of most Lib Dem PPCs was in danger of being taken for granted. Fortunately, I believe a modified policy is now in force whereby target seats still have priority but some funds and some support is held back to help other candidates. This seems a much wiser approach, and one which could over the long-term turn seats where the Lib Dems come second onto winners. However, although I was glad to stand once, my experiences during the last few months of the campaign, (albeit fighting a pretty unwinnable seat), were enough to put me off a second go. I know we ran a good campaign and I learnt a lot and enjoyed it. The fact is that if you stand for election in Windsor, with national policies that don't really resonate with the bulk of the local electorate, it's rather like climbing into a boxing ring with a heavy-weight champion. Once is sufficient.

Although I done a great deal of groundwork in the two years running up to the General Election, when it came to the final six weeks, I found myself fighting a well-resourced Tory machine more or less on my own. For example, when I went out canvassing in the evenings I never remember having more than four or five people with me and most times it was just me and a couple of others. In the event I lost by about 10,000 votes; however, had 3,000 people (out of an electorate of about 63,000) voted Lib Dem instead of Conservative then my scenario of turning Windsor into a Tory marginal seat would not have been far off the mark. The figures were as follows:

Adam Afriyie	Conservative	21,646 (49.54%)
Antony Wood	Liberal Democrat	11,354 (25.99%)
A N Other	Labour	8,339 (19.09%)

Others   2,354 (3.68)

(Swing to the Conservatives 1.22%; Turn out 63.98%)

So, at the end of a hard campaign, the Tories proved to be quite easy winners. If at the count that evening they were quite triumphalist, this was because initially they weren't really sure they were going to win.

As a candidate, you visit your local polling station early in the morning (about 7.00am). The day then continues with visits to most of the other locations, as well as regular calls into the campaign HQ (called the Committee Room) to see how the vote is going and to encourage everyone. The polls then close at 10.00pm and the count, which for me took place in the Montem Sports Centre, Maidenhead, will start after midnight, with the result declared about 3.00am, which makes for a long day. I made what I hope was a graceful speech conceding the result and pointing out that many countries in the world either have rigged elections or none at all. Our freedom to vote in secret for who we want was hard won and is not to be taken lightly. I also pointed out that as our new MP Adam Afriyie now represented everyone in the constituency, whether they had voted for him or not. And so with that my work as Lib Dem PPC for Windsor was done and with no regrets I left the field.

As this memoir comes to an end let me try and summarise what has happened to me on my journey. It began with a description of a nervy, dyslexic boy growing up in 1940s and 50s Britain, who was the product of a country vicarage and, sadly, a rather dysfunctional family. So much has clearly changed since those days and that's got to be good, because if my story is about anything it's about change and change for the better. Compared with my childhood experiences family life has become so much richer, thanks to a loving marriage and three wonderful children. I am in no way complacent about this and know how much good fortune is involved in these things. Anyone who feels loved can count themselves blessed and also I have, I believe, largely become the person I had it in me to be – self-actualisation, as the experts call it. Though I am neither 'good' nor 'great', after 70 years of being around I feel comfortable in my own skin. So if you were to meet me now I like to think that the old maxim 'what you see is what you get' would be true. I hope so.

Over the years I have kept much of what my parents lovingly offered me, indeed perhaps more than I know. However, I have also discarded some of the values and views which they, the Army, school, my peers and the Church would have expected me to keep. I am happy now to be liberal in thought, in politics, in my social views and in matters of religion. As a result I nowadays have real trouble with dogma, efforts by my peer group to influence me, fundamentalist religions (of all types), bureaucracy, and society in its acquisitive/aspirational mode.

We are all shaped by our experiences and how we deal with them. I have been in dangerous situations on active service with the Army. I have felt the cold wind of financial stringency and redundancy. I've had to learn how to earn my living and have always managed to pay my bills – despite five careers and umpteen jobs, or maybe even because of them. I've learnt to stop being in thrall to organisations or dependent on institutions, and instead have become entrepreneurial and have even been able to run a successful small business. To do this I've had to take some risks and to tough things out in an often adverse economic climate.

I grew up in a period of austerity, matured at a time of imperial decline and the background to much of my life has been one of considerable social change. Modern Britain is now, (even taking into account the recent recession), on a more even keel and unrecognisable from the country of my youth. A recent piece by Danny Finkelstein, writing rather beautifully in *The Times*, captures my feelings:

'Unlike those of us born here, my Father became British on purpose, as a conscious act, one that he had thought about deeply. He never thought Britain's leaders corrupt, or that the country was going to the dogs, or that our society was collapsing, undermined by its moral decay. He lived here proud of a nation that let him live, let him learn, let him teach, let him practise his religion. And ultimately let him die in bed, surrounded by his family.'

By far the most important element in my life and by definition the most influential in helping me make this journey has been my family, Ursula, James, Ellie and Hattie. I began with them and I would like to end with them as they are indeed my Alpha and Omega. They are now all married and our family has been enriched by George, Kathy and Ross – not forgetting four grandchildren. How simply incredible it has been, and is, to have such people in my life – to love them and be loved by them. Despite everything that has happened, good and bad, it is because of them that the 'sunny and lively' little boy who started this journey so many pages ago might possibly, just possibly, become a 'sunny' and lively' old man. I do hope so, and also that you have enjoyed the trip.

How I Wrote This Memoir
Without a Diary or Notes

I wanted to write this memoir a long time ago but over the years faced the usual inexperienced writer's problem of lack of confidence as well as a failure to find my 'voice'. How did these two blocks come to be removed?

The simple answer is by following the advice of a good and possibly great author. About five years ago I found a second-hand copy of Judith Cook's biography of J B Priestly, (aptly titled *Priestly*) and was struck by Priestley's productivity for he is reckoned by many to be the most prolific English author of the 20th century. The author quotes Priestly offering some advice to putative writers: 'Every morning you have to go in there and lift the elephant off the typewriter.'

Later when, Ursie and I were on holiday in St Ives, we went to visit an artist in her studio and she confessed to finding it difficult to get started on new projects. So I quoted Priestly's dictum about the need to get started and how I wanted to write a memoir. With a friendly smile but a slightly accusatory eye she then asked me how I was doing in terms of elephants and typewriters? It was enough and, taking the point, I began to write not long after.

I now want to turn to how I actually managed to put these pages together, bearing in mind that I kept no diary or logbook and most of my letters have disappeared. How has it been possible to remember and record events many of which happened fifty or sixty years ago?

About seven or eight years before I started this memoir I began a rough notebook in which I entered memories and recollections as they came to mind, and I tried to do this consistently for a few years. Sometimes, of course, I had to record things on a journey or away from home, so thoughts got quickly jotted into a small notepad to be transferred into my main notebook later. All through this period I clearly recall having the unsettling feeling that when I did eventually come to write I would not be able to remember enough of my life (especially the early bits) or, even worse, might have missed out some interesting incidents. As well as collecting enough material, I also had to work out how to actually write the thing. Indeed how to get the words onto the page and 'lift the elephant off the typewriter.'

Some people can type their first draft straight onto a laptop or PC, while others use their favourite notebook, pens and paper. My preferred modus operandi is to use an HB propelling pencil and to write onto wide-line ruled 80 gram paper – 80 sheets to a pad. I write on alternate lines, which leaves plenty of room for me to annotate or delete or change a line, and I also always keep a blank left hand page on which to scribble a late thought or rewrite paragraphs. I found these blank pages important – as you recall one memory or catch one idea this triggers off others and they must be captured instantly and in a place where they can easily be found. Numbering every manuscript page is useful too as it helps in finding your way around. The other advantage of a notebook or lined pad is that you can easily tear out pages. I'm actually writing these extra notes having reached Page 94 of my original draft (about doing athletics at Aldenham) but I have torn a blank page from the back of my pad and am doing additional notes for the Afterword, while the mood is on me.

Of course, I then have to get my words from their handwritten state onto the computer. For this memoir, I employed a typist, the good Suzanne, who is a PA at the clinic where Ursula worked and is consequently used to reading bad handwriting. Suzanne typed up all of the first draft and then sent me a copy on disc. My task was then to edit and to some degree rewrite the typed version of the memoir. So, the version on my PC was in effect a second draft.

Using a computer is ideal for this kind of work because the computer contains perfect devices for editing. You can check spellings; look up facts on Google; move great lumps of text around and edit text quickly and easily. Re-reading my first draft in typed form on the screen I can see I have left out important events, but adding them in is simple. In addition, some two years after starting to write, I realised I hadn't put in enough colour; details of my emotions at various times, descriptions of places, people – even the weather! Reading the second draft on my PC confirmed that this kind of detail is a minimum requirement if you are to keep people's interest. It's not enough to record the bare facts in the hope that family and friends will be interested, just because it's about you. If we assume that just the facts on their own will make our lives interesting, we may well justify T.S. Eliot's line about J. Alfred Prufrock: 'I have measured out my life in coffee-spoons'.

So there we are. I hope you have enjoyed reading the chapters about my life so far and that this last little bit has to some extent explained how the words got on the page.

Acknowledgements

Although books usually have one name on the front cover in fact they are nearly always dependent on help from other people. *Never The Same River* is no exception. Acknowledging the support, encouragement and good advice I have had actually understates this debt and I owe a number of people a big thank you.

When I was just going to write 'something for the family' Dan Clacher of Muddy Waters Publishing saw the manuscript and urged me to consider self-publishing. Without his enthusiasm I don't think anything would have happened.

Suzanne Turley was also in at the beginning of the process and turned my illegible scrawl into useable text. Gary Smailes at Bubblecow gently reminded me that 'less is more' and helped me remove unwanted material and unnecessary words.

Kate Hopkins spent many hours editing the first draft and also all my family have read and re-read the manuscript, giving excellent advice and encouragement. Crucially, at a point when I was floundering, I had invaluable help and professional advice from Richard Collins and his involvement has been a real joy.

My brother Michael kindly helped with the costs of production and his amazing memory has been essential in getting the earlier parts right, while Brigadier George Powell, Celia Ferguson and Chris Barrett have all made helpful comments.

ACKNOWLEDGEMENTS

My thanks are also due to York Publishing Services, and in particular to Clare Brayshaw, Paula Charles, and David Mercer who have held my hand during a journey into the unknown world of writing a book.